Early Years Policy and Practice

CRITICAL APPROACHES TO THE EARLY YEARS

You might also like the following books from Critical Publishing

Teaching Systematic Synthetic Phonics and Early English
Jonathan Glazzard and Jane Stokoe
978-1-909330-09-2
In print

Teaching and Learning Early Years Mathematics: Subject and Pedagogic Knowledge
Mary Briggs
978-1-909330-37-5
In print

Well-being in the Early Years
Ed Chelle Davison and Susan Waltham
978-1-909330-65-8
September 2013

The Critical Years: Early Years Development from Conception to 5
Tim Gully
978-1-909330-73-3
January 2014

Most of our titles are also available in a range of electronic formats. To order please go to our Website www.criticalpublishing.com or contact our distributor, NBN International, 10 Thornbury Road, Plymouth PL6 7PP, telephone 01752 202301 or email orders@nbninternational.com.

Early Years Policy and Practice

A Critical Alliance

Pat Tomlinson

Series Editors Chelle Davison & Susan Waltham

CRITICAL
APPROACHES
TO THE EARLY
YEARS

First published in 2013 by Critical Publishing Ltd

British Library Cataloguing in Publication Data
A CIP record for this book is available from the British Library

ISBN: 978-1-909330-61-0

This book is also available in the following e-book formats:

Kindle ISBN: 978-1-909330-62-7
EPUB ISBN: 978-1-909330-63-4
Adobe e-book ISBN: 978-1-909330-64-1

Cover and text design by Greensplash Limited
Project Management by Out of House Publishing
Printed and bound in Great Britain by T J International

Critical Publishing
152 Chester Road
Northwich
CW8 4AL
www.criticalpublishing.com

MIX
Paper from
responsible sources
FSC
www.fsc.org   FSC® C013056

Contents

Acronyms

CWDC	Children's Workforce Development Council
DCSF	Department for Children, Schools and Families
DfE	Department for Education
DfES	Department for Education and Skills
DWP	Department for Work and Pensions
EYFS	Early Years Foundation Stage
EYPS	Early Years Professional Status
EYTS	Early Years Teacher Status
QTS	Qualified Teacher Status
SEFDEY	Sector Endorsed Foundation Degree Early Years
TA	Teaching Agency

Terminology

Early Years Professional Status (EYPS) refers to the *graduate level professional accreditation programme for leading practitioners in the early years sector* (DfE 2012b).

For the purposes of clarity both the terms 'early years' and 'early education' are used to define *all children who are between the ages of 0–5 years 11 months* and who are *educated and cared for within the Early Years Foundation Stage framework.*

Meet the author

 **Pat Tomlinson's** working life has been spent developing, delivering or teaching aspects of children's policy. Her decades of experience and learning include school teaching in the 1970s, play development work in the 1980s, working as a university academic developing and delivering childhood studies graduate programmes through the 1990s to 2009 when she took up the position of head of the Early Years Programme at the Children's Workforce Development Council. Her interest in early childhood policy continues through involvement as governor of a large college and membership of a number of early years forums.

Meet the series editors

Chelle Davison is a Senior Lecturer of Early Years Professional Practice at Leeds Metropolitan University. Her role incorporates developing the critical understanding of early years pedagogy and its practical application in settings and schools. Chelle has recently made significant contributions to a range of policy documents and government reviews, and is a devoted supporter of the professionalisation of the early years workforce.

Susan Waltham is a Senior Lecturer teaching on a number of undergraduate and postgraduate courses in the School of Education and Childhood at Leeds Metropolitan University. Her academic expertise is in child psychology and human development, diversity and equality. Her research is centred on identity construction in young children in multicultural, multilinguistic settings. She also works as an independent consultant with organisations and early years settings in China, Pakistan and Malaysia.

Preface: introduction to critical thinking

What is critical thinking?

This introduction gives you the opportunity to learn more about critical thinking and the skills you will acquire as you use this series, introducing you to the meaning of critical thinking and how you can develop the necessary skills to read and research effectively towards a critical approach to learning and analysis. It is a necessary and wholly beneficial position to be starting with questions and finishing your journey with more questions.

> *Judge a man by his questions rather than by his answers.*
>
> François-Marie Arouet (Voltaire)

If you are already a professional within the early years sector, maybe as a teacher in a Reception class, or as an early years educator in a private day-care setting, you will no doubt have faced many challenging debates, discussions at training events and your own personal questioning of the policies faced by the sector as a whole. We want you to ask these questions. More importantly, we believe it to be an essential and crucial part of your professional development. You will no doubt be required to implement policies that might at first seem detached from your day-to-day professional practice. It is critical that you question these policies, that you understand their purpose, and moreover that you understand how they have come into being.

Often students are faced with complex definitions of critical thinking that require them to deconstruct the concept before they fully understand just how to 'do' the critical thinking in the first place. For example,

> *Critical thinking is the intellectually disciplined process of actively and skilfully conceptualizing, applying, analysing, synthesizing, and/or evaluating information gathered from, or generated by, observation, experience, reflection, reasoning, or communication, as a guide to belief and action.*
>
> (Scriven and Paul, 1989)

Rather than confusing you with specific academic definitions, it is our hope that as you read further and begin to understand this topic more, you will be encouraged to ask contemplative questions. Alison King emphasises the importance of students acquiring and cultivating a *habit of inquiry* to enable them to *learn to ask thoughtful questions* (King, 1995, p 13). Contrary to the standard methods of 'instruction' that leave the student as a passive recipient of information, King argues that where a student has developed the skills of critical thinking they become an 'autonomous' learner:

> *Such a habit of inquiry learned and practiced in class can be applied also to their everyday lives: to what they see on television, read in the newspaper observe in popular culture and hear during interaction with friends and colleagues, as well as to decisions they make about personal relationships, consumer purchases, political choices, and business transactions.*
>
> (King, 1995, p 13)

Consider the subject matter that you are now researching; you may have been tasked with the question 'How has policy changed over the past 25 years?' This is what King would suggest is a 'factual' question, one that may well have a limited answer. Once you have this answer, there is a tendency to stop there, making the inquiry fact-based rather than critical. If you were to follow up this first question with a critical question, King would argue that you are beginning to 'introduce high level cognitive processes such as analysis of ideas, comparison and contrast, inference, prediction [and] evaluation' (1995, p 140)

Example

Factual question	Critical question
How has policy changed over the past 25 years?	What has been the impact of policy change over the past 25 years?
Which policies have been introduced to support childcare and early education initiatives recently?	How has childcare and early education been influenced by recent policy?

Critical thinking has been described by Diane Halpern (1996) as

> *thinking that is purposeful, reasoned, and goal directed – the kind of thinking involved in solving problems, formulating inferences, calculating likelihoods, and making decisions when the thinker is using skills that are thoughtful and effective.*
>
> (Halpern, 1996)

The emphasis is on 'thinking' that alludes to the student pausing and considering not only the topic or subject in hand, but also the questions generated from taking an opportunity to ask those critical rather than factual questions.

To think critically signifies the ability to use 'a higher order skill' that enables professionals to act in a rational and reasonable manner, using empathy and understanding of others in a specific context, such as an early years setting. The rights and needs of others are always the priority, rather than blindly following established procedures.

A critical thinker:

* raises vital questions and problems, formulating them clearly and precisely; gathers and assesses relevant information, using abstract ideas to interpret it effectively;

* reaches well-reasoned conclusions and solutions, testing them against relevant criteria and standards;

* thinks open-mindedly within alternative systems of thought, recognising and assessing, as need be, their assumptions, implications and practical consequences;

* communicates effectively with others in figuring out solutions to complex problems.

(Taken from Paul and Elder, 2008)

Alec Fisher (2001) examines the description given by John Dewey of what he termed *reflective thinking* as *active, persistent and careful consideration of a belief or supposed form of knowledge in the light of the grounds which support it and further conclusions to which it tends*. Rather than rushing to discover what you believe to be 'the answer', consider disentangling the question and the 'right answer' before stating your conclusion. Could there be more to find by turning your factual question into a critical question?

Below are examples of a student discussing her recent visit to another early years setting. The first question is what King (1995) describes as a factual question, and you can see we have highlighted exactly where the facts are in the answer. The second question is a critical question (King, 1995), and again we have highlighted in the answer where the critical elements are.

Question (factual):

What did you see in the new setting that is different to your setting?

The equipment that was out didn't seem a lot [FCT], in my setting we have everything out [FCT] so the children can access it all, you know like continuous provision. In the other setting they had bare shelves [FCT] and they told me that new equipment was only brought out when the children had mastered those already out [FCT]. They didn't seem to be bothered about the EYFS either, like nothing in the planning was linked to the EYFS [FCT].

(Early childhood studies student, 2013).

Question (critical):

Consider the two different approaches, your setting and the one that you visited. What impact do you think they have on the children's learning and developing?

I suppose I can see that when we put toys and materials out, that there are always children who get things out but don't have a clue how to use it. I guess it would be better if there was less and that the things they did get out were right for the developmental level of each child [CRIT]. I suppose it is how we interpret continuous provision [CRIT]. I think as well that the other setting was using the EYFS to measure the development and learning of each child [CRIT], but they knew the framework and the children well enough not to have to write it all down all the time [CRIT].

(Early childhood studies student, 2013).

Another example of how you can become a critical thinker might be in asking yourself critical questions as you read and research a topic.

Thought provoking or critical questions require students to go beyond the facts to think about them in ways that are different from what is presented explicitly in class or in the text.

(King, 1995, p 14)

Stella Cottrell (2005) suggests that we must know what we think about a subject and then be able to justify why we think in a certain way *having reasons for what we believe ... critically evaluating our own beliefs ... [and be] able to present to others the reasons for our beliefs and actions* (Cottrell, 2005, p 3).

Five questions towards critical thinking

1. Do I understand what I am reading?

2. Can I explain what I have read (factually)? For example, what is this author telling me about this subject?

3. What do I think? For example, what is my standpoint, what do I believe is right?

4. Why do I think that way (critically)? For example, I think that way because I have seen this concept work in practice.

5. Can I justify to another person my way of thinking?

All that we ask is that you take the time to stop, and consider what you are reading:

What a sad comment on modern educational systems that most learners neither value nor practise active, critical reflection. They are too busy studying to stop and think.

(Hammond and Collins, 1991, p 163)

We encourage you to take time to ask yourself, your peers and your tutors inquisitive and exploratory questions about the themes discussed in this book, and to stop for a while to move on from the surface-level factual questioning for which you will, no doubt, only find factual answers, and to ponder the wider concepts, the implications for professional practice, and to ask the searching questions to which you may not find such a concrete answer.

For as Van Gelder so eloquently suggests, learning about it is not as useful as doing it:

For students to improve, they must engage in critical thinking itself. It is not enough to learn about critical thinking. These strategies are about as effective as working on your tennis game by watching Wimbledon. Unless the students are actively doing the thinking themselves, they will never improve.

(Van Gelder, 2005, p 43)

1 The tortoise or the hare: the shaping of early years policy since 1900

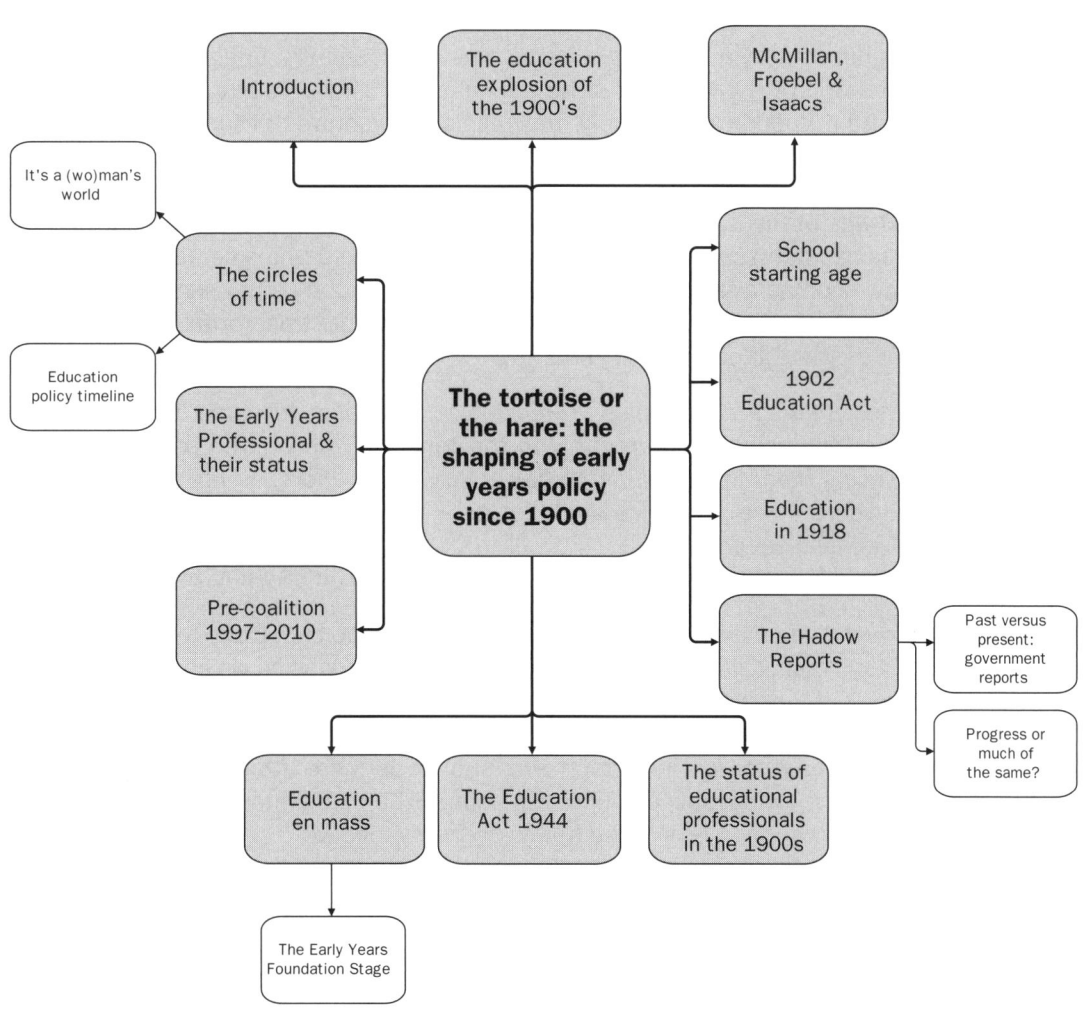

The mechanical teaching in many infant schools seems to dull, rather than awaken, the little power of imagination and independent observation which these infants possess.

(Board of Education, 1905)

Introduction

This chapter provides historical background to the evolution of early childhood education, specifically but not exclusively, how nursery schools developed in England and how the Early Years Foundation Stage curriculum came into existence. It briefly discusses the unique role of the Early Years Professional, renamed the Early Years Teacher from September 2013, a relatively new graduate status and a role that continues to undergo significant change as a result of the establishment of the coalition government. The chapter considers the origin of the Early Years Professional and how it is intrinsically linked to the evolution of early childhood education and care in England over the past one hundred years.

The education explosion of the 1900s

In the late eighteenth century and throughout the nineteenth century, England moved steadily towards the creation of a systematic state education structure (Anning, 1991). It was a movement away from, though not entirely, the religious structures of learning, towards a health-focused system that offered a safe environment as well as a place of learning for the country's youngest children. Not so far detached from the present day, the 'instruction' that children received was at the heart of the new education landscape where children, who for so many centuries had been seen as nothing more than a wage-earning commodity for their parents, were now seen as a tax-paying commodity of their country. They were regarded as vessels to be filled with skills and knowledge, which in turn would transform England's prosperity and pay for the next generation. A generation who sought to

> *implant in their minds the principles of Religion and Morality, revealed in the Holy Scriptures, and as inculcated agreeably to the tenets of the Church of England; ultimately placing them in situations, either at sea, or on shore, as far as may be practicable, where those principles shall not be endangered, and the prospect of an honest livelihood secured.*
>
> (see Figure 1.1, from Constitution of the Asylum, 1836)

Even now in the twenty-first century, the debate over where is the best place for a young child to be educated is still raging. Over 100 years ago, that same discussion was being had in the corridors of power. Part 2 of the Acland Report (1908) states very poignantly that the place of a child under five years of age was with its mother in a safe, secure, clean and loving home, to be educated and cared for by the person who should be more attached than any other to the child and to their overall success and well-being. When government contend that the best place for any child under five is in the home, so policy follows:

> *When the mother does her duty by her children; when she knows how to care for them properly and to make the best use of her narrow means; when her employment does not keep her away from home; when the home itself is clean, well-lighted, well-ventilated, and not over-cramped, and when the little children are within easy reach*

of some safe place to play in out-of-doors; in such circumstances the home affords advantages for the early stages of education which cannot be reproduced by any school or public institution. There is in the natural relationship between mother and child, and in the other influences of good home life, a moral and educational power which it is of high national importance to preserve and to strengthen, and which educational policy should be careful not to impair.

(*Education in England: The Acland Report*, Section 2.16)

CONSTITUTION OF THE ASYLUM.

NAME OF THE INSTITUTION.

1. That this Institution be designated the Merchant Seamen's Orphan Asylum.

DESIGN OF THE INSTITUTION.

II. That the design of this Institution be, to afford suitable Relief to the Orphans of Seamen in the Merchant Service, by rescuing them from vice and profligacy—by providing them clothing, maintenance, and education—by endeavouring to implant in their minds the principles of Religion and Morality, revealed in the Holy Scriptures, and as inculcated agreeably to the tenets of the Church of England; ultimately placing them in situations, either at sea, or on shore, as far as may be practicable, where those principles shall not be endangered, and the prospect of an honest livelihood secured.

OBJECTS OF THE ASYLUM.

III. That the legitimate Objects of this Asylum, be the destitute Orphan Children of Seamen in the Merchant's Service, whose Fathers are Dead.

RULES FOR ADMISSION OF CHILDREN.

IV. That no child can be admitted into the Asylum, who on the day of election is under the age of Seven years, or above the age of Ten years; nor any child be dismissed

Figure 1.1 *Extract from the Merchant-Seamen's Board of Managers' report on the welfare of orphaned children*

Critical questions

» *Consider the various childcare environments you already know. How can a baby be cared for and educated efficiently, successfully, purposefully and to an outstanding level when they are in a staff to child ratio of 1:3 in a setting, compared to 1:1 at home?*

» *Discuss whether home is the best learning environment for children under two years of age.*

» *Consider 'family-friendly' policies: are these implemented with the interests of the children at their heart?*

McMillan, Froebel and Isaacs

Famous names such as Margaret McMillan, Friedrich Froebel and Susan Isaacs are among the revered educationalists of the 1900s. They were individuals who fought tirelessly to provide better education, better access to health services and overall to develop the upcoming generation of workers (McMillan, 1911; see Figure 1.2). These individuals are still well regarded and respected for their early pioneering methods that led to the very first changes in government policy and altered the minds of parents and professionals alike about the benefits of education and good healthcare for the younger generation.

Margaret McMillan, a diligent campaigner for better environments specifically for very young children *constantly turned away from trivia to the clamouring needs of the poor. She longed to be involved in activities which realistically attempted to remove social injustices and liberate men from the shackles and humiliation of poverty* (Bradburn, 1976, p 17).

Moving an entire country towards the consensus that more needed to be done for young children was no small feat. I still recall seeing a photograph first published in an NSPCC magazine called *The Child's Guardian*, on the cover of a book by Peter Roche entitled *Unloved: The Story of a Stolen Childhood*, believing the image to have come from the early 1900s when in reality it was a photograph taken by Lord Snowdon of Peter Roche during the 1960s. I was amazed that this image had been taken some twenty years or so *after* the introduction of free healthcare in the form of the National Health Service (NHS). McMillan in 1911 stood up on the streets of Bradford pleading for a change in political ideology and for support in her open-air nurseries, and as I read accounts of her speeches, this child, Peter Roche, comes to mind even though the photograph was taken years later, in 1965. Had so little changed in 60 years to support families with small children?

I continue to be perplexed at how few policy shifts actually drill down to the street level, to a level that is required for government to change children's lives for the better.

Critical questions

» *Consider major cases such as Victoria Climbié, Sarah Payne, Soham and Baby P. Which policies are you aware of being implemented in settings as a direct result of these case reviews?*

» *Critically analyse each policy that you are aware of and reflect upon the impact for your own role/career.*

It is difficult to read the reflective accounts of teachers working within a Froebel classroom and not feel that while on the surface it appears much has changed since 1852 when Froebel was first gathering disciples of educational reform across the world, little has altered within

DEPARTMENT OF VISITING NURSING AND SOCIAL WELFARE

♦♦♦

IN CHARGE OF

EDNA L. FOLEY, R.N.

SCHOOL NURSING IN ENGLAND

By MARGARET McMILLAN

Member of the School Board, Bradford, England

To THE NURSES OF AMERICA, GREETING: Far away in Buckinghamshire, England, there is a mansion in a great park full of noble trees. From the outside the great rambling house looks plain enough, and not beautiful, but within there are vast rooms filled with things that have historic interest. The staircase, with its wide, low steps so wonderfully inlaid, is the work of Italian artist craftsmen who came hither long ago to execute it. This is Claydon House, the home of the Verneys. Florence Nightingale's sister was the wife of Sir Harry Verney, and for many years the queen of nurses used to spend a great part of her time here. In the hall is her marble bust given by the soldiers. Upstairs is the suite of rooms which bore her name. Here, in her declining days, she watched the sunset light fade behind the woodlands, and her influence is in every cottage home. It would be strange if Claydon House had no interest for nurses all over the world.

This home of beauty did not blot out from all who lived in it the vision of the world's sorrow. Florence Nightingale could hear through the whisper of stirred leaves, or the music of falling water in the quiet gardens, the groan of the wounded and dying in the field of battle; and the present lady of this home, one may add, has ears to hear the sob of anguish less remote, and even more hopeless. The present Lady Verney is one of our leading educationists, and she takes the keenest interest in the physical welfare of school children. What a rapid growth of consciousness we find in the people of to-day as compared with the people of fifty or sixty years ago. Formerly it was believed that the little aristocrat needed a nurse. Now we are all beginning to realize that all young creatures, the poor as well as the rich, need care. A laborer's baby is just as delicate as a princeling. He cannot " rough it " as is proved by the immense death-rate of infants in poor quarters. And yet there are myriads of priceless workers lost in this way every year; this wastage must cease.

Figure 1.2 *Margaret McMillan's observations of children's care*

the theoretical and philosophical debates around educational reform. Lawrence (1969, republished in 2011) posits *there is no centrally imposed curriculum or method; teachers are left free to work according to their own lights and the needs of their pupils, and the greater or lesser exigencies of an always impoverished service* (p 9). The national curriculum brought in by the Conservative government in the late 1980s largely opposes this late 1960s view of education in England, yet we find in 2013 free schools and academies appearing on the educational landscape, to challenge the independence and uniqueness of the independent schools sector for freedoms in the classroom much like those described in Lawrence's 1969 account of a Froebel led system. One might argue that as one static, state-imposed curriculum failed two generations, we are seeing a reversal of policies and a return to the pioneers of 1900s educational reform.

During the twentieth century progressive educationalists became aware of the Vygotsky construct of socio-cultural influences and how children might interact with their learning environments (Vygotsky, 1978). Pioneers of a new way to educate children began to connect a child's own experiences outside of the classroom with their ability to understand within. In the technological age of 2013 we still advocate the importance of the outdoors for our youngest children, endeavouring to utilise the outdoor environment for the learning and health of children, following the lead taken by Froebel and McMillan. Yet over 100 years on, the battles started by these prominent innovators are yet to be won. Of Margaret McMillan Bradburn writes:

> *soon she had clear evidence of the improved health of the children who attended her camp; the open-air lie seemed to build up their resistance to disease. This experience encouraged her to continue with her open-air ventures, which she later referred to as preventative medicine.*
>
> (Bradburn, 1976, p 33)

Lawrence describes how Froebel

> *likened the growth of a child to the growth of a plant, to be tended and cared for as the gardener cares for his seedlings and he emphasised the importance of play for the young child, leading to purposeful activity in the classroom. Above all, education should lead to harmony with God and nature.*
>
> (Lawrence, 1969, p 22)

Maria Montessori, another pioneering educationalist, wrote that:

> *Children have an anxious concern for living beings, and the satisfaction of this instinct fills them with delight. It is therefore easy to interest them in taking care of plants and especially of animals. Nothing awakens foresight in a small child, who lives by his rule for the passing moment and without care for the morrow, so much as this.*
>
> (Montessori, 2004, p 1)

The year 2013 has not brought about the progress one would have hoped for regarding classification of our children either. The newer curriculum that so much money is spent on implementing still offers an expectation of the 'average' child, something that many professionals struggle to consider objectively when assessing the children in their care through observation. It is also an area of difficulty for school teachers who can reel off by heart the national requirement averages for the end of Foundation Stage, the end of Key Stage 1 and the end of Key Stage 2. We should remember that while the government may well set these averages as a target for whole classes of children and thousands of schools, in reality a child remains just that, a child and not a number or statistic:

> *general characteristics of the Primary School period will not be shown fully by any one child. No real living child is 'typical' or 'average'. These notions are just useful tools to help us fix in our minds what there is in common between the actual children we observe … talking about the child almost as if there was some fixed real type that could in some mysterious way be distilled out from the actual children we know … leads to all sorts of rigid laws being laid down, and hard and fast notions of development being applied, which leave the practical person high and dry when he comes to deal with the living children in his class.*
>
> (Isaacs, 1965, pp 65–6)

Critical questions

» *Take one aspect from each of the early pioneers; can you critically reflect on your own practice making conclusive links between their ideologies and your practice?*

» *Who do you believe to be modern-day influences on early education policy?*

School starting age

The Education Act of 1870 determined the lower age limit of five years as being the appropriate age for formal schooling. The days were filled with tests and checks for government health monitoring, in an effort to reduce the mortality rate of children in England. The curriculum was centred upon the indoctrination of children within a specified religion, rather than the three R's (Bergen, 1982).

Within and among the changes in education, some of the UK's youngest children were routinely enrolled into schools, some from as young as three years old (Great Britain: Board of Education, 1905).

> *The great explosion of elementary education in England and Wales followed the Education Act of 1870, which divided the country into school districts, and created Local School Boards to administer local 'rates,' or taxes, in the expansion and operation of elementary education. The percentage of school-age children attending elementary schools rose rapidly, from 26% in 1871 to 46% in 1881. It continued to rise steadily, though somewhat less rapidly, to 57% in 1891, reaching 62% at the turn of the century, and 70% in 1911. (These figures are based on average attendance. The number of students registered is much higher.) There was a corresponding increase in the number of schools: from 9,521 in 1871 to 17,614 in 1881, to 19,508 in 1891, and to 20,100 in 1900. Similarly, expenditure on elementary education increased from 903,978 in 1871, to 2,854,067 in 1881, to 4,392,126 in 1891, and to 10,241,532 in 1900.*
>
> (Bergen, 1982, p 3)

The debate surrounding the appropriate school starting age has re-emerged (EPPE, 2004; Tickell, 2011). In 1870 one MP stated *Five is too tender an age for compulsory attendance* (cited in Alexander, 2009, p 16) while a second argued that although children contributed to the household income, they should be *beginning [school] early and ending early* (Whitbread, 1972, p 442).

1902 Education Act

The 1902 Education Act (Balfour's Act) decreed that all previous school boards should be replaced with Local Education Authorities (Education Act, 1902) as a means to reduce the financial burden of sustaining the pre-existing school boards. The changes also brought about local intervention for young children who were identified as needing additional support for both their health and education (Education Act, 1902). The government went on to hold an inquiry into the age a child should begin formal education and so commissioned a number of its female inspectors to carry out inspections of educational establishments, with the primary task of reporting on the educational appropriateness and success of placing children under five in formal education (Board of Education, 1905). One element of each report was unanimous, that young children of three, four and five do not make any headway or gain any 'intellectual advantage' from attending 'schools of instruction' (Board of Education, 1905; Blackstone, 1974).

CASE STUDY

Caroline's story

I have been caught up in the school starting age for years. My eldest is 9 and is a summer born baby. He always showed an interest in learning and I didn't really have any problem with him going to school at 4 while many of his classmates turned five before Christmas. Then I had two girls close together and despite my eldest girl being 5 in January, she didn't seem quite ready for school the following September. She was emotionally younger than her brother and I wasn't sure we should be putting her in a reception class. The following year my second daughter started school, her birthday is the last day of May. She is outgoing and boisterous, I still felt I didn't want her to start school yet but for different reasons to her sister.

Despite my reservations, their father decided they should be in school making friends and not 'dropped' into education in Year 1. I really didn't need to worry, both girls tested way ahead of the EYFS Profile. They were both visiting Year 1 classrooms for high achievers maths and literacy before the end of their first term. I sometimes wonder about our decisions nonetheless. My eldest girl is still emotionally immature and finds it difficult to be in large groups. She has one or two distinct friends rather than the whole class that both her siblings seem to have in their social groups.

Was I wrong to let her go to school too early? Maybe I will never know, but I am less inclined to believe children can struggle academically because of where their birthdays fall. Maybe we should go back to proper nursery schools where children can stay an extra year if they want to, or if their parents believe it to be beneficial. Where trained experts in early child development, can assess their readiness for school, and its institution-like environment. At the moment it feels a little bit like we pay for childcare and then rejoice when school comes along because it's free. I wonder how many other children should still be in a nurturing nursery school rather than a primary.

I think it's more to do with a lack of options, than the month of their birthday.

(Caroline 35, 2012)

Education in 1918

Further alterations were made to the English education system in 1918 when the school leaving age was increased. However, financial implications remained problematic and increased for some local authorities as the First World War continued (Education Bill, 1918). The debates within the House of Commons during 1918 deliberate the needs of young children and the potential contribution that they can bring to society:

> *We simply cannot afford to let our industries lack the better mental equipment which all those engaged in them will obtain if the main provisions of this Bill are carried out.*

(Education Bill, 1918)

The debate continued as a dialogue between ministers on the subject of the improvement of children's welfare and health. While education is the key subject matter being considered, this particular debate clearly identifies children's long-term health as being a central concern to government that might be expedited through improved educational consistency across local authorities.

> *I hope there will be in the course of our discussions no weakening of the provisions of the Bill affecting the physical welfare of children and young persons. I believe the whole House welcomes with both hands the provision bringing young persons up to eighteen years of age under the skilled attention of school medical officers.*

(Education Bill, 1918)

Critical questions

» *The school starting age is historical. Critically evaluate the decision to make formal schooling begin at five years of age in the early 1900s compared to the twenty-first century.*

» *Consider family-friendly policies (also discussed in later chapters). Are they family-friendly and child-friendly or do they simply facilitate more taxes being collected by the government?*

The Hadow reports

Sir [William] Henry Hadow, then Vice Chancellor of the University of Sheffield, published the first of six reports derived from committee-based consultations, at the request of the Conservative government (Hadow, 1923). Each consultation committee considered different queries, framed by the terms of reference, about the future of education in England. Reports included a proposal to differentiate the curriculum in schools for boys and girls

(Hadow, 1923 cited in Aldrich, 2002) and in 1931 the suitability of *courses ... for children (other than children in Infants' Departments) up to the age of 11 in Elementary Schools* (Hadow, 1931).

Significant to the history of early education in England, and specifically for children from birth to seven years, was the last of Hadow's reports. This was the first evidence that an early education might be of some consequence to a child's overall long-term well-being, apart from the generally accepted historical consensus that an infant's care, education and well-being were the responsibility and indeed the vocation of the child's mother, in the home (Hadow, 1933 cited in Gillard, 2006).

The Hadow reports can be accessed via the educationengland.org.uk Website, along with many documents covering important historical discussions from the consultative committee of the early 1900s that have been carefully transcribed.

Past versus present: government reports

One could be forgiven for confusion when considering the Hadow reports in light of the recent Graham Allen (2011) and Frank Field (2010) reports for the current coalition government; they both highlight intervention in the very early years of a child's life, both educationally, and with reference to health and well-being, as a crucial and necessary mediation by various professionals and outside agencies for the good of the child and the long-term benefit to society.

The terms of reference by which Hadow's committee were required to abide stated *consider and report on the training and teaching of children attending nursery schools and infants' departments* (Hadow, 1933). The report yields some significant indicators of early education policy as we know it today. For example, the suggestions that infant schools should be separate from primary schools (Hadow, 1933, p 176) and that laborious record keeping should be minimal (p 176), are both areas considered in recent times by Dame Clare Tickell (2011) in the Early Years Foundation Stage review.

Progress or much of the same?

The Hadow report of 1933 alludes to many of the key themes that are present in today's early education policy. These can be clearly identified through a simple comparison between the Hadow 1933 report *Infant and Nursery Schools* and more recent reports such as Frank Field's (2010) report into child poverty in England:

> *The treatment of children in the earliest years of life ... is of utmost importance if later emotional development is to be satisfactory.*
>
> (Hadow, 1933, p 179)

> *Early years (age zero to three in particular) are crucial and interventions early in a child's life are most effective in improving outcomes and life chances.*
>
> (Field, 2010, p 6)

Dame Clare Tickell published her recommendations in 2011 from a review of the Early Years Foundation Stage curriculum that came into force in September 2008 (Tickell, 2011). The

Tickell Review clearly acknowledged the importance of 'child-initiated' activities, a concept that was mirrored in the Hadow report (1933):

> oral lessons should be short and closely related to the child's practical interests.
>
> (Hadow, 1933, p 182)

> When working with young children, the exchange between adults and children should be fluid, moving interchangeably between activities initiated by children and adult responses helps build the child's learning and understanding.
>
> (Tickell, 2011, p 29)

One might be concerned that comparisons can be drawn between reports made in 1933 and those that have been compiled in more recent years; perhaps recommendations have not been fully integrated into policy for almost 80 years. When Graham Allen (2011) published his recommendations in *Early Intervention: The Next Steps*, to the coalition government in 2011, he reinforced Dame Clare Tickell's recommendation for *an integrated, professional approach that is designed to benefit all children, particularly the most vulnerable* (Tickell, 2011, p 49). This recommendation should not have come as a surprise: a united and cohesive approach to improving the educational and well-being outcomes for young children was considered in a similar recommendation made in Hadow's report (1933):

> effective cooperation between parents, teachers, doctors and school nurses has resulted in a marked improvement alike in the health and cleanliness of the children and urges that such cooperation should continue.
>
> (Hadow, 1933, p 176)

Graham Allen recently made a similar recommendation in his review of early intervention in the lives of our youngest children and those families who are classed by the government as being 'in need' according to the index of deprivation (English Indices of Deprivation, 2010). Allen proposed that the coalition support the *proper co-ordination of the machinery of government to put Early Intervention at the heart of departmental strategies* particularly in an effort to *raise educational achievement and ... support parents* (Allen, 2011, p xviii).

From just a brief comparison of early parliamentary debates and recommendations made by all the reports mentioned above and those which have been recently published such as Frank Field's (2010) review into poverty, Graham Allen's (2011) review into early intervention and Claire Tickell's (2011) review of the Early Years Foundation Stage, we can see that intervention in the early education and healthcare of young children has been seen consistently to be the vital element to successful and long-term outcomes.

However, when I read the parliamentary debates of the 1900s and then move to the increasing number of reviews carried out by the coalition government, I am less and less convinced that we have progressed the debate. Obviously schools have improved, the buildings have increased in number and training for our educators has become standardised and reflective of a profession and education has extended to all the population, with increases in statutory schooling. But early childhood education and care is still restricted for many, the quality remains variable and the workforce has yet to gain statutory professional status.

Critical questions

» *Critically compare the Field, Allen and Tickell reviews. Are these new recommendations or versions of something similar that have been before?*

» *It has been said that the youngest children of our society will become the answer to economic growth. Consider this as a political idea. What is your understanding of the underlying aims of new early years policy?*

The status of educational professionals in the 1900s

Significantly for early education policy as it stands today, the House of Commons discussion of 13 March 1918 included the status and conditions of work for teachers, a topic that is still vehemently debated today.

> *We want, for instance, surely a real improvement and development in the status, the salaries, and the conditions of work of the teachers of this country.*
>
> (Education Bill, 1918)

The teaching profession has become more robust throughout the past 100 years, and indeed is regarded by most as a respected and rewarding profession to be a part of. It has still been over 100 years from some of the first debates around the professionalisation of teachers to actually being seen as a profession in its own right. There is also a whole host of ongoing current debates and more modern concerns surrounding teaching being truly a professional career (Hargreaves et al, 2006).

Critical questions

» *Why does the professionalisation of teaching and early years matter?*

» *Critically compare the professionalisation of another sector (such as nursing) with that of early years.*

The Education Act 1944

The Education Act (1944) brought together all previous legislation and set the minimum standard for the structure of primary and secondary education in England. The Act also provided a duty on local education authorities to provide primary and secondary education separately:

> *It shall be the duty of every local education authority to secure that there shall be available for their area sufficient schools*
>
> *(a) for providing primary education, that is to say, full time education suitable to the requirements of junior pupils; and*
>
> *(b) for providing secondary education, that is to say, fulltime education suitable to the requirements of senior pupils.*
>
> (Education Act, 1944, 8–1)

The 1944 Education Act (C31) gave local education authorities the duty of making provision for children below the age of five. This was to be done using existing nursery classes within primary schools, or through the creation of new 'nursery schools' (Education Act, 1944, C31). Nursery schools were not the ideal solution for everyone: there were those who believed that to place young children into nursery schools at such a young age would undermine the wholesome and desirable learning environment of the home.

> it is no part of the Government's policy in promoting this Measure to supplant the home ... Family life is the healthiest cell in the body politic. It is the Government's desire that that family life shall be encouraged, and we hope to try and help children both in their physical, moral and religious development. I think it will be seen that we are trying to do our best towards this end and to fortify and buttress the influence of the family.
>
> (HC Deb, 19 January 1944, vol 396, CC207-322207)

Education en masse

The developed world has a long history of standardised testing in their homogenised curricula that is imparted to the children of each country, year on year by disempowered teachers, described by Kliebard (1987) as a *social efficiency movement*. The more children you can place into one classroom led by one teacher, the cheaper mass education will be. It is with resignation that I read current debates, articles and draft legislation leaning towards yet another *social efficiency movement* within early years care with the misguided suggestion that decreasing the staffing ratios for the care of young children will inevitably lead to cheaper childcare fees for parents and in turn, more parents returning to paid employment (McGurk, Mooney et al, 1995).

> This was supported by views expressed by private nursery staff. Staff expressed the view that more relaxed adult:child ratios would result in fewer interactions with children ... Staff expressed the view that relaxed adult:child ratios would not only result in fewer adult:child interactions but also the type of activities on offer to the children would change. Staff predicted that long-term changes in adult:child ratios would result in one-to-one interactions between children and staff being replaced by group activities. Staff would spend more time on supervision and less time interacting with the children. Relaxed ratios would reduce the opportunities for spontaneous activities and fewer creative, messy, art type activities would be available to the children.
>
> (Munton, Mooney et al, 2002, p 149)

Despite the overwhelming evidence to suggest that large class and childcare sizes are ineffective as methods for teaching and quality care (Munton, Mooney et al, 2002), government fails to see past the pound signs. Moving more children into the schools system may encourage more women into employment and cheaper early years care may encourage parents to place their children into mass educational facilities, but in the long term the potential damage to children will reverberate in the lines of unskilled and poorly educated adults of tomorrow.

> Public opposition to her plans has been overwhelming. The government's own advisor on childcare professor Cathy Nutbrown has said and I quote 'makes no sense at all' ... today the minister said that all of the evidence demonstrates that

what she's doing is right, who supports the proposals that she is making. Isn't this just another episode of bad policy making by the education secretary? And now we have a childcare policy rejected by parents, rejected by nursery providers and rejected by the governments own experts.

(Stephen Twigg, Shadow Education Secretary, Commons Debate, ITN, 2013)

The Early Years Foundation Stage

It was in 2001 that the government commissioned the creation of a framework that supported the very youngest children, from birth to three years of age. Designed as a result of the work of Lesley Abbott from Manchester Metropolitan University, the information and guidance pack would become the building blocks for today's statutory curriculum, the Early Years Foundation Stage (EYFS) (Table 1.1).

Table 1.1 *Birth-to-three curriculum (pre-EYFS)* (David and Britain, 2003)

Aspect	Component 1	Component 2	Component 3	Component 4
A strong Child	Me, myself and I	Being acknowledged and affirmed	Developing self-assurance	A sense of belonging
A skilful communicator	Being together	Finding a voice	Listening and responding	Making meaning
A competent learner	Making connections	Being imaginative	Being creative	Representing
A healthy child	Emotional wellbeing	Growing and developing	Keeping safe	Healthy choices

Critical questions

»   *Can you see similarities between the birth-to-three framework and the current EYFS curriculum?*

»   *The current EYFS has evolved from earlier policies and curricula. Consider which policies have led to a statutory curriculum for babies and young children.*

»   *If something evolves and is reviewed, like the EYFS, can it ever really be new or is it simply a reflection of new governments and new policies in wider society?*

The EYFS framework is a statutory document introduced as part of the British National Curriculum in 2008, which without specified exemption all early years settings and schools with fewer than five children must follow. The original EYFS document set out a detailed curriculum framework bringing together the Birth–3 Matters documentation and the Curriculum Guidance for the Foundation Stage.

By making the pre-school curriculum statutory, the state attempted to bridge the perceived gap between early years education and school-based education. There is a myriad of motives for such intense educational policy-making. Wood (2004) postulates that

> national education policies are also manifestations of global policy paradigms which may reflect similar issues, for example increasing economic competitiveness through developing a high-skills, knowledge based economy; improving levels of literacy and numeracy, responding to social and demographic shifts and to transformations in education and work through information and communication technologies.
>
> (Wood, 2004, p 3)

With EYFS governments began to micromanage early years. One need only take a look at Michael Gove's speeches to ascertain exactly why the early years sector continues to undergo such huge policy shifts:

> **What does it mean to be educated?**
>
> We've introduced a screening check at the age of 6 to make sure children are recognizing and blending letter sounds to read words fluently. It's designed to help identify those who may have reading difficulties and ensure they are supported in their reading ... We are introducing a basic test of competence in spelling, punctuation and grammar at the end of primary school ... Thanks to the work of Ian Livingstone, the British Computer Society and gifted teachers across the country excitement – and innovation – are returning to one of the most important – and testing – intellectual disciplines in modern education ... Technology will change our lives in ways we cannot anticipate in the years to come, and it will certainly transform teaching.
>
> (Michael Gove, Education Secretary, Speech, 9 May 2013)

Producing a curriculum designed to improve the outcomes of babies by the time they reach adulthood may be seen as laudable. However, without the high standard of graduates to deliver such a curriculum, one might be excused for believing it is a doomed system of educational reforms from the start. The curriculum emerged before the early years teachers to deliver it.

Pre-coalition 1997–2010

According to the Children's Workforce Development Council, Early Years Professional Status (EYPS) was the 'Gold Standard' of training for those leading practice as a graduate in the EYFS (CWDC, 2009; Teaching Agency, 2012). As part of the Labour government's (1997–2010) Ten Year Childcare Strategy (HM Treasury, 2004) that aimed in part to improve the education and childcare of nursery children, a number of enterprising and ambitious plans were announced alongside the pre-budget report of 2004. Significantly for those employed within the early years sector this meant that they would see an increase in the number of three- to four-year-olds receiving up to 15 hours of free childcare and education (HM

Treasury, 2004). This, along with the supplement of £125 million from 2006 towards assisting local authorities with increasing the number of childcare places available locally, meant that early years training became more affordable and often entirely subsidised (HM Treasury, 2004).

The Ten Year Childcare Strategy states that it aimed to *improve outcomes for children* (HM Treasury, 2004, p 31) and *engage the most disadvantaged families* (HM Treasury, 2004, p 37). One of the ways suggested to meet these goals was to create a new and innovative professional role within the early years sector. In 2006 the Early Years Professional Status training was piloted by a group of higher education institutions and private training providers (CWDC, 2006). By 2011 more than 8,500 Early Years Professionals had been trained (CWDC, 2011) and in excess of £55 million had been spent on funding the training and a variety of costs to employers for releasing staff members from their setting. The funding came first through the Transformation Fund between 2006 and 2008 and then from the Graduate Leader Fund from 2008 to 2011. From 2011 funding came through the Early Intervention Grant (DfE, 2011a).

The Early Years Professional and their status

Following on from years of debates as to what the most effective method of raising the long-term educational, social and economic outcomes for children might be, Labour's ten-year plan began a new and very ambitious strategy to use the improvement of child development and early education as the most cost-effective approach to achieving long-term positive outcomes for children and families (DCSF, 2009b), rather than attempting the remedial and counteractive methods of intervention later in life (Carneiro and Heckman, 2003; Field, 2010).

In addition to a change in childcare provision Labour launched the Sure Start strategy which was aimed at disadvantaged families with children under three (Moss, 1999).

Moss (1999) and Lumsden (2012) argue that prior to 1997, when the New Labour government came to power, there was not a consistent approach towards the unification and integration of all the services available to families with young children (Moss, 1999, p 230), and that rather than 'reformation' the government should have been more ambitious and completely transformed the early years sector and with it improved the long-term outcomes for disadvantaged children and their families (Moss, 1999, p 231).

Echoed in the policy commitments of the current coalition government that has seen the Chancellor, George Osborne, announce that they will double the funding available for two-year-olds to access free early education places (HC, 29 November 2011), New Labour, like the current coalition government, also faced a number of problems regarding the implementation of their childcare strategy, not least how to generate the places for all of the three- to four-year-olds who would be entitled to free nursery places (*Nursery World*, 2011) and securing all of the highly qualified staff who would care and educate these children. In an attempt to support early years settings in the expansion of their provision, Labour pledged £305 million towards *developing, attracting and retaining Early Years Professionals* (DCSF, 2009c) and a further £642 million to *support settings to make adjustments to the flexibility of their settings to increase access for all children and improve the quality of provision* (DCSF

2009d). This was the first time that any government had pledged such a high level of funding to the improvement of the early years sector.

As it stands today, the coalition have held steadfast to the funding of free places for two- and three-year-olds but not the continuation of the EYPS.

Although the coalition have removed all targets since taking office, initially Labour, in partnership with the Children's Workforce Development Council (CWDC), aimed to have *an Early Years Professional in every full day-care setting by 2015* and *to raise the qualification levels of the sector to level 3 or higher* (HC CM Select, 2007).

It was this particular policy aim that has generated over 12,000 Early Years Professionals since 2006 (Teather, 2011). When the coalition took office, they stated that, rather than place an Early Years Professional in every setting by 2015, their goal is to place an Early Years Professional into settings where there are high levels of disadvantage (DfE, 2012; appendix 3), thus attempting to ensure that the highest qualified professionals are working with the most disadvantaged children; in keeping with over 100 years of government debate and independent research to employ *A highly skilled early years workforce is critical if we are to combat inequality, help tackle poverty and improve the life chances of the most disadvantaged children* (DfE, 2011).

The Early Years Professional as it then was, was assessed against 39 standards. These standards have been reviewed and implement from September 2012 (*Nursery World*, 16 January 2012; DfE, 2012). When, in 2011, CWDC began the tendering process for new contracts to deliver the EYPS training, they also announced a change to the method of training and the pathways that candidates would take. As Lumsden (2012) points out, in 2006 and in 2011, the design and implementation of the Early Years Professional Status training *was not only formal recognition of the importance of a qualified workforce in the early years at a graduate level but intervention at a government level in the professions* (Lumsden, 2012, p 10). 2013 sees implementation of the coalition's version of this graduate status, with a third set of 'Early Years Teaching Standards' designed to bring Early Years Professionals in line with qualified teachers. Three years; three sets of standards; six cohorts of professionals assessed against three sets of standards; and myriad confused employers and head teachers left wondering who they should be employing and what they should be paying. Align this to three agencies with responsibility for early childhood education and care (ECEC) in less than a year and uncertainty for the future of the professional is exacerbated. In April 2012 the Teaching Agency, an executive arm of the Department for Education, took over ECEC from the Children's Workforce Development Council. In April 2013 the National College for Teaching and Leadership was formed following the merger of the Teaching Agency and the National College of School Leadership.

Government impact on early education practice was slow and the sector still struggled to compete professionally alongside teachers (*Nursery World*, 2011). When the coalition came to power, only a fraction of previous funding was announced for the continuation of Early Years Professional training, with a deadline currently standing at 2013.

The government announced in 2013 that the EYPS would be replaced, though without any major change, to become the Early Years Teacher Status, aligned further to the teaching profession.

There is an argument that suggests that Early Years Professionals have had a significant impact on practice in early education (Lumsden, 2012; Hadfield, Jopling et al, 2011) and indeed on the professionalisation of the sector as a whole; however, without further research and a continuation of the training, the full impact of the Early Years Professional might never be known.

CASE STUDY

Sharon's story

I wanted to encourage my team to up skill and move towards being a graduate. I had spent over 30 years training people in the civil service and I knew the importance of a graduate education. The difference it can make on practice day to day is enormous. Parents and children could see the difference in my nursery as soon as we started training. No one could have predicted the impact that the training could have had, we were in an environment where we were taught to think outside of the policies that were 'done' to us and were top down. We would read a magazine article or we would receive a letter from the local authority explaining yet another new early years policy that we had to implement. Before the training we just set about implementing the change. Now we were questioning it and wondering why they wanted to make the change. It wasn't that we were not going to do it, it's just we wanted to understand the reasons behind new curriculum or new training. We were learning to be critical thinkers and in turn we were teaching the children to be critical thinkers too.

(Sharon, Nursery Manager and Early Years Professional, 2012)

The circles of time

The history of early education in England is long and repetitive, different governments making very similar recommendations and continuing pilot initiatives culminating in new policy and statutory requirements placed on local authorities; an example of this can be seen in the review of the Early Years Foundation Stage (EYFS) curriculum by Dame Claire Tickell (2011).

In 2006, the Childcare Act placed specific onus on local authorities to provide childcare places where the Early Years Foundation Stage is offered. The EYFS amalgamated the *Curriculum Guidance for the Foundation Stage* (DFEE, 2000), *Birth to Three Matters* (DfES, 2002) and the *National Standards for Under Eights Day Care and Child-minding* (DfES, 2003).

It was the unification of all of these previous documents, combined with the ongoing desire to improve outcomes for young children that set England on a course that resulted in the creation of a new, graduate level professional (Hevey, Lumsden and Moxon, 2007). This new and innovative role can be seen in terms of all other professions as an integrated approach to Children's Services and one that *occupies a new professional space with flexible borders located at the intersection of education, health and social care* (Lumsden, 2012, p 6). Lumsden clarifies the distinctiveness of the Early Years Professionals role further (see Figure 1.3) by highlighting just how the Early Years Professional can act as the source of dramatic, long term holistic change for young children and their families.

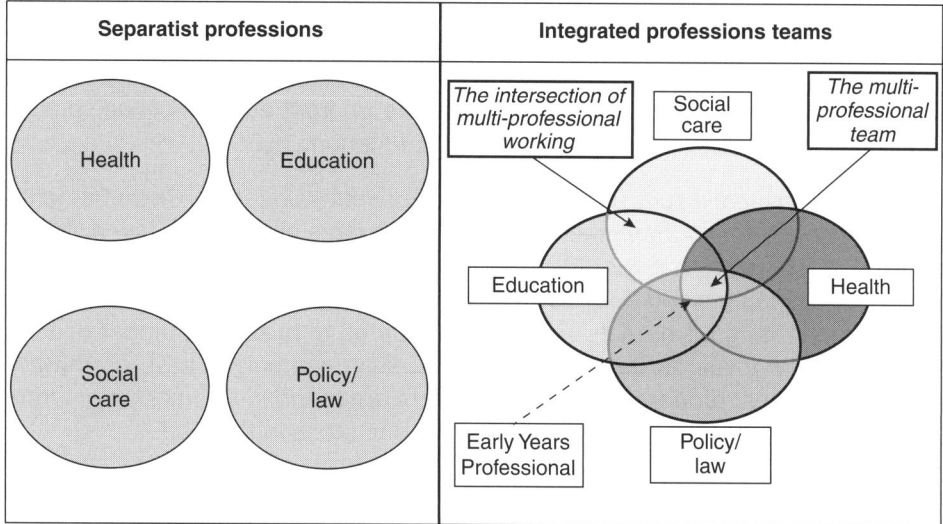

Separatist professions	Integrated professions teams

Figure 1.3 *Separate and integrated professions in Children's Services* (Lumsden, 2012, p 19)

The ingenuity of the Early Years Professional as a tool in the advancement of early years practice and the improvement in the quality of practice, can be recognised even in the early stages of the evaluation of the profession: *The EYPS programme has had a substantive impact on practitioners' ability to effect change. The most positive responses were in terms of identifying areas of effective change and communicating these to other staff in the setting* (Hadfield et al, 2010, p 35)

Unfortunately, the progress that Early Years Professionals have made since the very first undertook the training in 2006, has been stained with misgivings and confusion, with the training initially being sold to the workforce as being equivalent to Qualified Teacher Status (QTS) without attracting any of the pay and conditions afforded to QTS graduates (Lumsden, 2010, p 174). As far back as 2008, clarification was sought on numerous fronts to explicate the role and status of the Early Years Professional.

It's a (wo)man's world

The gender balance of the early years sector has consistently favoured women, having far more women than men employed to work with young children. This is evidenced when one considers the findings of the interim report produced by Hadfield et al (2010) at the request of the devolved CWDC:

> *a composite snapshot, based on information on the practitioners who have achieved EYPS and using the most popular indices, a typical practitioner would be white British (87 per cent), female (98 per cent), aged between 36–45 (31 per cent), established in her career (34 per cent 8–15 yrs. experience).*
>
> (Hadfield et al, 2010, p 9)

Early years education has been predominantly a female profession for over a century. In 1905 it was female inspectors who were commissioned by the Board of Education *'in an inquiry relative to the age of admission of infants to Public Elementary Schools and the curriculum suitable for very young children'* to investigate the appropriateness of the schools where young children attended (Great Britain: Board of Education, 1905).

In *Men in the Nursery Revisited: Issues of Male Workers and Professionalism*, Claire Cameron (2007, p 4) describes the female-dominated early years workforce as *extreme*. Owen (2004, cited in Cameron, 2007) states that the 2001 UK census revealed that only a little over 2 per cent of the entire childcare workforce (266,700) were male. There have been numerous campaigns and targets from governments who have attempted to raise the number of male workers in early years; however, as Cameron highlights, such campaigns have not always been successful –*the highest proportions of male workers are found in Denmark* (Cameron, 2007, p 5) – with trends in many countries actually mirroring those in England.

Perhaps the most significant aspect of Claire Cameron's research is that she identifies how European countries have made a success of their various advertising campaigns and efforts to recruit men into the early years sector, through what she terms *professionalisation in terms of extensive training, a unique body of knowledge and a distinctive occupational identity* (Jenson and Hansen, 2003 cited in Cameron, 2007).

Critical reflections

Key findings

» Intervening in the early education of children below state school age has been seen as a positive notion for over 100 years.

» Children who attend high quality nursery settings have improved health, well-being and long-term educational success.

» Funding for early education from central government has been inconsistent, ranging from very minimal support to hundreds of millions of pounds.

» The Early Years Professional is not a new vocation but struggles to be recognised as a professional status similar to teachers.

» The status of teachers has been a key aspect of government policy and has been a topic of debate in Westminster for over 100 years.

» The early years sector remains disconnected from education policy as a whole.

» 98 per cent of Early Years Professionals are female, men being attracted as professionalisation is strengthened.

It would appear that professionalising the early years workforce by means of education alone has proved unsuccessful in the main, despite £555 million being spent on raising qualifications; Early Years Professionals are still underpaid and unrecognised in comparison to those with QTS (Hadfield et al, 2010). This was a concern long before the conception of the Early Years Professional. Angela Anning (1991) argues that in some respects the very nature of what it means to be an employee within the early years sector, and a woman, has compounded the failure of governments to succeed in making the early years a recognised profession:

> to some degree it must be acknowledged that early years practitioners themselves have been to blame. They have been reluctant to articulate their professional knowledge. Early years cliques have tended to feed on their own shared understanding.
>
> (p 46)

As the history of early education policy is unpicked, it become a self-evident that governments in general are less than clear as to how to proceed in the best interests of the youngest children. In addition, and regrettably, within some policies it appears that the success, and by default, the failure, of society as a whole is somehow linked to the success, or failure, of children before they reach statutory school age:

> These results also show that children in the lowest achieving fifth in terms of their learning and development at the end of the Early Years Foundation Stage (EYFS) are six times more likely to be in the lowest fifth at Key Stage 1. Children's experiences in their early years provide the essential foundations for both healthy development and their achievement through school ... These clear links illustrate why it is important to ensure that children's early experiences equip them with the skills that they need for life – a fact underlined recently by the Frank Field review on poverty and life chances and the Graham Allen review of early intervention.
>
> (Tickell, 2011, p 8)

Education is always a key political struggle and is one of the main driving forces behind much of the old and new policy as governments come and go. Since Labour began to focus heavily on the importance of very early education in the ground-breaking ten-year strategy and other innovative plans, the early education of children from birth to five has remained a significant element of the coalition government's agenda.

In the past 12 months five major reviews have taken place. Collectively, these form the largest review of early childhood education for a hundred years. What makes them so significant is that early childhood has been seen in isolation from compulsory education, but with an underpinning recognition that what happens in the early years has a significant impact on later years; therefore getting well-trained professionals to work with children under five is paramount and essential.

The professionalisation of teaching, which itself has almost 75 per cent bias towards female teachers (DfE 2012), has still not been resolved over a hundred years after it began; it is crucial that the professionalisation of the early years sector, and the professionals within that sector, are not disregarded less than ten years into the creation of this new profession. The essential differences between the EYPS programme delivered from 2006–11, the EYPS programmes run between 2012–13 and the EYTS programmes run from September 2013 are set out in Table 1.2.

The essential differences between the EYPS programme delivered from 2006–11, the EYPS programmes run between 2012–13 and the EYTS programmes run from Sept 13 are set out in the table below:

Table 1.2 *Adapted from www.education.gov.uk/childrenandyoungpeople/earlylearningandchild-care/delivery/b00201345/graduate-leaders/eyps/information [accessed 2 May 2012]*

Change	EYPS in 2006–11	EYPS in 2012–13	EYTS in 2013 onwards
EYP Standards	All candidates were assessed using the 2006 EYPS Standards	No change. A review of the EYPS standards was completed in 2012. This took account of emerging policy and government reviews: in particular *Supporting Families in the Foundation Years* and the review of Early Years Foundation Stage (EYFS). The review aimed to produce a revised set of EYPS standards for implementation by training providers delivering the EYPS by September 2012.	All changed. A review of the EYPS standards is under way. The review seeks to shape the old standards to fit a similar format to those of the general primary and secondary teaching standards, moving early years teaching into the initial teacher training category of professionalization.
Funding sources	CWDC had funding monopoly	The Teaching Agency will provide a funding allocation to all training providers. In addition to this, training providers will be encouraged to develop new self-funding sources (eg individuals, employers, local authorities and corporate sponsors).Training providers will be able to charge fees to candidates not covered by Teaching Agency funding.	The Teaching Agency will provide a funding allocation to all training providers. In addition to this, training providers will be encouraged to develop new self-funding sources (eg individuals, employers, local authorities and corporate sponsors).Training providers will be able to charge fees to candidates not covered by Teaching Agency funding.
Pathways	Five pathways: • Validation (3 months) • Short (6 months) • Long (15 months) • Full (12 months) • ECSD (12-20 months)	Four pathways: • Graduate Practitioner Pathway (GPP, 6 months) • Undergraduate Practitioner Pathway (UPP, 12 months) • Graduate Entry Pathway (GEP, 12 months) • Undergraduate Entry Pathway (UEP, 24 months).	Four pathways: • Graduate Practitioner Pathway (GPP) • Undergraduate Practitioner Pathway (UPP) • Graduate Entry Pathway (GEP) • Undergraduate Entry Pathway (UEP)
Minimum intakes	No minimum intakes	Minimum capacity set for prime organisations.	Minimum capacity set for prime organisations.
GCSE requirements	GCSE English and maths was required on completion.	GCSE English and maths will be required on entry.	GCSE English, Science and Maths will be required on entry, in line with general teaching entry requirements.

Table 1.2 (cont.)

Change	EYPS in 2006–11	EYPS in 2012–13	EYTS in 2013 onwards
Fitness requirement	Candidates required to be 'physically and mentally fit to work as an EYP'.	There will be no fitness requirement but guidance will be provided.	There will be no fitness requirement but guidance will be provided.
Overseas candidates	Candidates were required to be able to 'live and work in the UK'.	Candidates must have the right to work in the UK for at least the duration of their pathway.	Candidates must have the right to work in the UK for at least the duration of their pathway. Candidates must demonstrate they are able to read effectively and communicate clearly in English.
Funding amounts	There was a standard funding amount for each pathway place.	Funding amounts have been reduced in recognition of market conditions and efficiency gains required by government. A component of funding will be dedicated to degree top-up on the UPP.	There is a standard funding amount for each pathway place in line with teacher education.
Method of procurement	Training providers were procured through an open tender.	Contractors procured through the National College's collaborative framework agreement.	Contractors procured through the National College's collaborative framework agreement.
Deferral	Candidates allowed to defer for an unspecified duration.	Contractors will be required to employ formal procedures and stringent monitoring of deferral. Deferral will be time limited and at candidates' formal request.	Contractors will be required to employ formal procedures and stringent monitoring of deferral. Deferral will be time limited and at candidates' formal request.
Outcomes	Candidates that received a 'not met' outcome were able to start a pathway with full funding an unlimited amount of times.	Candidates that receive a 'not met' will be unable to receive funding to undertake a pathway again but will be able to self-fund.	Candidates that receive a 'not met' will be unable to receive funding to undertake a pathway again but will be able to self-fund.
Recruitment	Universal within settings parameters.	Focus on disadvantage and underrepresented groups across all settings.	Focus on disadvantage and underrepresented groups across all settings.
Selection criteria	None	Required to enable recruitment to funded places to meet policy needs.	

Education policy timeline

Table 1.3 *UK education timeline*
www.educationengland.org.uk

1902 *Education Act 1902*: the 'Balfour Act' established a system of secondary education integrating higher grade elementary schools and fee-paying secondary schools; abolished school boards and established local education authorities (LEAs).	1904 Secondary Regulations: introduced a subject-based curriculum.
1905 Board of Education report by women inspectors on the admission of infants to public elementary schools.	1906 *Education (Provision of Meals) Act 1906*: allowed LEAs to provide meals for undernourished elementary school children.
1906 Dyke Report *Questions Affecting Higher Elementary Schools* (Board of Education Consultative Committee): made recommendations regarding the role, staffing and curriculum of higher elementary schools.	1907 Elementary Code: improved quality and aims of elementary education.
1907 *Education (Administrative Provisions) Act 1907*: among other things, this Act introduced a scholarship/ free place system for secondary education and required LEAs to provide medical inspections of elementary school children.	1908 Acland Report *School Attendance of Children Below the Age of Five* (Board of Education Consultative Committee): made recommendations regarding the provision and content of nursery school education.
1909 Acland Report *Attendance, Compulsory or Otherwise, at Continuation Schools* (Board of Education Consultative Committee): argued that LEAs should be empowered to require under 17s to participate in some form of post-elementary education.	1910 *Education (Choice of Employment) Act*: foundation of careers service.
1911 Acland Report *Examinations in Secondary Schools* (Board of Education Consultative Committee): this was the Consultative Committee's second report on exams (the first – not online – was published in 1904). It argued that the existing system needed simplifying.	1913 Acland Report *Practical Work in Secondary Schools* (Board of Education Consultative Committee): argued that secondary schools should provide teaching in 'some branches of Educational Handwork', and should make them an integral part of the curriculum.
1914 *Education (Provision of Meals) Act 1914*: extended the powers of local education authorities to provide meals for undernourished elementary school children.	1917 Lewis Report: proposed school leaving age of 14 with no exemptions, followed by attendance for at least 8 hours a week or 320 hours a year at day continuation classes up to age 18.
1918 *Education Act 1918* (Fisher): wide-ranging Act extending education provision in line with recommendations of 1917 Lewis Report.	1919 Burnham Committee: established to decide on teachers' pay.
1921 *Education Act 1921*: consolidated all previous laws relating to education and raised school leaving age to 14.	1921 Newbolt Report *The Teaching of English in England*.
1923 Hadow Report *The Differentiation of the Curriculum for Boys and Girls Respectively in Secondary Schools*.	1923 Secondary education for all became Labour Party policy.

Table 1.3 *(cont.)*

1926 Hadow Report *The Education of the Adolescent*: proposed junior and senior schools with transfer at age 11, secondary education for all, and increase in school leaving age to.	1931 Hadow Report *The Primary School*: set out the committee's vision of primary education.
1933 Hadow Report *Infant and Nursery Schools*: the last of the six Hadow Reports.	1936 *Education Act 1936*: raised school leaving age to 15 and authorised building grants of up to 75 per cent for new denominational 'Special Agreement' senior schools.
1937 *Factories Act 1937* wide-ranging Act including limitations on the employment of young people in hazardous environments.	1941 Board of Education Green Paper *Education after the War*.
1941 Rab Butler (Conservative) appointed President of the Board of Education.	1943 Norwood Report *Curriculum and Examinations in Secondary Schools*: backed the tripartite system recommended by the 1938 Spens Report.
1943 White Paper *Educational Reconstruction*: formed the basis of the 1944 Education Act.	1946 Free milk provided for all pupils.
1947 Clarke Report *School and Life*: the first report of the newly-created Central Advisory Council for Education (England) was an inquiry into the transition from school to independent life.	1947 School leaving age rose to 15 and came into effect.
1948 *Nurseries and Child-Minders Regulation Act 1948* laid down rules for the regulation and inspection of child minders.	1948 Clarke Report *Out of School*: the second report of the Central Advisory Council for Education (England) looked at facilities for out-of-school activities.
1951 General Certificate of Education (GCE) introduced.	1957 'Leicestershire experiment' began: reorganisation of schools.
1958 Carr Report: employers overwhelmingly opposed to vocational instruction provided by schools.	1958 White Paper *Secondary Education for All: A New Drive*.
1959 Crowther Report *15–18*: recommended raising the school leaving age to 16 and the provision of further education for 15–18 year olds, questioned the value of day release provision for apprenticeships.	1960 Beloe Report *Secondary School Examinations other than the GCE*: the report of a Committee appointed by the Secondary School Examinations Council which led to the introduction of the Certificate of Secondary Education (CSE) in 1965.
1962 *Education Act 1962*: required LEAs to provide students with grants for living costs and tuition fees; placed legal obligation on parents to ensure that children received a suitable education at school or otherwise – failure to comply could result in prosecution; made LEAs legally responsible for ensuring that pupils attended school.	1964 *Education Act 1964* the 'Boyle Act' allowed the creation of middle schools
1967 Plowden Report *Children and their Primary Schools*: arguably the best known of all education reports, it promoted child-centred education and was much maligned by traditionalists.	1968 *Education Act 1968*: laid down rules about changing the character of a school (eg to comprehensive).

Table 1.3 *(cont.)*

1968 *Education (No.2) Act*: required polytechnics and other LEA colleges to have governing bodies.	1968 Middle schools: the first opened in Bradford and the West Riding of Yorkshire.
1971 *Education (Milk) Act 1971*: limited the provision of free milk in schools (and led to the jibe 'Thatcher, Thatcher, milk snatcher').	1973 School leaving age raised to 16.
1978 Waddell Report *School Examinations*: recommended a single exam at age 16 to replace the GCE O Level and CSE. (The first GCSE exams were taken in 1988).	1978–85 HMI surveys: in response to Plowden's suggestion that the quality of education in England should be reviewed every ten years, HMI produced, between 1978 and 1985, five major surveys covering the whole school age range. 1978 *Primary education in England* 1979 *Aspects of secondary education in England* 1982 *Education 5 to 9* 1983 *9-13 Middle Schools* 1985 *Education 8 to 12 in Combined and Middle Schools*
1986 General Certificate of Secondary Education (GCSE): common 16+ exam system replaced GCE O Level and CSE.	1987 *The National Curriculum 5–16*: the consultation document in which the government set out its plans for the introduction of the national curriculum and associated assessment procedures.
1990 Rumbold Report *Starting with Quality*: Committee of Inquiry report on the education of 3 and 4 year olds.	1994 Dearing Review *The National Curriculum and its Assessment: Final Report*: the Tories' National Curriculum and assessment arrangements were hopelessly complicated. Ron Dearing was called on to sort out the mess.
2000 City academies: David Blunkett announced the government's intention to create a network of academies – effectively private schools paid for by the state.	2003 Green Paper *Every Child Matters*: led to the 2004 Children Act
2004 *Five Year Strategy for Children and Learners*: formed the basis for the 2005 White Paper *Higher Standards, Better Schools for All*.	2006 *Childcare Act 2006* new rules relating to the provision, regulation and inspection of childcare.
2007 School leaving age: government announced its intention to raise the SLA to 18, possibly in 2013.	2007 *The Children's Plan*: ambitious plan for all future government policy relating to children, families and schools.
2008 *Education and Skills Act 2008* raised the education leaving age to 18; Key Stage 3 SATs effectively abolished.	2008 Academies: 51 opened in September.
2008 Tories' free schools policy announced by Michael Gove (shadow education secretary).	2008 IRPC Interim Report *Interim Report of the Independent Review of the Primary Curriculum*.
2009 Cambridge Primary Review *Towards a New Primary Curriculum* (interim reports): *Past and Present* and *The Future*.	2009 *Apprenticeships, Skills, Children and Learning Act 2009*: created a statutory framework for apprenticeships.

Table 1.3 (cont.)

2009 White Paper *Your Child, Your Schools, Our Future*: wide-ranging proposals including the removal of central government prescription of teaching methods and reduction in the use of private consultants to improve schools.	2010 *Academies Act 2010*: provided for massive and rapid expansion of academies.
2011 Tickell Report *The Early Years: Foundations for Life, Health and Learning*: made recommendations relating to the Early Years Foundation Stage.	2012 *Statutory Framework for the EYFS*: setting the standards for learning, development and care for children from birth to five.
2013 *EYFS Profile Handbook* published by the Standards and Testing Agency.	

2 Family structures, status and public policy

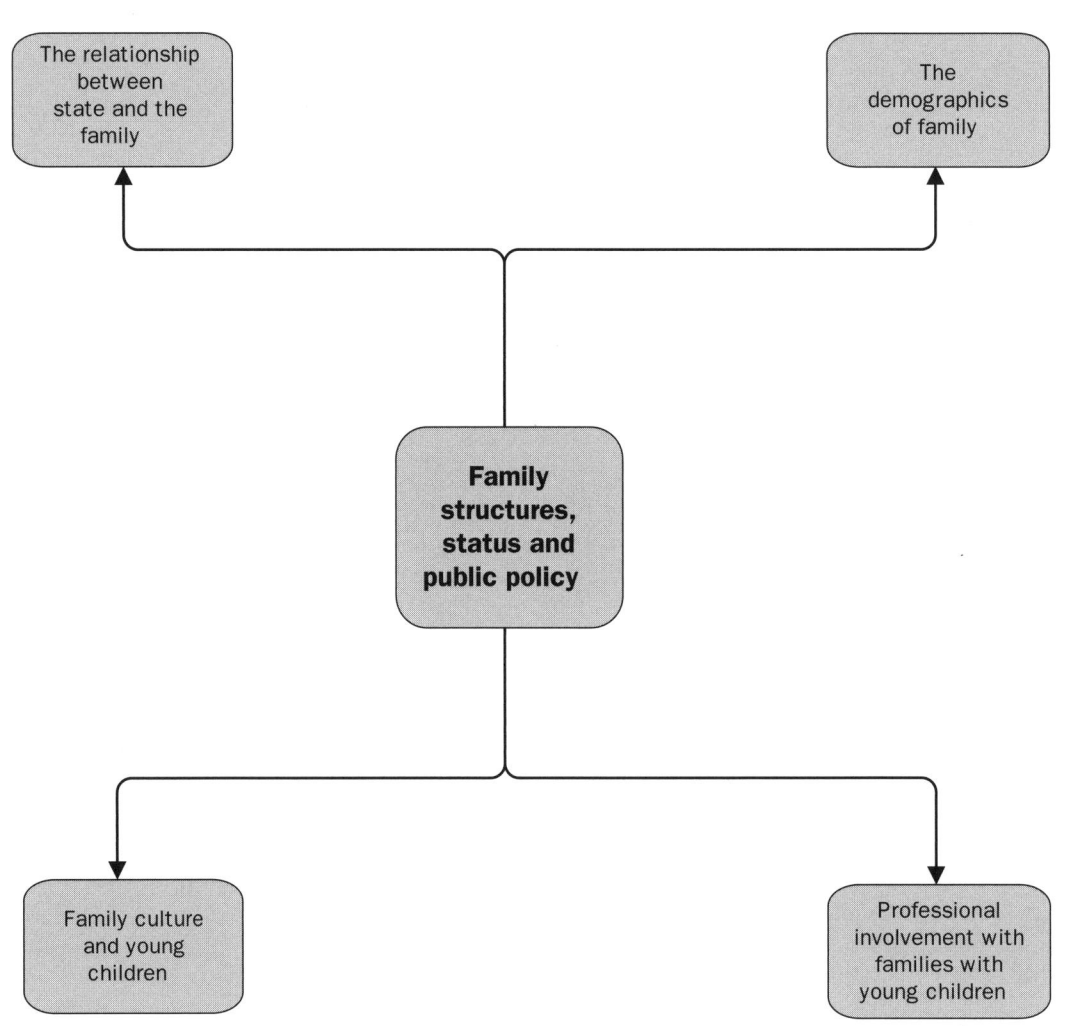

The relationship between state and the family

The demographics of family

Family structures, status and public policy

Family culture and young children

Professional involvement with families with young children

Introduction

Families come in all shapes and sizes. There are large extended families with multiple generations actively involved with each other on a daily basis and small nuclear families self-contained and distinct from their wider group of relations and many more besides. Whatever the dimensions and cultural norms of families the concept is intrinsically linked to child-rearing, almost universally seen as the right place for children to be born and brought up. Daniel and Ivatts (1998) emphasise that children are often invisible within the concept of family, highlighting the common notion of '*starting a family*' as a euphemism for having a baby. As the articles of children's rights become more prominent in our ideas of children and social constructs of childhood emerge in literature and research, children may no longer be invisible within families but they are certainly indivisible from them. The United Nations Convention on the Rights of the Child (UNCRC) sees family as the rightful place of children for their care, protection and developmental needs. The United Kingdom (UK) government, in common with many other countries, views the family as sacrosanct. Essentially it is a private entity where parents make choices for their children and take responsibility for them, where intervention by the state is limited and autonomy only overridden when children are at risk.

However, the state does have an influence on families through fiscal and economic policies and education and healthcare legislation as well as in many other ways. It is this aspect of family the chapter considers, exploring the interrelationship of influence and the drivers of change in family policy and the effect on young children. The discussion critically analyses how social and economic change in family structure and status has influenced or been influenced by the development of political ideology and policy manifestos. The chapter examines the demographics of early childhood in families in the UK and the status of young children in families in societies and diverse cultures. It considers the diverse roles played by professionals working with families with young children and how policy trends affect and change working practice.

The relationship between the state and the family

According to the UNCRC article 18,

> *Both parents share responsibility for bringing up their child and should always consider what is best for the child. Governments must support parents by giving them the help they need, especially if the child's parents work.*

The statement identifies a clear relationship between the state and families with children. It is simplistic in its interpretation, as inevitably it has to be, in that it implies two parents taking an active role in child-rearing. As we see later in the chapter this assumption is challenged by the changing demographics of family life. Most governments around the world have ratified the UNCRC (see Chapter 4, *The status and rights of young children as political and policy influencers*) which suggests that most governments take responsibility for supporting parents. The model of family life within many societies is a hierarchical, patriarchal and economic one where the family comprises a male head of the family whose role is to provide financially for the family, the breadwinner function, and a female carer of the breadwinner and nurturer of any children. This is a long-established model only recently challenged in some countries as concepts of equality and rights of individuals have become more dominant in political discourse.

Breadwinner model

The predominant feature of the breadwinner model is its focus on gainful employment. The family unit is expected to provide an adult working male who has an obligation, through selling his labour, to sustain his family and home. The breadwinner is 'king of his castle' and those in it are dependent on him for their welfare. State intervention is limited in such models and tends towards external affairs such as land or property disputes, compliance within the prevailing laws and collection of taxes rather than domestic matters of care and welfare. Thus women and children are deemed insignificant and lack influence on matters affecting their lives. This does not mean that women do not work; often they are the primary food producer and provider for their families. Women create and sustain homes and care for other family members' needs. In many societies this will include not only the male bread-winner and the young but also elderly relations. This model dominated UK society until late into the twentieth century. Even the advent of the British welfare state in 1945 held on to many of the facets described above. Gender differentials prevailed with benefits based on men as the primary earner and beneficiary of welfare. The focus on participation in full-time gainful employment as the major contributor to welfare entitlements dominated the welfare system in the UK. Entitlements were based on financial contributions made through the pay-roll system – National Insurance contributions as they are known. These contributions enti-tled the individual to certain benefits in specific circumstances during a working life and a pension on retirement. The benefits included allowances for dependants, these being wives and children. The entitlement for a wife was less than that for the male benefit recipient. A woman could earn her own independent benefits the same as a man if she worked full time. This was, of course, unlikely to be possible if the woman was in a family with children, as she would have the primary role of child carer and home maker. Indeed for many years (until 1977) married women who worked were able to pay the 'married woman's stamp' which was a reduced National Insurance contribution rate which lacked any entitlement to welfare benefits in case of sickness or unemployment and did not contribute to a state pension (HM Revenue and Customs, 2013). For many women on low pay and in part-time work this was seized on as a way to maximise income in the short term. However, it kept married women in an inferior position and maintained the notion of dependency on the main breadwinner, the husband. It also reinforced the idea of women's primary role as child carers and home makers whose work was subordinate to that of men. In the 'breadwinner' model of family, generation of income is of primary importance in the family and the state's role is largely an economic and fiscal one. The main aim of capitalist, industrialised countries, for example, is to generate investment and growth in economic activity to create employment and to use taxation, largely through employment, to service other government policies. Care and home making is predominantly seen as a private matter within the family and as such attracts less interest in political and policy terms (Finch, 2003).

> *By placing emphasis on paid work as opposed to care, the male was taken as the norm of the citizen – women and children, by definition were not full citizens and were therefore not entitled to social benefits.*
>
> (Finch, 2003, p 2)

The concept of the breadwinner model is still a common feature of social welfare states across Europe. However, the challenges created by equality and feminist agendas since the early 1970s have had an impact to a greater or lesser extent.

Critical question

» *In UK society there are changing models of family life. Reflect on your family relationships and analyse for examples of the breadwinner model in your immediate and wider family. From your experience critically evaluate the impact of the breadwinner model on your expectations of family life. Changes to family life, especially to the 'breadwinner' model, imply changing roles for mothers and fathers. How might an early childhood education and care professional support young children living in diverse family structures?*

Women, childcare and work

The progress of women's issues and the advent of equality and rights legislation and policies have created a shift in the relationship between state and family in many European countries, although the extent of the change is different across countries. The Nordic countries, such as Sweden and Denmark, have moved to a model of citizenship, and care has taken a dominant role in state welfare. These countries have high levels of state provision of good quality childcare offered to children from one year old. Women play an active economic role in society and family care and welfare is viewed as a shared responsibility of all parties, including the state. These societies have high expectations of women returning to work a year after childbirth. Paternity leave is well established; in Sweden 16 months is allowed for parental leave, and childcare costs are directly related to ability to pay and maintained at a low percentage of family income (see also Chapter 5, *Education and care for early learning and development*). In the southern countries of Europe, especially Italy, the picture is different. Here social welfare models are somewhat contradictory. While the equality and rights agendas have been articulated in state policy they are not backed up by facilitative provision. Care is still viewed as a private family matter within a context of wider family involvement. Women in Italy find it difficult to return to work without extensive intergenerational family support and if they do so it is with little protection of employment status and social support. Policy-making and provision are locally determined and there are wide discrepancies, but overall childcare is limited in the private and public sectors. For example, public childcare provision in the north of Italy may be as high as 20 per cent and in the south as low as 2 per cent of eligible children (Plantenga and Remery, 2009).

Such differentials reflect established cultural perspectives of societies on family and the care of children within it, which in turn are reinforced in political attitudes and debate and social policy initiatives. The incidence of informal childcare in the early years provides an indicator of family structure in European society. Figure 2.1 shows the percentage of families in selected countries using friends or extended family members to provide childcare for under two year-olds.

The three Nordic countries reflect the culture of working women and expectations of strong state support for mothers returning to work. Dependency on the wider family network is marginal as most women will be working, including grandmothers and female friends, who in many cultures are the prominent providers of informal childcare. A very different approach is reflected in Greece and the Netherlands where there is a strong tradition of grandparents caring for very young children at home. In Greece it is common for three generations of family to share a home, which can provide an immediate and convenient source of childcare. A high proportion of the population of the Netherlands lives in rural communities with extended

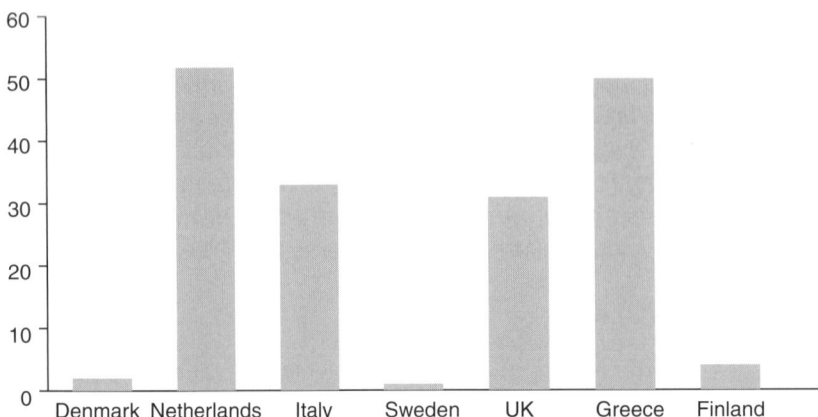

Figure 2.1 Percentage use of family or friends for childcare of under two year-olds
Source: Adapted from data in Plantenga and Remery (2009).

family connections close by. These demographic conditions, together with extended closure of childcare facilities during holiday periods, increase the dependency on family networks of care (Plantenga and Remery, 2009; Lloyd, 2009).

Critical question

» *Different notions of family childcare are evidenced above. Compare and contrast the different approaches and identify the strengths and weaknesses of these approaches, for the young child, the parents and the carers.*

Political agenda

Family constructs are influenced by political ideology and policy. If a government is particularly focused on labour market development, or views worklessness as an important problem to address, then childcare policy may take a quite different form from that of a government that is primarily concerned with participation and equality rights for women and children. The first imperative may be subsidised childcare to facilitate access to work with emphasis on availability and access rather than quality and standards. In contrast, childcare provided as a commitment to equality and rights is more likely to focus on the quality and nature of provision that facilitates a value-added experience for children in the family.

> *In the United Kingdom an estimated half of non-working parents said they would take up employment if they could obtain good-quality, affordable and reliable childcare.*
> (Plantenga and Remery, 2009, p 23)

The UK coalition government childcare policy flies in the face of these comments. The cost of childcare in the UK is higher than in most other countries in the European Union (EU). The coalition is in the throes of increasing ratios of children to staff for child-minders and is moving further towards a demand-led form of provision as in the Dutch model (see Chapter 5, *Education and care for early learning and development*). A pre-budget announcement in March 2013 indicated tax relief of up to £1200 per child per annum for childcare costs, further reinforcing the demand-led model. As discussed in Chapter 5, this approach is viewed as an attractive one, putting purchasing power in the hands of parents but it has serious flaws in demographic availability and quality. The relief is not available to families with a parent who remains at home and will not be introduced until 2015. From the first year of operation, all children under five will be eligible, and it is intended that the scheme will build up over time to include children under 12. To be eligible, families will have all parents in work, with each earning less than £150,000 a year, and will not already receive support through tax credits and later, Universal Credit (HM Revenue and Customs, 2013).

Welfare to work

In the UK between 1997 and 2010 a policy priority was social exclusion and the Labour government made a commitment to end child poverty in the UK by 2020. Family policy was targeted on those in poverty. Evidence demonstrates that participation in the labour market reduces the risk of poverty and that improved economic well-being of parents reduces child poverty and improves future outcomes for children. Therefore a main thrust of Labour policy was getting families working. To this end a series of policy initiatives were implemented including working family tax credits, Sure Start schemes, which included childcare, funding for Children's Centres in areas of disadvantage and the New Deal for Lone Parents. As women formed the significant majority of lone parents such an initiative sought to change the role of mothers from dependent carer and home maker to that of breadwinner. Similar programmes were being pursued in other countries, for example in the USA where the Personal Responsibility and Work Opportunity Reconciliation Act was launched in 1996 which sought to impose work requirement on lone parents. It was a compulsory programme that withdrew welfare if work was not obtained. Critics of the New Deal were fearful that rather than being a voluntary initiative as stated by government, it might become compulsory and add draconian measures such as those of the US programme. There were questions over the morality of the situation and how much pressure was put on lone mothers to become employed at any cost (McCulloch, 2006). However, for the first time here was a policy initiative that challenged the prevailing model of family life. From a dominant culture of benefit or absent-parent dependency, the aim was to facilitate independence and full participation in the family.

The family policy agenda of the Labour government was very wide. It had ambitions to address child poverty, improve parenting and create social inclusion. The aims were laudable if rather ambitious. The focus went beyond aspirations for structural change into the realms of culture, attitudes and beliefs. Family policy under Labour was built on a philosophy epitomised by a wealth of policy. Some may have missed the mark but nevertheless the strategy was coherent, if complex, and sought to establish a holistic approach. The coalition government, probably by the very nature of its formation, did not articulate a coherent family policy. It instigated a number of reviews related to family issues immediately after its election, for example the Field review on poverty and life chances (Field, 2010), the Munro review of child protection (Munro, 2011) and the Allen review on early intervention (Allen, 2011). Field says in his introduction:

> *It is family background, parental education, good parenting and the opportunities for learning and development in those crucial years that together matter more to children than money, in determining whether their potential is realised in adult life.*
> (Field, 2010, p 5)

The statement is open to critical debate but nevertheless indicates the changing policy approach of the coalition.

Critical question

» *The Labour government took a strong economic approach to alleviating social exclusion, through welfare to work programmes. Field seems to be suggesting that income is not such a priority in influencing life chances. Consider the two perspectives and critically evaluate each in relation to young children's experiences and prospects in later life? (You might consider the discussion in Chapter 6, Poverty as part of the early years experience.)*

Social justice

The coalition continued some of the initiatives started by the Labour administration and has now developed a strategic approach to family policy. The ideology underpinning the policy is built on the value of:

* a two parent family;

* marriage as a cornerstone of successful family life;

* family autonomy and economic viability;

* welfare focused on the disadvantaged.

In *Social Justice: Transforming Lives* (DWP, 2012), the government sets out the principles and strategy for families. There are seven main aspects:

1. supporting family formation;

2. promoting positive relationships between parents;

3. emphasis on early intervention;

4. supporting parents and young families;

5. tackling domestic and sexual violence;

6. turning around the lives of the most troubled families;

7. the adoption and care systems.

Supporting family formation

Government views the welfare system as penalising couples, suggesting that it is more financially beneficial to be living apart than together. It has introduced Universal Credit as a means of reducing this penalty for low earning families by enhancing the *earnings disre-gard* (DWP, 2012, p 18) and reducing the tapering off to allow more couples to keep more of their income from work. There is also greater parity between the personal allowances for single people and couples on out-of-work benefits. While many agencies involved in family work, such as Family Action and the Chartered Institute of Housing, welcome the principles underpinning the strategy they are concerned that implementation under the proposed pro-cedures will not achieve the aims and that by 2015 some of the most vulnerable families will be worse off. There are growing concerns that some of the most vulnerable families, such as those with children with disabilities, may lose income as the cash replacement for tax credit is lower than the existing tax credit allowance (Family Action, 2012).

Universal Credit reflects one of the main thrusts of coalition policy to reduce the plethora of welfare benefits and bring a uniform and universal approach to recipients of welfare. The introduction of Universal Credit does away with the existing benefits of:

*   income-based Jobseeker's Allowance;

*   income-related Employment and Support Allowance;

*   Income Support;

*   Child Tax Credits;

*   Working Tax Credits;

*   Housing Benefit.

The Department for Work and Pensions (DWP) believes that the new Universal Credit system will incentivise work, create smoother transition in and out of work, help produce a dynamic labour market and simplify the system which makes it easily understood and cheaper to administer. However, as highlighted there are flaws in the proposal and question marks over its ability to support those families in most need. The coalition took a different approach when reforming child benefit. In this instance it took a universal non-means-tested benefit and turned it into a means-tested one. Child benefit has been withdrawn from families who earn beyond a specified threshold. This benefit has been contentious for some time with advocates of non-means-tested welfare strongly promoting it as an important resource for families with children and dissenters challenging the value and costs of supporting the children of high earners out of the public purse. There was a degree of furore around the cuts, especially over how the earnings threshold was applied and some accommodation was made by government, but the change has now been implemented.

Promoting positive relationships between parents

The coalition government views marriage as an important part of family life. It is keen to encourage and support it. It is funding relationship support for couples and marriage preparation and first-time parenting courses. It also supports services for separated and separating parents. The aim is to support the best interests of the child through financial, emotional and practical support for parents and simplify systems of family justice and child maintenance. The coalition is clear that it is seeking to *drive cultural change* (DWP, 2012, p 18) in family relationships. The aim is to keep families together in stable relationships but alleviate the damage caused to children if families separate.

Emphasis on early intervention

The coalition sees early intervention as central to its family philosophy. It set up the Early Intervention Grant (EIG) early in its administration and withdrew the Graduate Leader Fund (GLF). GLF was a ring-fenced fund aimed at promoting professional development in the early education and care workforce. Replacing it with the EIG, which was not ring fenced, allowed local authorities to determine how best to support early intervention for families.

The flexibility created opportunities for local authorities but coincided with reductions in central government funds that left many local authorities trying to fill gaps in existing services rather than enhancing them. The Sure Start scheme, started by the Labour administration and focusing on work with expectant and new parents and very young children, continues but its remit has been narrowed to areas of disadvantage. To support parental work in the early years the number of health visitor professionals was increased. The coalition promoted health visitors as an important professional resource in early intervention work with families. These initiatives have been in operation for a short period and at this stage it is too early to make an informed evaluation of whether they are achieving the policy objectives.

Supporting parents and young families

Many of the policy initiatives to support parents and young families such as the Sure Start and health visitor programmes and parent support, guidance and training services have been mentioned in earlier sections on social justice. A schedule of reforms has been launched including:

- doubling the capacity of the family nurse partnership programme to help improve a range of health issues for young families;

- projects to facilitate increased take-up of relationship support for first-time parents;

- extending free early education provision to the most disadvantaged two year-olds;

- increasing free early education for all three and four year-olds to 15 hours a week;

- additional indicators to the public health outcomes framework relating to specific health issues for pregnant and new mothers.

The underpinning ethos of these reforms and programmes is that of early intervention as considered in the Allen report (Allen, 2011). The intention is to counter the disadvantage faced by many children in the early years and the actual and subsequent detrimental impact on their childhood and adult experience.

Aspects 5–7

The social justice family agenda goes on to address specific issues including domestic and sexual violence and the adoption and care systems. The policy also launches a project focused on *Turning around the lives of the most troubled families* by the end of the 2010–15 Parliament (DWP, 2012, p 22). The project will identify 120,000 of the most troubled families and seek to intervene with a range of strategies to effect change. Local authorities are being asked to identify the families and appoint a co-ordinator to ensure they get the intervention they need. Government has identified a range of behaviours it wishes to turn around. These include poor school attendance, worklessness and criminal and anti-social behaviour. It will be interesting to observe the experiment. The essence of the intervention seems to lie in small scale one-to-one interventions. One of the case studies identified clearly indicates the approach.

CASE STUDY

Turning around the lives of troubled families: the LIFE programme

The aim of the programme is to work with families to support them in identifying the change they wish to bring about and making it happen. The programme is the initiative of Swindon Council and partners and draws on the Community Fund to resource it. The team will work with families who are in *chronic crisis* and have consistently failed to facilitate change despite multiple interventions from a number of agencies. The case study goes on to identify a particular example of the programme's potential.

> *Rob and his partner Rachel were well known to local agencies: they rarely managed to pay their rent, their children were not attending school and were close to being taken into care. Members of the LIFE team came to the family home where Rob and Rachel interviewed and selected their own caseworkers.*
>
> *Rob explains: 'There was an endless list of problems and I couldn't see how to deal with them. But LIFE gave us the space to think about them and the skills to solve them.*
>
> *We started by looking at getting the kids to school. Members of the LIFE team helped us to see that we could get the school clothes ready the night before, getting books ready, putting the shoes somewhere we'd remember. Once we got that sorted the kids started going to school, we were all happier and we moved on to the next problem.'*
>
> *Rob adds: 'The majority of people want support, they just don't know how to do it. The simple things we learnt through the LIFE programme saved our family and show other people that they can turn their lives around like we have.'*
>
> (DWP, 2012, p 22)

Critical question

» *The message of the case study is that with some personal practical help people can turn around their lives. However, social research demonstrates the significance of structural circumstances that affect people's lives. Reflect on the initiative and the broader context of people's lives to explore the prospects and constraints of such an approach.*

Social research shows that inadequate housing and socio-economic circumstances have real impact on children's ability to thrive developmentally. Inadequate housing not only affects children's physical health, such as increased risk of meningitis, respiratory illnesses and slow growth, but educational attainment too. Overcrowding at home is linked to delays in cognitive development and behavioural problems in childhood. Homeless children, those in temporary accommodation, are two to three times more likely to miss school and develop disruptive behaviour (Harker, 2006). Only 25 per cent of children receiving free school meals gain five good GCSEs or equivalent, compared to over half of the overall population (DfES, 2006). Very young children's language and literacy development is linked to family income and their mothers' educational qualification. Lack of maternal educational qualifications and poor socio-economic circumstances have strong influence on children's competencies at age three and on entering primary school (Hartas, 2010). Turning around the lives of troubled families is likely to demand significant structural change if it is to be sustained. Intervention of the sort identified in the case study can be helpful but the importance of socio-economic status and home and neighbourhood environment cannot be underestimated and ought to be part of any 'turn around' strategy if it is to have the best chance of success.

Henricson (2012a) suggests that any new policy should

> *specify the integrated promotion of family wellbeing from cradle to grave, across the full range of perspectives, some aligned and some divergent, that constitute family life.*
>
> (RSA, blog posting, 2012)

She suggests that such a policy should deal with all gender and generational issues within a human rights framework. She highlights areas of mental health, relationship interaction and tensions and morality as being important aspects of family policy alongside more commonly accepted social welfare elements such as education, child protection and housing. Clearly the social justice agenda and the early intervention approach acknowledge some of the wider aspects of Henricson's proposition but tend to focus on selected elements rather than a holistic approach.

Critical question

» *The coalition government has focused on strengthening family relationships and early intervention in much of its family policy. The 'turning around' strategy is a cornerstone of coalition government policy. Critically evaluate the prospects for achievement. You could use a SWOT (identifying the Strengths, Weaknesses, Opportunities and Threats) analysis to assist the evaluation.*

The demographics of family

The traditional two-child family remains the most common family type in England and Wales, with 38 per cent of women born in 1966 having two children (see Tables 2.1 and 2.2). Childlessness is the second most common family size for the 1966 cohort. This is a recent development first encountered among the 1964 cohort, whereas for those born between the late 1930s and early 1960s, three children was the second most common family size. A woman born in 1939 was more likely to have one, three or four or more children than not to have any. Only one in ten women born in 1966 had four or more children, compared with nearly one in five in the 1939 cohort (see Tables 2.1 and 2.2).

The data demonstrate the relatively new and rapid changes to family constructs since the second half of the twentieth century, and in particular from the 1960s onwards. While families of two heterosexual parents married with a couple of planned children seems to prevail, the diversity of family life is extensive and substantial numbers of children are growing up in very different family arrangements and building friendship networks that reflect this diversity.

Table 2.1 Number of families with dependent children, UK, 1996 and 2012

| Family type | Thousands | | | | | |
| | 1996 | | | 2012 | | |
	With dependent children	Without dependent children[1]	Total families	With dependent children	Without dependent children[1]	Total families
Married couple family	5,223	7,418	12,641	4,610	7,575	12,185
Civil partner couple family[2]	N/A	N/A	N/A	6	60	66
Opposite sex cohabiting couple family	539	920	1,459	1,131	1,761	2,893
Same-sex cohabiting couple family	..	15	16	6	64	69
Lone parent family	1,631	814	2,445	1,986	989	2,975
All families	7,393	9,167	16,560	7,739	10,449	18,188

[1] Families without dependent children have only non-dependent children or no children in the household.
[2] Civil partnerships were introduced in the UK in December 2005.
.. indicates that estimates are not sufficiently reliable to be published.
Totals may not sum due to rounding.
Source: Labour Force Survey, Office for National Statistics.

Today's families are more complex than the tables suggest. For example, two-parent households may be the result of two families coming together after divorce or separation and its members may be step-parents and children. Two- or one-parent families may have fostered or adopted children as well as contain birth children. Many more families with children do not undertake marriage and the number of children living in cohabiting households doubled in the 16 years between 1996 and 2012. Family is fluid in the twenty-first century. It can change many times over its lifetime, and not just in the ways routinely experienced, such as from non-dependent to dependent children and back again. Couples separate and divorce,

Table 2.2 *Percentage of dependent children in the UK: by family type, 1996 to 2012*

	Percentages	
Number of dependent children	1996	2012
One child	42	47
Two children	41	39
Three or more children	17	14

Source: Office for National Statistics licensed under the Open Government Licence v.1.0.

moving from joint to single parenthood and step families. Gay and lesbian couples create families with dependent children through surrogacy and adoption and looked-after children become members of more than one family for short or long periods of their lives. This is a far cry from some of the traditional rhetoric of pundits across the media and politics who wish to 'preserve' family life as some form of sacrosanct formula and status. Such a suggestion, based around the notion of married parents and birth children, is offensive to the many successful lifestyles of families with different arrangements. It is also incumbent, in a democratic society, on politicians to ensure family policy reflects the demographics and supports family well-being at its most diverse.

Marriage or cohabitation

Marriage remains the most common form of partnership in the UK, with 52 per cent of men and 50 per cent of women being married in 2006. However, marriage is waning and has been on a downward trend for many years, in 2005 reaching its lowest since statistics began. It is projected that by 2031 there will be as many never married as married women. Couples living together before marriage have increased from virtually nothing in the 1950s to 77 per cent in 1996 and for those cohabiting prior to a second marriage the figure is higher. There are a significantly lower number of cohabiting couples staying together after the birth of their child than married couples. Some 26 per cent of cohabiting couples have experienced some form of separation by the time their child is three as opposed to 7 per cent of married couples. Such statistics tend to be promoted by advocates of marriage. However, it is wise to be cautious as different sorts of people with different social, cultural and economic situations choose to marry or cohabit which is likely to influence sustainability of the relationship. For example, Goodman and Greaves (2010) identify a number of circumstances in their research that are more likely to be present in cohabiting relationships than in married ones and are known to affect outcomes for children. There is a differential in educational attainment with married couples more likely to have attained high levels of education; married couples are more likely to have higher incomes and professional occupations and to own their own home; married couples may have lived together for some time prior to the birth of the first child and have planned the pregnancy; and mothers in married relationships tend to be older when the first child is born. These socio-economic factors may be overlaid with cultural ones such as religious beliefs being more common among married couples and some ethnic communities which may or may not promote and support marriage. Within this context Goodman and Greaves advise:

Our findings suggest that while it is true that cohabiting parents are more likely to split up than married ones, there is very little evidence to suggest that this is due to a causal effect of marriage. Instead, it seems simply that different sorts of people choose to get married and have children, rather than to have children as a cohabiting couple, and that those relationships with the best prospects of lasting are the ones that are most likely to lead to marriage. Our analysis suggests, therefore, that if more cohabiting parents decide to get married, it is very unlikely that a significant number would become more likely to stay together.

(Goodman and Greaves, 2010, p 1)

Evidence shows a gap in cognitive, social and emotional development of children aged between three and five born to cohabiting parents and those born to married parents. However, once differences such as those highlighted above of education, occupation, income and housing tenure are accounted for, the gap becomes insignificant for cognitive, and falls dramatically for social and emotional, development. If pregnancy planning and relationship quality is considered, differences in social and emotional development become insignificant (Goodman and Greaves, 2010). Research such as this carries important messages for the development and design of family policy to enhance children's life experiences and chances. It strongly suggests a focus on socio-economic policies to alleviate disadvantage within families whatever the make-up rather than the promotion of marriage per se.

Changing patterns of family life

The concept of family is changing. Although we still see a prevalence of married couples with children, there are growing numbers of families that reflect changing views and values in UK society. Civil partnerships were introduced in the UK in December 2005 and same-sex couples now enjoy a legally recognised status as a family. The incidence of lone parent families rises steadily year on year whether through personal choice or couple break-up (Table 2.3).

Table 2.3 *Families by family type in the UK, 1996 and 2012*

			Millions
Family type	With dependent children	1996	2012
Married or civil partner couple family	With dependent children	5.2	4.6
Cohabiting couple family[1]	With dependent children	0.5	1.1
Lone parent family	With dependent children	1.6	2.0

[1] Cohabiting couples include both opposite- and same-sex couples.

Source: Adapted from data from the Office for National Statistics licensed under the Open Government Licence v.1.0.

Lone parents

Lone parents look after nearly a quarter of children across England and Wales. It is estimated that approximately 11 per cent of households comprise a lone parent and dependent children and that 25 per cent of children are being brought up by a sole parent compared with approximately 7 per cent in 1971. There is often a stigma attached to lone parents. They are seen as benefit-dependent and lacking in parenting skills. Such perceptions do not take account of the circumstances of many lone parents and misunderstand the issues faced by large numbers of single parents in UK society. As Reeves (2013) points out, the demographics of lone parenting show young mothers with few educational qualifications and low earnings prospects. In such circumstances it is perhaps unsurprising that large numbers of lone parents seek welfare benefits and housing support. Low socio-economic status is associated with developmental delay and low achievement of children in families; therefore it is not surprising if the children of lone parents experience difficulties. However, we must not assume that single parenthood is the causal factor but need to explore the social and cultural elements that prevail, as Goodman and Greaves (2010) have done when looking at marriage and cohabitation.

The reasons for low achievement among children in lone parent families are complex. Many lone parents are poor, for example:

- around 4 in every 10 children in single parent families as opposed to 2 per 10 in couple families are poor;

- 23 per cent of lone parent families with a part-time worker are in poverty;

- 39 per cent of single parents say the money runs out before the end of the week as opposed to 19 per cent of couple families;

- 63 per cent of lone parent families have no savings as opposed to 34 per cent of couple families.

Many single parents experience difficulties managing work and childcare:

- 59 per cent of single parents work;

- 46 per cent rely on informal childcare such as grandparents or ex-partners;

- 32 per cent of single parents find difficulties meeting childcare costs as opposed to 20 per cent of couple families.

(Source: Gingerbread, 2010)

Lone parents take on all roles within families – breadwinner, carer and home maker – frequently in less than adequate economic circumstances. For low-paid parents with young children the ability to work full time and sustain childcare either personally, or through a third party, is nigh on impossible. The provision of early childhood education and care is costly in the UK and provision may not be accessible to those who need it most. The challenge to lone parents to raise personal educational attainment, while raising children and in all likelihood working, is a tough one. Reeves (2013) promotes the notion of a symmetrical family, ie one where gender equality is sound, men take all the family roles as a norm and parents, be they absent or not, contribute actively to child-rearing and family life. Social and fiscal policy reflects some aspects of the premise with moves towards paternal as well as maternity leave and equality and equal pay legislation. However, for many lone parents the halcyon notion of shared parenting is not an option. Families split and form new families, parents avoid continued contact and financial support for their children, for widows and widowers it is not an option and, for some, contact with the absent parent may be dangerous.

Looked-after children

In 2011 there were 65,520 looked-after children in the UK. During the year ending 31 March 2011, 3,050 looked-after children were adopted and 26,830 children ceased to be looked after. Of those children who started to be looked after during 2011, 54 per cent were provided with a service because of abuse or neglect. This percentage has increased each year since 2008 when 48 per cent of children were provided with a service for this reason. Of those children who were looked after at 31 March 2011, 74 per cent were in a foster placement (Glendenning, 2011) (see Figure 2.2).

The impact of foster families on children is difficult to ascertain but studies suggest that the predominant reasons for children experiencing cognitive and emotional difficulties and delay are their experiences prior to foster care rather than the foster care experience. Emotional and mental health differs depending on the age of the child when becoming looked after, with seemingly little effect if before six months of age (Wilson et al, 2004). In some instances the fostering family environment does little to alleviate and change the situation; for example, in terms of educational achievement there are significant differences and shortfall in GCSE achievement between looked-after children and all children (see Chapter 4, *The status and rights of young children as political and policy influencers*).

Critical question

» *Children in single parent households or who are 'looked after' often do not achieve educationally compared to all children. Examine and analyse conditions that are likely to result in detrimental educational experiences for these children and consider what elements of social, economic and educational policy would help change underachievement to success.*

Mothers, fathers and child behaviour

The demographics show changing patterns of motherhood since the Second World War. Mothers in employment tripled between 1950 and 2008 and the trend continues. Seventy-two per cent of mothers in cohabiting and married families are working and 56 per cent of mothers in single parent families. Mothers are still mostly responsible for home making and childcare and in spite of working spend three times more time with their children than they did in the 1970s. Fathers are more involved in family life, spending over 200 per cent more time with their children in 2000 than in the 1970s – 25 minutes a day rather than eight minutes (Family and Parenting Institute, 2013) The Institute highlighted:

> *A survey of 16 industrialised countries found time devoted to childcare for married fathers in full-time employment with children under five had risen from 0.4 hours per day in 1960 to 1.2 by 2000. Fathers said that they found the time to do this because they gave up on personal pursuits (mainly sleep) and because they are trying to cut down work.*
>
> (Family and Parenting Institute, 2013)

Patterns of child-rearing are changing with children being regarded as individual members of the family. The focus has moved towards negotiation rather than discipline and today parents view themselves as less strict than their counterparts. However, in many families,

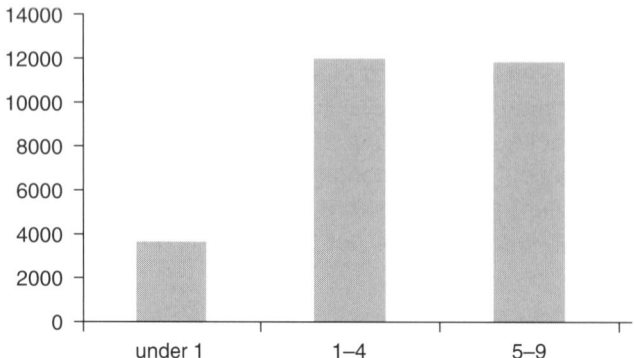

Figure 2.2 Number of looked-after children in the UK (2011)
Source: Glendenning, 2011.

children have less freedom and choice in where and who they spend their time with, with informal street play being heavily curtailed.

In the UK women are having children much later in life, and fewer of them. This coincides with people living longer, creating the so-called 'beanpole' effect of more generations alive but with fewer aunts and uncles. The pressure on grandparents is growing as older mothers wishing to continue and develop their careers are seeking the help of retired but active grandparents.

CASE STUDY

Grandmother's role

Marina recently retired from full-time work with a view to spending time with her husband in pursuing activities and holidays they had been unable to undertake when working. Within three months of doing so her daughter, Annie, became pregnant with her first child at the age of 35. Marina had often said she would help with childcare if Annie chose to have a child but was rather surprised at being called on to do so. Her daughter is a health professional who wants to pursue her career, and her partner works out of town Monday to Friday. The advent of the child has had little impact on the father's life but for Annie her day is filled with work and evenings and weekends with childcare. Marina and her husband have become full-time child carers and all intended post-retirement activities have been put on hold.

Critical question

» *Consider the impact of the case study family on the young child. What issues may arise for family members from this arrangement? Early childhood education and care professionals and teachers would need to be sensitive to these arrangements. What professional practice principles would you employ in dealing with parents and carers of the child?*

This is a growing phenomenon in UK family life, where couples often work long distances from home due to employment opportunities and career demands, leaving in effect a single parent to manage on a day-to-day basis. Grandparents are becoming commonplace carers with the

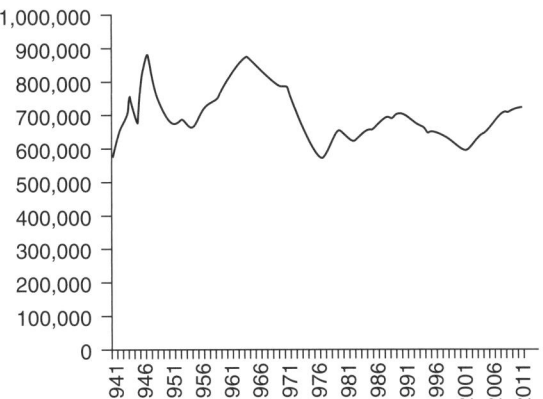

Figure 2.3 Number of live births England and Wales
Source: Adapted from data from the Office for National Statistics licensed under the Open Government Licence v.1.0.

full duties of childcare for children from a very young age. Meanwhile fathers still tend towards a single primary role of worker as demonstrated by the statistics and case study.

Family culture and young children

The UK is experiencing a mini baby boom as fertility rates have increased year on year since 2001 (see Figure 2.3).

There were 808,000 births in the UK in 2011, composed of 612,000 births to UK born women and 196,000 births to non-UK born women. Twenty-four per cent of births in 2011 were to non-UK born women, an increase of two percentage points since 2007. This increase is caused by a 24 per cent rise in the number of women of childbearing age who were born outside the UK and a fall of 5 per cent in the number of UK born women of childbearing age since 2007. Poland is the most common non-UK maternal country of birth in the UK, with around 23,000 births in 2011. It is the most common in each of the four UK countries and in London, reflecting the wide geographical distribution of women born in Poland. The top five non-UK born mothers' countries by number of births (Poland, Pakistan, India, Bangladesh and Nigeria) show that women born in Pakistan have the highest fertility rates of the five individual maternal countries of birth examined, with around 180 births per thousand women in 2011, compared to around 60 births per thousand for UK born women (adapted from data from the Office for National Statistics licensed under the Open Government Licence v.1.0).

The data indicate the ethnic diversity of children's lives in the UK. Very young children often experience different cultural approaches to child-rearing in families and communities than in society at large. The way members of society interact with each other and the environment is influenced by the traditions, norms, values and practices that families and communities believe and demonstrate (Thomas, 1998). Young children meet and engage with children of diverse ethnic backgrounds and cultures at pre-school provision and on entering school. Families may hold on to traditional child-rearing practices that do not always reflect the society within which they reside and what professional training advocates. Refugee families, for example, may be unaware of the norms in the host society and not understand the nature and operation of provision and services that exist in the community. Research shows that development in young children is influenced by experiences related to the child's close and extended environment, such as the relationship with parents and wider social, cultural and socio-economic influences (Bronfenbrenner, 1979). Culture and society are strong determinants in the development of the individual, particularly because they affect child-rearing practices (Harkness, 1980). If the interrelationship between family and society is at odds then young children can experience tension between the expectations and norms of their family environment and those of their peers and wider society.

Spicer's survey of different racial and ethnic parenting beliefs (2010) highlights the existence of different cultural perspectives of child-rearing and children's development. He surveyed African-American, Hispanic and White parents in the USA and found that different ethnic groups viewed parenting differently. For example, White parents were more likely to view as important rule-setting and enforcement and comforting an upset child than either African-American or Hispanic families. African-American and Hispanic families were more inclined than White families to the view that children from six months are able to feel emotions of sadness and fear or sense these emotions in others. Parents in different ethnic groups also had different ideas on school-readiness. For Hispanic and White parents, being able to play well with others was important, whereas African-American and Hispanic families viewed the ability to sit still and pay attention as a primary ability. While other socio-economic aspects of the parents in the study must be considered and the differences in approach are not unanimous in each ethnic group the results of the survey do suggest the importance of understanding cultural influences on young children's experiences in the family.

De Gioia (2009) in her study of parents and childcare staff expectations of continuity of child-rearing practices between home and childcare settings highlighted important differences in feeding and sleep patterns. Her study uses the ecology framework of Bronfenbrenner to explore the relationship beyond the family and in childcare settings. De Gioia found that often parents were specific on the ways in which children were prepared for sleep and the process of feeding. She highlights research showing sleep time as a sensitive experience for young children and that the processes engaged in preparing children for sleep, and the confidence they have in the experience, are major influences on children's ability to make a comfortable transition from home to childcare environment. For immigrant children this may be particularly important as sleep practices are the last thing to adjust in the new environment. Cultural norms of eating for young children are diverse. For some communities fingers are the dominant utensil, whereas other communities may see the use of cutlery as an important development for young children. In some instances parents may desire and provide an interactive eating regime with their young child while others promote independence as early as possible. It is important for the well-being of the child that professionals interacting with young children and parents are sensitive to these practices and provide continuity of experience. Some parents view their cultural practices as non-negotiable while others take a more flexible approach. In some instances the childcare centre ethos prevails and is implemented without the knowledge of the family. Such an approach does not allow for diversity and does not respect the value of cultural norms and practice. To work effectively and be in the best interests of the child, care providers need to be sensitive to and support family values (De Gioia, 2009).

Critical question

» *As a professional working with young children and families what would you want in your professional toolkit to enable you to appreciate and reflect the cultural diversity of those with whom you work?*

Professional involvement with families with young children

Professionals involved with young children and their families need to be informed and sensitive to the context of childcare and practice in the family home and community. For young children continuity of care is important to support well-being and development. As shown in De Gioia's study, the most basic needs of the child – food and rest – require careful handling to avoid detrimental effects and development delay. Professional practitioners may have a wealth of learning and experience to hand in terms of early childhood education and care but if by implementation it ignores the wishes of the family and the expectations of the child it could have a negative effect. It is essential that professionals working with children ensure their safety and well-being but they must also listen to and address the cultural values of parents and family and unless there is a danger to the child, take account of them.

Providers of early education and childcare and school services for young children should ensure that staff reflect the diversity of children's cultures in the provision and beyond.

CASE STUDY

Cath and Veronica's story

Cath and Veronica were enthusiastic entrants to one of the first childcare courses run in their area. They were keen to learn and committed to work as volunteers in their locality. They had set up a pre-school playgroup which was well attended and in demand by the young families in the community. Each week they eagerly took new ideas and ways of working back to the playgroup to share and try. So the tutor was thrown by Cath and Veronica's response to the session on diversity and cultural sensitivity of *We don't need to do that*. When asked for more explanation they said that there were only White children and families in their neighbourhood so issues of cultural awareness and ethnic diversity were not relevant.

It took extensive debate and many examples for Cath and Veronica to begin to see that complexion was not the only potential indicator of cultural diversity and that within a diverse ethnic society such as the UK awareness and appreciation of diversity was beneficial to the young children and families with whom they worked. Staff attitudes are significant determinants of continuity of cultural practice between home and early childhood education and care settings or school. The presence of staff from representative cultures can build the link, providing insight for the setting and empathy with the family.

Critical question

» *Understanding demographic and cultural situations within and beyond communities is essential knowledge for professionals working with children and families. How might you ensure knowledge and cultural awareness of the communities within which you exist and work? What impact would this have?*

Good quality communication between professionals and families is essential to avoid misunderstandings and facilitate negotiated practice in the best interests of the child. Staff must make efforts at drop-off and collection times to talk with family members, sharing knowledge and seeking advice or opinion. Providers ought to offer opportunities for family members to air and share their views and discuss the ethos of the setting: in essence to build a partnership of care for the child. This is true for all professionals working with young children be it in health, education, care or protection.

Critical reflections

Family in all its forms

The relationship between family and the state is a complex one. Personal, cultural, ideological and pragmatic views and opinion create a heady mix for policy-makers and professional practitioners involved in family work. Many people hold idealised or uncompromising perspectives on family structure, which affect approaches to provision and services and influence the experiences of families that do not fit the particular model identified. The turmoil of change in social mores since the 1960s has seen changing iterations of family. The concept of family as a married heterosexual couple with two, three or more children has shifted considerably. Fewer couples are marrying and more living together, family size is reducing and mothers are having their first babies at a much later age. As equality and diversity have become significant social requisites families have started to reflect changing attitudes. Homosexual couples create families and have dependent children. Fostering families are the norm for looked-after children and adoption by gay and lesbian couples and single people is now possible. Single parenthood is increasing steadily year on year and the stigma attached to it less than 50 years ago has gone. This is not to say that prejudice does not exist and that the variety of family models is easily maintained and accepted. There are still strong advocates of marriage as a prerequisite for family and it is still the main family model in UK society. Lone parents are often disadvantaged economically and looked-after children still perform below their potential educationally.

In most societies children are viewed within the context of family and family is seen as the primary entity with responsibility for children. However, how children experience their family lives is influenced by government, through economic, fiscal and social welfare policy and legislation, for example child benefits and family tax credits, employment legislation such as maternity and parental leave and childcare provision. The family political agenda of many European countries is being reshaped, largely due to rebalancing the policy mix between service provision, public and private costs and individual participation. For example, there is debate about demand- and supply-led childcare (see Chapter 5, *Education and care for early learning and development*) and flexible working. The world of work is changing for families as both parents become more involved in childcare and women want and expect to continue their careers after having children. A recession and changes to welfare policy have pushed the agenda of 'welfare to work'. The political rhetoric is strong in this arena with pithy nomenclature and strap lines related to getting people away from benefits and into work. The New Deal for Lone Parents was the Labour administration's initiative to encourage lone parents into employment. For many this has been low-paid and part-time work, making it impossible to sustain family life on earned income alone. The coalition government has maintained Labour's theme of 'making work pay' with the Prime Minister, David Cameron, using the more draconian approach of cutting welfare *so it pays to have a job* but as Garvin and Lewis (2012) state, for millions of people, work does not pay. Wages do not cover household bills or basic family needs and the worst-hit families are resorting to food banks. The minimum wage is at its lowest level since 2004. This, in a country where bonuses of over £1 million are being received by some of the wealthiest people and with a government that is reluctant to support the European Union's proposal to curb excessive bonuses, seems to be somewhat of a dichotomy.

Children's status in families is changing; from being invisible they are regarded as independent members of the family, with welfare and participation needs and rights (see Chapter 4, *The status and rights of young children as political and policy influencers*). Children in families in developed countries are largely viewed as social investments attracting significant amounts of family income, time and resources; however, in other parts of the world children are viewed as important economic assets, able to support and provide family income and care. These two stark contrasts demonstrate the wide differences in family status and circumstances of children across the world. For young children family life is mostly one of dependency and little autonomy. The cultural context in which they reside has a direct impact on their childhood experiences and future prospects. Young children in poor families may fail to thrive, with health and development issues affecting their life chances (see Chapter 6, *Poverty as part of the early years experience*). Cultural norms and values affect young children at the most basic level of needs such as sleeping and eating and their experiences will be influenced by the priorities and preferences of child-rearing that dominate adult family life.

For policy-makers and professionals, cultural diversity is an important consideration in family policy. In diverse ethnic societies such as the UK it is imperative that professionals understand and take account of cultural values and practices. For early education and childcare professionals and early years teachers cultural contexts should inform and influence practice in the best interests of the child and to enable strong partnerships to be built between family and professional practitioners.

Further reading

Graham Allen MP (2011) *Early Intervention: The Next Steps*. London: HM Government.

> This report is a review of the rationale for early intervention and recommendations for policy development. It considers aspects of early childhood and care. Allen introduces the review with the following:

> *Early Intervention is an approach which offers our country a real opportunity to make lasting improvements in the lives of our children, to forestall many persistent social problems and end their transmission from one generation to the next, and to make long-term savings in public spending.*

> (Allen, 2011, p vii)

The review makes a link between economic and social welfare. It was completed at the request of the coalition government with a view to it informing policy development.

Caroline Bryson, Anne Kazimirski and Helen Southwood (2006) *Childcare and Early Years Provision: A Study of Parents' Use, Views and Experiences.* London: National Centre for Social Research.

This report provides current information on parents' use, views and experiences of childcare and early years provision in the UK. It is the third in a series of surveys relating to childcare and parent choice and demands. It provides insight and data into early years education and care provision used by parents and provides useful data to evaluate policy interventions. The survey draws on quantitative and qualitative data by following up selected case studies from the original survey.

Department for Work and Pensions (2012) *Social Justice: Transforming Lives.* London: Department for Work and Pensions.

This is the coalition government's strategy for *transforming lives*. It covers family policy among other areas and is an important document for understanding policy direction in early years and family work.

Richard Reeves (2013) *The Symmetrical Family, Families@30.* London: 4Children.

This is a polemic on family definitions and purpose and the role of male and female members within it. Reeves articulates the main trends in changing family life. He considers the current challenges for families and goes on to propose the agenda for the next 30 years. His assumptions are based on male–female couplings. This is an interesting premise worthy of consideration and critique.

3 Cultural and social aspects of the health and well-being of young children

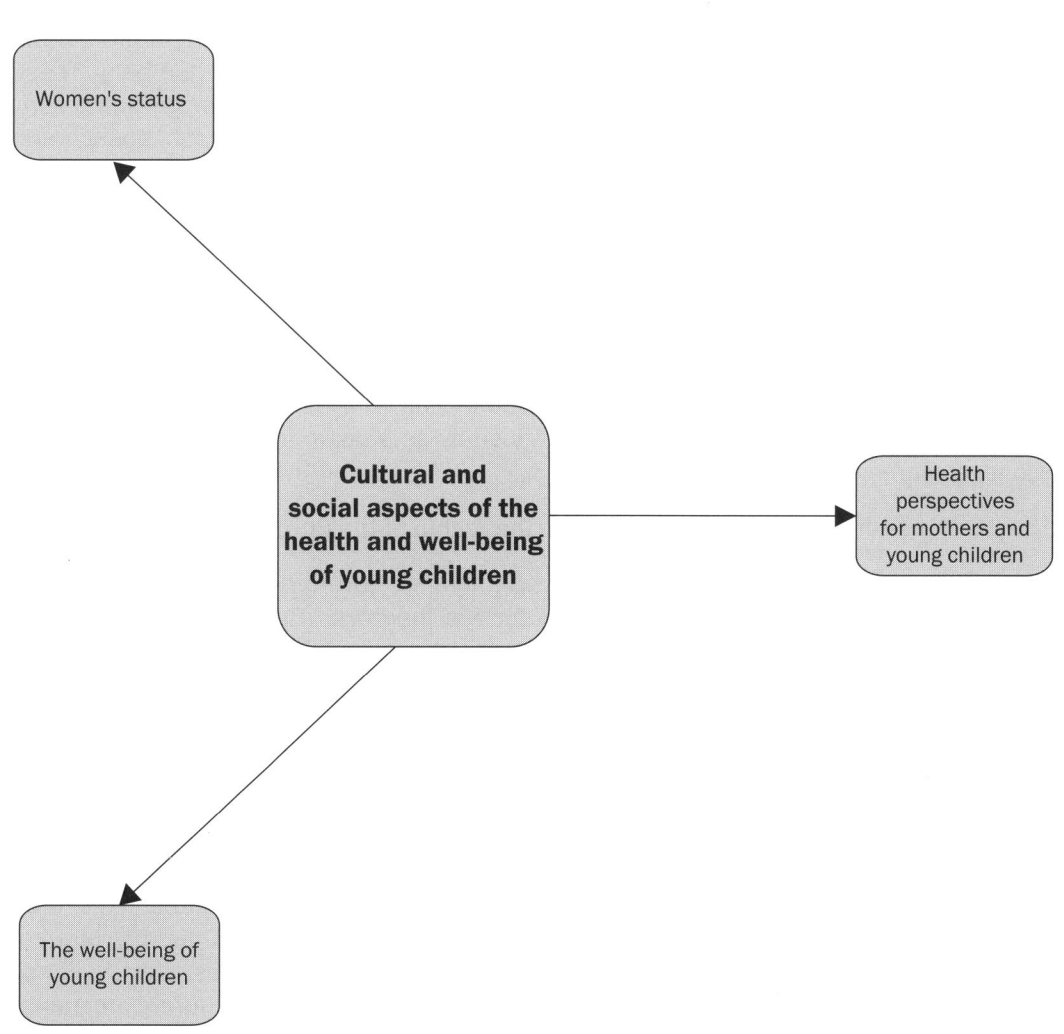

Women's status

Cultural and social aspects of the health and well-being of young children

Health perspectives for mothers and young children

The well-being of young children

Introduction

This chapter engages in a critical discussion of health and social services for pre-birth and early years: comparing and contrasting diverse social and cultural approaches. It considers public and institutional attitudes towards specific situations relating to health and well-being in respect of young children and examines the tensions and contradictions evident in a range of policy areas. These include infant health, family planning and pregnancy, safeguarding of young children from abuse and neglect and the status and treatment of disability in early childhood. Throughout the chapter discussion embraces the diversity and role played by professionals working with parents and young children and how policy trends affect and change working practice. It provides the political and policy context of health and well-being that is discussed in detail in relation to child development and professional practice in critical perspectives of well-being in the early years that is part of this series.

The health of pregnant mothers and babies and young children is generally viewed as important and of concern to society. Within the UK we spend significant amounts of public finance – £2,629,977,000 in 2011–12 (source: Department of Health Annual Report and Accounts in Hansard, 2012) – on maternity and baby care and have created a network of professionals whose role it is to provide good pre- and postnatal services for mother and baby. These include midwives, obstetricians, paediatricians and health visitors. As babies grow into early childhood these services extend to paediatric, community and school nurses, speech and language therapists, child psychologists and other allied health professionals. The services of such professionals are mostly welcomed by users and contributions from the public purse are largely positively perceived. This socio-cultural perspective on child health is constrained by the social paradigm that all children are wanted, all babies are welcome and with a little help all mothers are instinctive capable parents. Once we venture into the unsavoury world of unwanted pregnancy, dysfunctional parenting and disadvantaged families, and beyond to child abuse and neglect, this positive perception is tested and challenged. It is then we bring in concepts of 'responsible parenting' and 'deserving families'. Public attitudes in such situations can be widely divided and are influenced by persuasive institutions of the state, religions, commerce and the press.

Article 24 of the United Nations Convention on the Rights of the Child states:

> *Every child has the right to the best possible health. Governments must provide good quality health care, clean water, nutritious food and a clean environment so that children can stay healthy. Richer countries must help poorer countries achieve this.*

The convention was ratified by the UK in 1991, and to date by all but two countries, yet health inequalities still exist across the world and within the UK. In England children under five years living in deprived areas are 8 per cent more likely to be obese; 9 per cent more likely to be of a low birth weight; and 12 per cent more likely to have an accident than those living elsewhere (Audit Commission, 2010). Research into early childhood consistently shows a relationship between the experiences of very young children and positive outcomes in later life. This is as true for health outcomes as for educational and economic ones. The Marmot Review into health inequalities in England identified giving children the best start in life as its greatest priority, suggesting that health inequalities must be addressed during pregnancy and the early years if society is to eliminate inequalities in later life (Marmot, 2010).

Women's status

In wealthy industrial nations such as the UK, family size has reduced over the twentieth century and in the twenty-first century families are having children later and some not at all. This has been influenced by many and diverse factors, including improved survival rates of children, industrial transitions and technological developments and the role of women in the family and workforce. When I was a young woman in the 1960s and 1970s, social and cultural norms changed extensively with women's issues high on the political agenda.

CASE STUDY

Women's rights in the 1960s

In my early years of work, in the late 1960s, it was common practice for prospective employers to ascertain the marital status of women and question their intentions about having children. As a married woman of childbearing age I could not obtain a mortgage, despite earning more than my husband. When I applied for a promotion within the Civil Service, my employer at the time asked when I intended starting a family, obviously questioning my commitment to the job and worthiness of promotion. When I applied to university in 1972, many admissions tutors could not comprehend that I was living independently and would not be willing to reside in halls of residence. This attitude had a significant influence in my final choice of establishment. Such situations pervaded women's lives in the 1960s and 1970s.

The feminist movement, together with social reformers across the western world, made great strides in economic and political equality and was ably supported by technical developments in contraception and legalisation of abortion. For the first time, women of all social classes were able to manage their pregnancies and control their family size. Such transitions were not easily gained and the institutions of state, religion and commerce did not yield without resistance, some of which still remains in the twenty-first century. Some religions still oppose particular forms of birth control – for example, Pope Benedict XVI in 2012 left unchallenged the Human Vitae edict of Pope Paul VI in 1968, maintaining that interventionist methods of birth control were wrong. This edict, which is challenged by many of the Catholic faith and its officials, seems outmoded in the twenty-first century. In Ireland the government has yet to reform its abortion laws, which prescribe an almost total ban on abortion. Human Rights Watch (HRW), an independent international organisation, called on the Irish government in 2010 to

> take all necessary steps, both immediate and incremental, to ensure that women have informed and un-coerced access to safe and legal abortion services within Ireland as an element of women's exercise of their reproductive and other human rights.
>
> (HRW, 2010, p 3)

The apparatus of the state has often lagged behind legislation. For example, there are concerns over the parlous level of reporting of sexual assaults on women and inadequate police investigation and criminal prosecution of those that are reported (Morris, 2013). In commerce, having achieved equal pay legislation in the 1970s (reformed in the Equality Act, 2010) women were still fighting cases of inequality in 2011. Birmingham City Council lost its appeal against an equal pay decision in November 2011. Former staff who worked in mostly women's low paid jobs such as cooks, cleaners and care staff had discovered they had been denied bonuses given to colleagues in traditionally male-dominated roles such as refuse collectors and street cleaners (BBC, 2012).

Within the complexity of social and cultural transitions, women's health and well-being and that of their children are inextricably linked.

•   A woman's economic and social circumstances through pregnancy, her age and lifestyle and access to maternity support have an impact on her child.

•   During infancy a mother's feeding preferences and child-rearing abilities affect her child's health and growth.

•   In the early years, mothers make a significant contribution to their children's well-being in all aspects of their growth and development.

Critical question

»   *Critically analyse the policy influences on women's role and status in UK society in the last 50 years and the impact on child-rearing practices and expectations. Take an example of child-rearing you are familiar with and consider how the mother's situation has influenced the child's well-being and future prospects.*

Health perspectives for mothers and young children

As highlighted earlier there are a plethora of maternity and child health services dedicated to ensuring positive health outcomes for children. These services have been developed to deal with a range of child health issues. Maternity services are provided to enable safe pregnancy and birth. Health visitors operate within communities to support and monitor health and development in infancy and early years. Paediatric services specialise in overcoming childhood disease and illness.

Infant mortality

Levels of infant mortality were still high at the end of the nineteenth century across most of Europe and there were wide variations across countries. Some of the Nordic countries had the lowest incidence at around 100 per 1000 live births compared to the worst such as Germany, Austria and Russia at 250 per 1000 live births. By the turn of the century numbers had fallen and in the early 1900s began to converge to reach between 20 and 50 per 1000 live births in the 1950s. This was paralleled with a fall in fertility rates and increased life expectancy. The facts are known but the reasons for the improvements are not so clear. We can presume that health and hygiene improvements for individuals and communities made a contribution, not least the availability of clean water, adequate sewers and measures to prevent and treat diseases. As demographic studies have progressed it has become apparent that feeding patterns within communities and regions have a significant impact on infant mortality, so that countries where prolonged breast-feeding was the norm enjoyed lower infant mortality rates than those where it was not (Corsini and Viazzo, 1993). However, this in itself is unlikely to account for the rapid reduction and convergence in the first half of the twentieth century. Population distribution also influenced the incidence of child mortality with urban areas having poorer survival rates than that of rural populations in the nineteenth century. This was largely due to the inadequacies of urban living, such as overcrowding and poor sanitation allowing disease to spread, rather than the benefits of a rural environment. As urban living became the norm and brought improvements in health, hygiene and lifestyles, infant mortality declined. Social and economic circumstances played a part, with women's labour patterns, household structures and incidence of illegitimacy having an impact on infant mortality. Social class as a determinant of infant mortality levels was not without its contradictions, especially in the nineteenth century where wealthy gentry and professionals experienced higher levels of infant mortality than the peasantry, ascribed largely to lack of sustained breast-feeding within such families (Corsini and Viazzo, 1993). However, there was a strong inverse correlation between infant mortality and social class at the end of the nineteenth and beginning of the twentieth centuries in the UK, which had a strong class differentiation. In the USA, with a less-defined class system, differences were located around ethnic communities. The impact of social change and scientific understanding raised expectations of infant survival and reformers, scientists and politicians among others believed that many infant deaths could be prevented. In 2012 infant mortality across the European Union was 4.4 deaths per 1000 live births (www.cia.gov/library/publications/the-world-factbook/rankorder/). The precipitous drop in the last 40 years has been due to neonatal survival rates with the development of a panoply of procedures, medications, interventions and care that has reduced mortality rates of children in the first four weeks of life from 6 to 3.6 (ie by 40 per cent) per 1000 live births in high income countries such as the USA, Australia and most of north and western Europe and from 20 per 1000 live births to 10 (by almost 50 per cent) across eastern Europe (Oestergaard, 2011).

Infant mortality rates are changed when a diverse range of social, health, economic, population and lifestyle factors come into play. Fluctuation and rates of change can be affected by any or all of these factors to different degrees in varied circumstances. It is clear that feeding patterns within families and communities hold great sway and that welfare and hygiene reforms among populations have extensive impact. Wide-scale prevention and treatment of childhood disease and illness affords reduced rates, and as overall death rates fall specialist procedures and care have incremental impact. For those countries with high infant mortality the priority is for structural health and social reform and investment in breast-feeding as the norm. In those societies with low infant mortality rates further reduction is most likely to occur through specialist improved procedures, such as neonatal care or early intervention to facilitate changes to personal and familial lifestyles, such as teenage pregnancy.

Critical question

» *Survival rates for infants in wealthy industrialised societies are largely influenced by lifestyle choices and conditions. What can professionals working with mothers and babies do to support the further reduction of infant mortality and evaluate what strategies they might use?*

Mother and baby care

Experiences in early childhood have a real influence on life chances throughout life. Evidence shows that brain development is affected by external environments and circumstances. Therefore a healthy start for mother and baby is essential if children are to have successful lives and achieve their potential as adults. In the UK midwives play a pivotal role in pregnancy and birth, one that is acknowledged by the Department of Health in its 'Healthy Child Programme' (2009). Indeed, midwives are viewed as playing the lead or co-ordinating role throughout pregnancy. However, midwife training and recruitment have not kept pace with demand and serious concerns were being expressed as early as 2000. Reduction in funding for training providers and trends towards hospital-based services, alongside increasing birth rates, the trend towards older mothers with more complex pregnancies and increases in multiple births have resulted in a growing shortfall between actual and required numbers of midwives. David Cameron made a pre-election pledge to increase midwife numbers, yet in spite of over 5,000 new midwives since 2001 to over 20,000 in 2012 it is anticipated that this still leaves a shortage of almost 5,000 trained midwives in 2012–13. Attempts are being made to reduce the gap and calls by the Royal College of Midwives for government to maintain the current high numbers in training have been heeded. From a nadir of only 1,800 students in training in 2005–6 we have seen an upward trend with trainee numbers reaching around 2,500 per year since 2009–10 (Royal College of Midwives, 2012).

The role of midwives is changing. Policy directives place midwives in the vanguard of pregnancy services, taking the lead in straightforward pregnancies and co-ordinating the multidisciplinary team when they are more complex. Policy has shifted and the trend over the past 10–15 years towards predominantly hospital-based midwives has moved in favour of community-based and focused practice. Midwifery services are expected to provide information and support beyond the mother and baby to fathers and extended family members, as appropriate, and to support mothers and babies post-birth through the early weeks of life. The Healthy Child Programme (2009) suggests that:

> the midwife role, in addition to assessing health and social needs, is to ensure that all screening tests are understood and available to all women. They make sure that pregnancy is monitored through to delivery of the baby. They may maintain contact for up to 28 days after delivery, as necessary.
>
> (Shribman and Billingham, 2009, p 71)

Midwives are anecdotally seen as a force for good. I was amazed, when out with a good friend who was a community midwife, at the number of times she would be approached by women to comment on and thank her for her role in their pregnancies, often embarrassing older children by introducing her as the midwife who delivered them. This is reflected in studies comparing midwifery to other forms of maternity services. The Cochrane collaboration (Hatem et al, 2009) reviewed 11 trials involving 12,276 women that compared midwife-led models of care with other models of care for childbearing women and found a number of benefits of midwife care, including less use of general anaesthesia and instrumental births, mothers feeling in control of the process, more spontaneous vaginal births and initiating breast-feeding and shorter stays in hospital. The authors found no adverse effects and concluded that midwife care should be the norm, except where there are medical or obstetric complications (Hatem et al, 2009).

Critical question

» *If primary care during pregnancy and the first few weeks of life is the job of the midwife as lead and co-ordinator, what do you think is the role for the early childhood education and care professional during infancy and babyhood? Develop and evaluate strategies to facilitate good practice.*

Childhood illness and disease

Advances in medicine and vaccination together with improvements in nursing care have reduced morbidity across many childhood illnesses and disease. The reduction in death rates has increased the percentage of children with chronic disorders. There is little statistical evidence, but indicators suggest that chronically ill children account for somewhere between 1 and 4 per cent of healthcare needs in a developed country such as the USA (Stein and Jessop, 1982). Since the mid-twentieth century medical professionals have been discussing the approach of health professionals towards chronically ill children. The essence of the discussion has ranged between advocates of a 'medical' model of treatment, care and support and a 'social' model. The medical model dominated in the nineteenth and early part of the twentieth century with the focus on the disease or specific condition and its treatment or cure, almost irrespective of the impact on the child's experience and family life.

CASE STUDY

Linda's hospital experience

Linda, my cousin, was in the local children's hospital when she was four and I was five. Indeed, I remember vividly waving to her in her bed on the balcony of the hospital from the roadside. Apart from her mother and father no one else was allowed to visit, and even parents were limited to a maximum of two hours a day. Children under 12 were not allowed on any hospital wards, even when it was a parent who was ill. Linda was not allowed personal items from home to comfort her and spent a week confined to bed without playthings to occupy and distract her. The bed was wheeled on to the balcony in the belief that fresh air was important for recovery, which was her only distraction from the bare walls of the ward. The focus was on the physical health of Linda with little regard for her emotional needs. No one thought to challenge this regime and accepted the restrictions imposed without question.

This is a far cry from the lively playful wards in children's hospitals in Britain today, where family visiting is positively encouraged and parents can stay overnight with their children. In most children's hospitals or wards, hospital play workers are employed and medical staff brighten the wards and treatment rooms with interesting distractions and comforting playthings. By the 1980s enlightened professionals were promoting a holistic approach whereby the health, support and care of the child encompassed all aspects of physiological and psychological needs within the context of social life. A non-specific approach to chronic conditions was promoted alongside advances in disease epistemology. Advocates claimed that there were common problems and needs associated with any chronic condition beyond disease-specific requirements that had an impact on children and their families. Stein and Jessop (1982) identified a number of generic issues that required consideration if appropriate support was to be established. These included:

*   the visibility or otherwise of the condition;
*   the nature of the condition, be it stable, life-threatening or unpredictable;
*   whether the condition affects mental, sensory or motor capacity;
*   whether it required intrusive or routine care.

Their view was that by focusing on the wider dimensions of personal needs a more sensitive and effective programme of care could be established. As they say,

> *the effect on children of repeated hospitalizations and days lost from school can be examined regardless of whether the hospitalization was because of crises associated with asthma or sickle cell anaemia.*
>
> (Stein and Jessop, 1982, p 355)

The social model has developed since then with advocates promoting the active voice of children in determining health and care regimes and enabling full and integrated participation in society. The social model was not readily accepted by all. Specialists in specific diseases and those involved personally or professionally with promoting research and support for specific conditions were at times suspicious of the 'generic' approach, anxious that the search for remedies might be sidelined and care undermined by non-specialist staff. In today's climate of holistic and multidisciplinary approaches to healthcare previous attitudes may seem somewhat blinkered. However, the recent report of the Children and Young People's (CYP) health outcome forum on long-term conditions, disability and palliative care (2012) identifies the 'single disease' model as detrimental to the health and well-being of the child arguing, as did Stein and Jessop over 30 years ago, for comprehensive quality assessments, taking account of children's multifarious needs and views in liaison with parents and focusing on positive developmental outcomes.

Disability

Changing notions of disability rather than handicap have challenged public perceptions of children who experienced disabling conditions. Disability was prominent on the political agenda from the 1970s onwards on the heels of race and sex issues and consequent anti-discriminatory legislation. Disability legislation to prevent discrimination first appeared in British statute in 1995 and the Act has been extended over time. People with disabilities have challenged negative perceptions and made their voices heard. People with disabilities are ensuring they are engaged in all aspects of society and represented in the public domain. The coalition government undertook a consultation exercise in 2012 about ways to offer appropriate support for children with special educational needs (SEN) and disability (DfE, 2012c) and launched its resulting Children and Families Bill on 5 February 2013. The primary tool for identifying the needs of children with disabilities will be through *education, health and care* plans (EHC). These plans must take account of parents' and children's voices and provide safeguards to educational access and experience within schools. The main focus in the bill is educational needs and opportunities for SEN and children with disabilities. There is some small reference to health issues but little in relation to cultural or social engagement. Thus, very young children in particular may fall through the safety net of this bill. Some reference to early childhood education and care could have strengthened their position and ensured the provision of services to meet their special needs.

The benefits of statute are in the implementation, and to date disability services for young children have been patchy. The Children and Young Persons (CYP) health outcome forum subgroup highlighted a number of problems for children with a disability or long-term condition. These include difficulties in accessing services, inconsistent quality and quantity of services and variability of practice (CYP, 2012).

Unless the EHC plans and the processes for managing them address the issues raised there will be little change and the 700,000 children with a disability in England (Hansard Column 358W, 28 June 2012) will not receive the support they ought to be able to expect. The report for government highlights some strategic areas for change with specific recommendations within them. They are:

* providing a quality integrated assessment;

* providing a quality service;

* enabling the child's voice;

* managing transitions in the child's life;

* supporting a functioning family;

* making the system work. (CYP, 2012)

These reflect the basic tenets for good practice across all health and well-being work with children.

Critical question

» *What strategies would you develop and put in place to meet the recommendations? Critically analyse your proposals for feasibility in practice. You might want to consider the range of professionals needed to facilitate implementation and determine the issues they might face.*

Healthy child policies

The Audit Commission estimated that there were 20 policies related to the health of children under five developed by the UK government between 1999 and 2009. It estimates some £10.9 billion has been spent. Table 3.1 provides headline figures in relation to key areas of health initiatives. The impact of this investment has not produced radical results in improving child health and in terms of narrowing the gap for disadvantaged young children has had virtually no impact at all (Audit Commission, 2010).

Table 3.1 *Under-fives health initiatives*

Funding 1998/99 to 2010/11	
Under-fives Sure Start and Children's Centres (capital and revenue)	£9,906,000
Under-fives health visitors (revenue)	£3,670,000
Other funding with impact on under-fives' health	£19,051,000

Source: Audit Commission (2010).

In the first years of the Labour government, health policy for the early years was funded largely through Sure Start. As discussed in detail in Chapter 6, *Poverty as part of the early years experience*, Sure Start was launched in 1998 with the aim of giving young children the best start in life. It supported childcare, early education and health and parenting issues. Sure

Start was community based and engaged multidisciplinary teams with strong emphasis on supporting and improving parenting. Most Sure Start schemes offered early childhood education and care (ECEC) and in time became linked to Children's Centres. Children's Centres, when fully functional, provided integrated early learning and care for children from birth to age five; a range of family support and health services including antenatal and postnatal advice; employment and training advice for parents; and support for families with special needs. (For more details see Chapter 5, *Education and care for early learning and development*.) Other health policies developed between 1998 and 2003 covered the population as a whole. From 2004 until 2009 a plethora of child health policies prevailed, as shown in Table 3.2.

Many of the policies and statutes had a broad remit beyond the obvious health parameters linked to medicine and disease into areas of well-being such as safety, lifestyle and familial circumstances. For example, the Children Act 2004 and Every Child Matters (2004) are extensively occupied with safeguarding. Despite the extent of policy and funding, the health of young children falls woefully short of desired outcomes. Both the Audit Commission (2010) and the Children and Young People's health outcomes forum (2012) highlight many of the same concerns. These include:

- disparity of services across demographic and geographic communities;

- weak and inconsistent management of service provision at all stages and levels;

- poor data collection, monitoring and evaluation of provision and funding;

- ill-trained clinical and other relevant professionals;

- not enough attention paid to inequalities of health;

- insufficient attention paid to the voice of the users.

The CYP health outcome forum report, commissioned by the Secretary of State for Health in January 2012, was submitted to the Department in July 2012. It contains salutary reading and makes extensive recommendations to improve provision and health outcomes for children. The forum emphasises the importance of a child- and family-centred approach to provision and service. It identifies essential aspects of achieving this:

- acting early and intervening at the right time – for example setting performance standards of speed of referral to treatment and being responsive to different stages and transitions in children's lives;

- integration and partnership – promoting multidisciplinary teams including non-health professionals such as ECEC staff and teachers;

- safe and sustainable services – ensuring they are age appropriate and facilitate transitions in young children's lives;

- workforce, education and training – health education should prioritise children and develop a safe and sustainable workforce for children;

- knowledge and evidence – such as including children in NHS surveys and population-based surveys; monitoring data in age appropriate bands and comparative monitoring and evaluation, nationally and internationally;

Table 3.2 *UK child health policies 2004–2009*

Year	Policy			
2004	Every Child Matters			
2005	Child Health Promotion Programme	Children Act	Children's NSF and core standards	Sure Start and Children's Centres
2006	Childcare Act	Healthy Start scheme		
2007	Children's Plan			
2008	Healthy Child Programme			
2009	Healthy Child Programme		Healthy Lives, Brighter Futures	

Source: Audit Commission, 2010.

- leadership, accountability and assurance – including outcome measures for diverse health conditions, appointing clinical leads for child health services and ensuring safeguarding measures are sound;

- incentives – by promoting integrated services and developing quality measures for performance and funding. (CYP, 2012)

The report is extensive and the list above provides only a flavour of the diversity and depth of the proposals.

Healthy Child Programme

Since 2009 the main policy and guidance document for health commissioners has been the Healthy Child Programme (HCP) (Shribman and Billingham, 2009). The programme focuses on pregnancy and the first five years of a child's life and provides a schedule of *the stand-ard for an evidence-based prevention and early intervention programme for children and families* (p 63). The guide is for commissioning agents within the National Health Service and Integrated Children's Services. The specifications of the programme are extensive and include a schedule of age- and stage-related protocols.

Early identification of need and risk is viewed as a key requirement for both populations and individuals. The programme stipulates health reviews covering assessment of risk using a range of social, psychological, demographic and economic factors. There is an extensive screening schedule based around significant stages through pregnancy and up to a child's fifth year. Prevention of risk and promotion of good practice underpins the guidance. The HCP schedule provides details for commissioners of services. The following is a short extract from the overview of the HCP schedule.

- *Emotional and psychological problems addressed*

- *Promotion and extra support with breastfeeding*

- *Parenting support programmes, including assessment and promotion of parent–baby interaction development, including language*

- *Additional support and monitoring for infants with health or developmental problems*
- *Common Assessment Framework completed*
- *Topic-based groups and learning opportunities*
- *Help with accessing other services and sources of information and advice.*

(Shribman and Billingham, 2009, p 32)

The guidance also covers infrastructure standards such as information, data collection, governance, estate and resource needs and allocation and quality measures.

Even a simple analysis shows a high level of comparability between HCP policy and the recommendations of the CYP health outcome forum report (CYP, 2012). It tends to support the Audit Commission's finding of limited progress when three years on from inception the same issues that need addressing are reported to government. One explanation for the tardiness of implementation is that while commissioning agents are aware of the health issues of the early years this is not always reflected in strategic planning or given priority in local area agreements (ibid).

It was Tony Blair, British Prime Minister from 1997 to 2007, who promoted the phrase 'joined-up thinking' but the notion of multifaceted policy development and working had been around for some time. The policy and professional agenda is littered with phrases promoting such an approach. Some progress has been made, for example with Children's Centres as indicated earlier. However, it seems that the rhetoric is more prevalent than practice. The bringing together of government departments under the umbrella of children, schools and families by the Labour administration was an attempt to make headway but the Department of Health remains stubbornly distant. This separation is reflected in many areas of child health with Primary Care Trusts being heavily focused on a medical model in delivery of services to children. General practitioners and hospital doctors are prominent, if not dominant, in the health service hierarchy and tend towards disease-focused practice. The culture of the medical professions in the UK is one of specialism and hierarchies where distinct knowledge and skills are seen as most important. In common parlance we talk of 'specialists' in health and attach greater significance to their views than a humble GP or nurse. While high levels of expertise are required to manage specific disease it is also crucial that health professionals take a holistic approach to a child's health needs.

Critical question

» *What do you view as the role of ECEC professionals in supporting the Healthy Child Programme? Critically appraise the contribution an ECEC professional can make to a multi-professional team.*

The well-being of young children

The well-being of babies and young children is most often viewed within the context of family life, and while for most children this is the case, for a significant minority it is not. There are over 89,000 looked-after children in the UK, that is, children in the care of the local authority. The reasons for such circumstances are many but for over half of these children it is a result of neglect or abuse (NSPCC, 2013).

The situations of young children within families can be vulnerable and require intervention. For many, external factors create the greatest vulnerability, as discussed in Chapter 6, *Poverty as part of the early years experience*. Economic conditions, be they global, national or local, can leave families with young children in deprived circumstances. Adult employment status, levels of income and availability of assets have significant influence on whether a child strives or thrives. Fiscal and social policies can alleviate or strengthen difficult circumstances. As discussed in Chapter 6, wage and benefit legislation can enhance or diminish a child's life. Commitment and support for equality and reduction in disadvantage affect well-being. Societies with little or no social care agenda severely affect disadvantaged children and diminish their emotional, social and cognitive development.

Social care policy

The ways in which the social care agenda is developed and delivered has an impact on levels of success. The Labour administration (1997–2010) put social exclusion high on its political agenda and produced extensive policy documents to help achieve its goals, *Narrowing the Gap* (DCSF, 2007a) and *The Children's Plan* (DCSF, 2007b) being two examples. Both policies reflect the centralised approach to performance goals and strongly directed performance and procedural protocols. The difficulty with such an approach is in managing the implementation at such a high level and distance from service delivery and persuading implementers that this is the best way to do things. Highly centralised policies tend to operate on the basis that 'one size fits all'. Yet, in most user and provider consultations it is local initiatives reflecting community circumstances and needs that are praised and requested. Anecdotal examination of successful cases studies demonstrates the importance of the local context. Successful models of intervention such as teenage pregnancy reduction programmes and improving early years parenting are local initiatives that focus on user needs.

CASE STUDY

Redbridge Children's Centre

The Audit Commission highlights the example of the Redbridge Children's Centre as an effective use of public finance. The Centre developed services for the Roma community in its area, ensuring Romanian language speakers were involved in delivering front-line services. It runs three sessions a week with Romanian-speaking staff, and a health visitor runs post-natal classes once a week. Over the two years of its existence Roma families have come to value the resource and from small beginnings it now has well over 400 children involved. The initiative has grown from strength to strength and helped improve pregnancy and early years outcomes for the community. The Audit Commission found that *Local parents who use the groups found them to be helpful for their children's mental and physical health, and an important forum for their community to discuss issues relating to their children* (Audit Commission, 2010, p 6).

Despite the status given to social exclusion, the Organisation for Economic Co-operation and Development (OECD) analysis puts the UK, along with the USA, low in achieving child well-being among 30 of the richest nations of the world. Nordic countries such as Denmark and Sweden are highly placed. The UK starts from a lower base with larger numbers of disadvantaged and low income families as a percentage of the population than these countries (www.indexmundi.com/map/) largely due to their greater social welfare and wealth distribution programmes. However, the circumstances of social exclusion are similar but the approach to the problem is rather different. Cultural norms in Nordic countries see state intervention as a positive thing and child-rearing as shared between family and the state. Professionals such as social workers and social pedagogues are viewed as helpful experts. The UK and USA perspective tends towards state intervention as intrusion and remedial rather than developmental. Cultural perception in British society is that parents have the right and responsibility for child-rearing and should be held to account if things go wrong. It is not surprising that those with the remit for righting these wrongs, such as social workers and other professionals are often viewed as interfering and with suspicion by those in need (C4EO, 2011). Scrutiny of the popular media shows this to great effect: I am aghast at the number of occasions in soaps watched by millions where social workers and related professionals are presented as troublesome, feared and interfering, and they are often vilified publicly when high profile real-life cases hit the headlines. Thus any government seeking extensive, radical and highly directive social change may meet wariness at best and resistance in some instances.

Big society

The highly centralised and top-down approach of Labour changed with the election of the coalition government. David Cameron's notion of the 'big society' was a cornerstone of the Conservative manifesto in 2010, and the emphasis on local and community decision-making and action would suggest devolution of policy and practice determined through a local agenda. There are difficulties with such an approach, however, if government has a social agenda that is at odds with local wishes. A government promoting early intervention and a desire for resources to be aimed at the disadvantaged must seek ways to ensure the agenda is shared and implemented and funds directed accordingly. The complex nature of disadvantage across UK society and the multifarious intervention needs are unlikely to be met by local activists, volunteers and charitable organisations without radical changes in funding and training. To deal with issues such as child protection, developmental delay and lifestyle issues such as obesity and teenage pregnancy requires a highly trained and qualified workforce with sound professional credentials working in multidisciplinary teams. On the one hand the coalition government (HM Government, 2010) is seeking to pull back from state intervention in family life and promote a greater role for citizens in conjunction with the voluntary and private sector, while on the other developing extensive intervention policy, reforming rather than eradicating many Labour initiatives (Churchill, 2011). Rowlands (2010) suggests that specific interventionist remedial programmes are unlikely to have much impact on fundamental inequalities in society and that a more holistic and universal developmental approach, such as that of Nordic countries, is more likely to succeed. He identifies the Sure Start programme as coming closest to this approach but that restricting its remit to disadvantaged families and localities undermines the importance of universality in social welfare.

Safeguarding children

The impetus for child protection policy and strategy tends to run in cycles and review, change and intensity of policy and strategy is often linked to high profile and tragic incidences of child abuse or neglect. During the 1970s through to the early 1990s there were a number of high profile cases of young children dying through abuse and neglect by their parents or primary carers. From Maria Colwell in 1973 to Rikki Neave in 1994 these serious cases highlighted weaknesses in the child protection system. A lack of inter-agency communication and dominance of silo working was consistently raised as a contributing factor of failure to protect children. There was a prevalence within health and social services of risk avoidance and defensiveness and a culture of blame (Parton, 2011). Indeed, there was a shift from intensive intervention and removal of children from their homes as a reaction to failure in child protection such as that of Maria Colwell to the other end of the spectrum when cases of removal of children were challenged by parents and brought to the public's attention such as those of Cleveland (1988) and Orkney (1991). Social work was in a dilemma, damned if it did not respond to children in danger and damned if it did and got it wrong. Such knee-jerk reaction is not helpful to a service that is at the sharp end of child protection. But problems do exist. Virtually every inquiry from Colwell to Climbié found inherent systems failures and structural inadequacies across the services.

CASE STUDIES

Child deaths by parental abuse

- Maria Colwell, aged seven, died at the hands of her stepfather in 1973. The inquiry identified a lack of communication between agencies and failure to see the child alone. It also found that the decision made to return Maria to her parents was flawed. All agencies involved in the case were criticised (Shaw, 2011b).

- Jasmine Beckford died in 1984 and had been in the care of social services for two-and-a-half years before she died, after her stepfather was convicted of assaulting her younger sister. She was seen by a social worker only once in 10 months (Batty, 2003).

- Heidi Koseda died in 1984 when her stepfather starved her to death. A private inquiry into her death found that the voluntary sector inspector allocated to her case failed to investigate a complaint of child abuse made by a neighbour. He also tried to cover this up with a fictitious account of a visit to see the child (Batty, 2003).

- Tyra Henry was 21 months when her father killed her in 1984. The inquiry suggested social workers were too trusting of the adults in the family.

- Kimberley Carlile was four when she died in 1986. Her stepfather received a life sentence for her murder while her mother was given 12 years' imprisonment for assault and cruelty. The inquiry concluded that the death was avoidable by intervention of appropriate agencies (cited in Munro, 1999).

- Doreen Mason died of neglect in 1987 after her mother and her boyfriend were violent towards her and then failed to have her injuries treated. Doreen was 16 months old and on the 'at risk' register from birth. A report said her social worker was inexperienced and given no proper training or supervision, and that the social services department suffered from a *siege mentality* and *destructive mistrust* between senior managers (Laurance, 2003; Shaw, 2011).

- Leanne White was three in 1992 when she was beaten to death by her stepfather. An inquiry concluded that her death could have been prevented if social services had responded properly to reports that she was at risk (Lambert, Independent, 2013).

- Rikki Neave was six when he died in 1994. His mother was convicted of cruelty. She had asked a succession of social workers to take the boy off her hands and told one she would kill Rikki if they did not do something. A report by the Social Services Inspectorate three years later said that fault primarily lay with senior management in the social services department (Central Inspection Group, 1998).

- Chelsea Brown, aged two, was killed by her father in 1999. The girl's social worker visited the family 27 times in the 10 weeks before her death. She took Chelsea to a paediatrician who said that six out of nine areas of bruising *had no plausible explanation* and at least one was deliberately inflicted. These findings should have triggered police involvement and a multi-agency case conference, but neither happened (Steele, 2001).

- Victoria Climbié, aged eight, died from hypothermia in 2000. Her aunt and her boyfriend were both jailed for life. A public inquiry into her death began in September 2001. Lord Laming who led the inquiry identified gross failure of the system, expressing amazement *that nobody in any of the key agencies had the presence of mind to follow what are relatively straightforward procedures on how to respond to a child about whom there is concern of deliberate harm* (Laming, 2003, p 4). He also identified *widespread organisation malaise* (p 4).

This catalogue of potentially avoidable tragedies had many causes and no one specific action or individual can be blamed. The list demonstrates inherent system failure, poor leadership and management, insufficient training and practitioner support and lack of inter-agency communication and collective action.

Child protection returns

Child protection and children's welfare were high on the political agenda by 1989 when the Children Act, 1989 became statute. This Act was a radical step in bringing together, under one piece of legislation, the basic tenets of children's status and family context. The notion of parental responsibility rather than authority and the supremacy of the child's needs and welfare obliged agencies with responsibility for children to promote their welfare and keep them safe. The notion of safeguarding rather than protection moved centre stage (Children Act, 1989) and dominated policy and strategy from 1990 to 2008. As a result of the Climbié inquiry there was extensive review of child protection policy and strategy. This resulted in the launch of Every Child Matters, a Green Paper consultation in 2003, and consequent legislation in the Children Act, 2004. The Act sought to *create clear accountability for children's services, to enable better joint working and to secure a better focus on safeguarding children* (explanatory notes, Children Act, 2004).

The social exclusion programme influenced child protection perspectives to become that of safeguarding. The emphasis was on supporting parents, a state and family partnership with a shared welfare remit. The move towards early intervention to overcome disadvantage across the spectrum of life, be it economic, educational, geographic or demographic, tended towards universality and social pedagogy, as identified in Nordic countries. The notion was to narrow the gap in equality and provide improvements for all. The policy achieved some degree of success and raised ever increasing expectations and demands of parents and families for early childhood education and care and support services for parents and families.

Some argued this undermined child protection and marginalised social workers who had a statutory responsibility for child protection. Certainly there was a general perception that the social exclusion agenda was the way forward. By 2008 public funds were under pressure as were the staff providing safeguarding services. The death of baby Peter Connelly (Baby P) hit the headlines in that year: another example of a tragic case of neglect and abuse. The Secretary of State ordered an inquiry into the local authority and a public war of attrition ensued with accusation and counter-accusation among the services and individuals involved. Once again Lord Laming was asked to report on the child's death. His findings identified positive developments in policy and strategy for the welfare of children but a lack of progress in key areas related to child protection. He found weaknesses in inter-agency collaboration and working practice and managerial support. He criticised poor training of front-line staff and over-heavy caseloads curtailing the time and attention required for child protection work. He suggested this was in part due to ineffective inspection regimes (Laming, 2009). All told, the report contains 58 recommendations which were accepted in full by the Secretary of State in March 2009.

Munro Review

Changing economic circumstances and the impact of the Peter Connelly case began the move towards social work reform and yet more refinement and expansion of systems and procedures. The Children's Workforce Development Council (CWDC) was remitted by the then Labour government to strengthen training and induction for new social workers. The Social Work Task Force was established and then the Social Work Reform Board in 2010. One of the first tasks of the coalition government was to request a review of child protection. The Munro Review (2011) made a number of recommendations bucking the trend over the past 20 years for greater reporting and recording mechanisms. Munro suggests that part of the problem has been over-bureaucratisation of child protection emphasising procedural and recording processes rather than building expertise of professionals working with children and families. It may be that procedures rather than practice have come to dominate safeguarding work but it is timely to remember that in the last century significant contributions to poor outcomes for children who needed protection were unsatisfactory reporting systems, lack of communication within and across agencies and inadequate historical and comprehensive information on individual cases. As Munro suggests, and the coalition government agrees, over-dependency on procedures must not detract from direct work of professionals with children and families. However, good quality, informative and timely reporting ought to be part of practice and provide helpful communication for all agencies involved. Perhaps the main problem is not the procedures themselves but the culture that surrounds them. If reporting is seen as 'checking up' and testing competency within a context of defending one's practice if things go wrong then the system will come to dominate rather than facilitate the child protection process. Many researchers and reviewers of child protection within the UK have identified the defensive nature of agencies delivering the service (Munro, 2011; Parton, 2011) and organisational theory identifies three key aspects of defensive organisations, ie avoidance of action, blame and change (Ashforth and Lee, 1990). These result in a culture of stultifying action, covering one's back and reluctance to take initiative. Munro concludes that policy-makers and strategists should rethink the place of regulation and procedures and base requirements on a learning rather than compliance culture that informs and helps collective understanding and allows greater flexibility for local expertise to inform the process.

Critical question

» *What is your view on the place of regulation and procedures in professional practice? Assess the risks involved with over-regulation and procedural compliance and those associated with reduced regulation and greater flexibility for professionals in protection work. Evaluate the analysis and determine your stance and reasons for it.*

Social work training

Professional training and development of social workers is a cornerstone of Munro's recommendations. The review indicates that the spectrum of need and provision in relation to the well-being of the child has led to uncertainty in child protection matters, with many non-social work professionals lacking the confidence to make informed decisions due to inexperience and insufficient training. Her findings suggest that the presence of a *skilled and experienced social worker* (Munro, 2011, p 132) in multi-agency teams improves the quality of analysis and decision-making in child protection matters. Munro criticises the prescribed and centralised approach to social work education and training. The highly centralised and prescribed system of recent years, developed in response to concerns over standards and practice for reasons discussed earlier in the chapter, has led to a focus on assessment of the child's situation rather than alleviation of it. This has stifled innovation and confidence in expertise. In a damming statement she claims:

> *The prescription of how to practice has sapped the profession's ability to develop its own knowledge and skills base. Most worryingly, there has been so much focus on improving social work skill in the timely assessment of children and families, that insufficient attention has been given to providing social workers with the knowledge and skills to help them. In the light of the growing body of evidence about the effectiveness of methods of solving problems and changing behaviour, this omission is grave.*
>
> (Munro, 2011, p 133)

Government's response has been to continue the existence and work of the Social Work Reform Board (SWRB) and endorse the recommendations of the Social Work Task Force (SWTF) to improve social work training and strengthen practice. The Board has representatives from interested parties including educational institutions, service providers and the profession. The SWTF report (2009) recommended improvements in training for social workers, in particular practice learning, and the establishment of a national social work college to promote high quality social work. Placements have been problematic for some time. In the 1990s when I worked in a university providing social work training, students were often unable to access social work placements of any quality never mind good ones. I well remember colleagues frantically searching at the eleventh hour for placements even if only tangentially linked to social work for trainees. The SWTF report (2009) suggests that this remains a problem with high quality placements being limited throughout undergraduate training. In a letter to the SWTF the Secretaries of State for Children, Schools and Families and Health said,

> *This means that higher education institutions (HEIs) must work together, with employers, and with the GSCC through its accreditation of courses, to ensure ...*

that high quality placements and academic education prepares them for the jobs they will go on to do.

(Balls and Burnham, 2009)

The coalition government has continued to endorse the recommendation, a national social work college has been set up, and from 2013 changes to social work education and training and practice learning come into effect. A new professional capabilities framework (PCF) is now in place that will be used to assess the quality of graduating social workers and continuing professional development. There are nine stages in the framework and a variety of pathways for achievement. Munro (2011) fully endorses this work as a means to ensure the profession takes charge of the professional learning it needs. The impact of these changes will take time to be realised and sufficient high quality placements will not appear overnight. The developments remain highly centralised and, as we have seen many times, reform from on high does not always translate to changed and improved practice at the front line. Perhaps the most important aspect of Munro's comments on front-line staff is that they should have time to work with the children and families in their care and to liaise sufficiently with other agencies and individuals involved. This means proper levels of resourcing, sensible case loads and cover and frequent and regular supervision. Without this, high quality training will be wasted and children will not get the best deal.

Multi-agency involvement

Child protection does not fit into neat parameters of single agency working, neither for that matter does any aspect of children's well-being. Whether in relation to health or education issues, welfare or lifestyle, many agencies and professions must be involved to support the best outcomes for children. In child protection matters awareness and concern may be raised in any number of ways. For young children, midwives and health visitors are obvious sources as are Early Years Professionals and teachers. They also have a role to play in the protection process and outcomes. Unfortunately, as case reviews and research show, they are not always as knowledgeable as they need to be, at times sidelined or ignored and often not seen as part of a holistic approach to resolution. The Social Services Inspectorate identified similar weaknesses in collaborative working when inspecting Cambridgeshire County Council's child protection service at the request of the Secretary of State as a result of the death of Rikki Neave. Inspectors reported:

Initial and review child protection conferences and core groups had frequently been postponed because they were inquorate. We were not satisfied that there was sufficient understanding of the importance of child protection issues amongst all relevant agencies at operational level including some staff in paediatric and psychiatric services for both children and adults. It was reported to us that in some parts of the county some agencies were reluctant to become involved in child protection work for fear of being involved in areas of difficulty and possible public concern.

(SSI, 1998, p 10)

Munro addresses the issue of multi-agency working but largely from a systems aspect and not that of professional expertise and integration. She recommends strengthening the Local Safeguarding Children Boards (LSCBs) to monitor the help given by agencies in prevention and remedial capacities. LSCBs have the function of bringing together agencies such as police, health, education and social care to ensure effectiveness of safeguarding. They have a statutory role in agreeing local safeguarding policy and procedures on how different agencies will work together. LSCBs undertake Serious Case Reviews (SCR) and prepare annual reports on safeguarding. Munro advises a change of approach to SCR analysing *why* a situation occurred not simply how, so that lessons can be learned and implemented. Government has responded positively to these recommendations and directly supports LSCBs to improve effectiveness (DfE, 2012b). This does not address the fundamental issues of inadequate training and collaboration. It may go some way to assist but there are more significant aspects to be addressed. These include more than a cursory look at safeguarding in generic training of other professional and vocational areas. Training and continued development need to consider the extent practitioners may be involved in safeguarding, prevention or remedial work and adjust programmes accordingly and, linked to Munro's findings of the value of experienced social workers in multi-agency teams, senior front-line social workers might beneficially engage in such continuing development. People can be made to work together and policy-makers can prescribe processes and procedures to facilitate it but no one can make multidisciplinary teams effective. They have to want to do it themselves and see a purpose in doing so. The best incentive for effective multi-agency working is successful outcomes and all participants feeling they have made a valued contribution. These are the personal factors influencing good collaboration. Policy-makers can identify and desire the function and strategists can plan and determine protocols but only practitioners can make it effective. The environment needs to be conducive to such collaboration. Leaders and managers across all agencies need to facilitate and believe in the idea. Participants need to respect each other's professional and vocational status. Staff need time and opportunity for it to happen. Without these elements multidisciplinary work is unlikely to be effective.

Critical question

» *What education and training do you believe would help ECEC professionals gain knowledge and confidence in child protection matters and how could this be best achieved?*

Critical reflections

Shared issues and common remedies

The history and culture of health services and professionals is different to that of well-being services such as social care, yet the requirement to collaborate, combine and communicate is essential if they are to best serve children's needs. Traditional paradigms in professional areas, such as the 'medical' model have been challenged and new ideas tried, such as the 'social' model. The more evidence collected the clearer it is that single disease methodologies in health and centralised and prescribed policies in social care for children do not work. A holistic perspective and integrated functions are the way forward. However, we must not lose sight of specific needs and circumstances in this mix. Children do need specialised treatment for illness and focused protection when at risk of abuse or neglect. This is truly a holistic and integrated approach.

Current government appears to be addressing such matters in a variety of ways. In its response to the Munro Review it covers a wide and diverse set of expectations. Within health services it expects reform to ensure effective early intervention in the Foundation Years especially for families with greatest need. It is looking for an expanded health visitor workforce and greater collaboration between health and social care professionals. It wants professionals to support effective transitions in children's lives from babyhood to early years and starting school. It wants schools to be safe havens for children, with teachers well versed in child protection and school nurses able to support transition from early years settings into school. It will provide greater professional autonomy but increase accountability across health and social services. It is strengthening the police with specialist agencies to fight child abuse and exploitation and reviewing how the family justice system can be more effective for children and families (DfE, 2011).

To achieve this, resource supply must meet demand. More midwives are essential in the changing demographic of a UK 'mini baby boom'. More good ECEC facilities will be required and well-qualified staff to run them. Changing patterns of family planning and improved survival rates of children with differing abilities will need enhanced services and knowledge, skill and understanding of all professionals whether teachers, ECEC staff, health visitors or social workers. The highest standards of education and training are required for professionals and society should expect the highest standards of practice in return. As assets for the health and well-being of children and families a society must respect professional expertise and have confidence in their ability to do the *right thing* (Munro, 2011, p 6). Policy-makers and service providers must give the workforce the time, training and tools to do the job. In return we should expect openness and honesty and a desire for accountability.

If this sounds utopian then so have been most of the authoritative reviewers and leaders of inquiries mentioned throughout the chapter because in essence these are the recommendations they make. Indeed, the proliferation of policies since 1997 related to young children tends to reflect this summary, and although not always followed through in resource terms or implementation, have reflected the significance of health and well-being in pregnancy and early childhood for the political agenda.

Further reading

Children and Young People's Health Outcomes Strategy (Report of the Children and Young People's health outcomes forum, CYP, 2012).

> A comprehensive report that is relevant to those with an interest and professional responsibility for children's health and well-being. It considers and makes recommendations about children's health beyond the traditional boundaries of health professionalism, taking account of the contribution to be made by those in education and social care. It takes account of the voices of children and families and how their views can be met in health policy.

Professor Eileen Munro (2011) *The Munro Review of Child Protection* (final report). London: The Stationery Office.

> Professor Munro subtitles her report a *child-centred system*. She argues for less regulation and centralised management and greater autonomy for social workers to get on with their job. She discusses the dilemmas for front-line staff and makes recommendations for change to the current safeguarding approach. An important read to understand the changes happening across the safeguarding system.

Nigel Parton (2011) Child Protection and Safeguarding in England: Changing and Competing Conceptions of Risk and their Implications for Social Work. *British Journal of Social Work*, 41: 854–75.

> This paper critically reflects on policy developments and debates in England in relation to child protection and safeguarding over the past 20 years. It links it to policy and practice from the early 1990s to late 2008. It provides a stepping stone for critical understanding and discussion of the issues and provides a context for changing policy.

4 The status and rights of young children as political and policy influencers

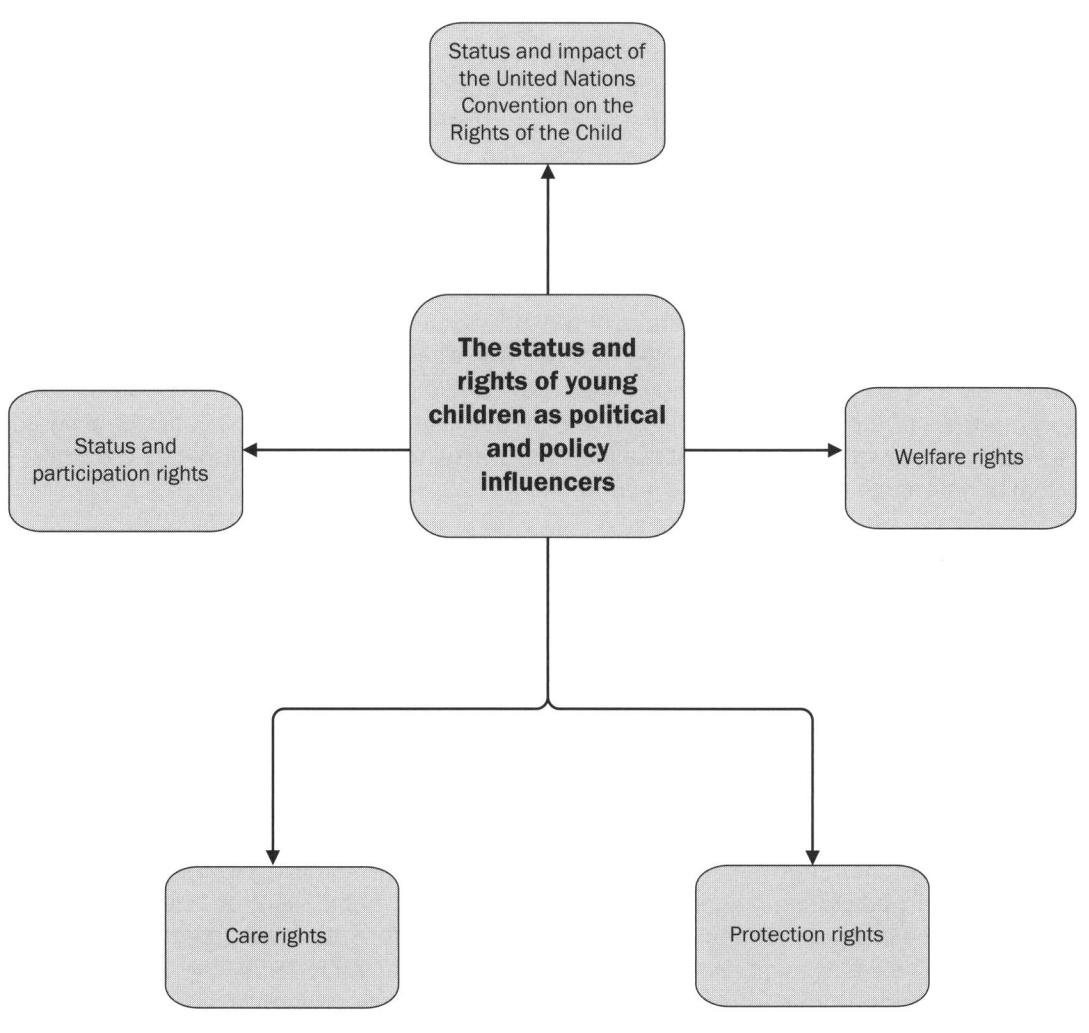

Introduction

The chapter takes a critical look at the current status and impact across the world of the United Nations Convention on the Rights of the Child (UNCRC). It discusses the rhetoric and reality of rights for young children, paying particular regard to participation rights. It considers the implications for young children within western democracies who have welfare rights but few liberty rights. As part of the discussion the chapter examines the notion of 'best interests' of children by adults. Throughout, the chapter engages in a critical debate on the value of rights within poor communities, chaotic political systems and severe economic conditions.

The concept of rights is a relatively new one, particularly for children. The idea sits within a context of childhood as a socio-cultural concept and a distinct and different state of being in the human cycle: an autonomous and independent experience rather than merely a preparation for adulthood. The concept is well documented and known but not necessarily widely shared. Thus rights that involve participation and independent decision-making do not sit easily with widely held views of children as dependent beings under the care, guidance and protection of adults. There are many occasions when children have not been considered or have been ignored in decisions that affect their daily lives. Situations such as the family moving to a new area or choice of school are frequently taken with little or no account of the child's opinion and wishes, or where the determination of the foster carer for a looked-after child is largely decided by adults. These decisions can have a great impact on children's experiences and achievements and affect them as adults in later life. As adults we tend to view these decisions as for the benefit of the child but as we know from high profile media cases and personal and professional experience this is not always the case. In some instances such decisions going against the child's wishes can be severely detrimental psychologically and developmentally. Protection rights, such as from danger, abuse and exploitation and welfare rights such as health, nutrition and education are more easily absorbed by individuals and governments as being things they can determine, control and facilitate in the best interests of the child. This approach to rights tends towards the perspective of children as passive recipients rather than active citizens, of children who have yet to gain the wherewithal to determine their needs and wants.

Status and impact of the United Nations Convention on the Rights of the Child

The notion of rights for children has been enshrined in the United Nations (UN) since 1989. It is separate to and distinct from the Declaration of Human Rights adopted by the UN in 1948. The focus of the declaration is liberty, the freedom to choose and determine one's life circumstances without coercion or oppression. The focus of the UNCRC is on protection and care to ensure the *best interests* of the child. While both the declaration and convention are concerned with political, social, economic, cultural and lifestyle circumstances there is a clear differentiation between the human rights of self-determination and the child rights of responsibility placed on others, that is adults, to enable them. There are elements of the UNCRC that indicate autonomous action, for example freedom of expression, thought, belief and religion and association. However out of 45 articles (UNICEF, 1989) the overwhelming majority put the onus on parents or governments to enable the right. Such a framework puts a moral responsibility on governments to provide policies, provision and services that support the achievement of the rights and political, economic and social conditions that are not detrimental to the 'best interests' of children. The UNCRC requires parents and carers of children to provide family and community conditions that support their rights and not exploit or oppress them.

Since 1989 many positive actions have taken place throughout the world. UNCRC has instigated changes to legislation and programmes of health and protection for children. In Brazil in 1990 legislation was approved for children and adolescents based on UNCRC principles. In South Africa UNCRC's ratification led to prohibition of corporal punishment for children and a separate juvenile justice system, and Morocco set up a national institute to monitor children's rights. Of course, these few examples do not reflect a worldwide situation. A number of countries still exploit children, through enforced labour, sexual abuse and as soldiers in armed conflict. Many children are still considered the property of adults to use as they see fit. Large numbers of adults still question the rights of children to be active participants in decisions affecting their lives (Seymour, 2009).

Current status of UNCRC

Most countries of the world have now ratified the convention. Only Somalia and the USA have yet to do so. Ratification means that a country is obliged to bring appropriate legislation, policy and provision of services to support the convention and ensure that children are not prevented from experiencing the rights prescribed. Countries report on progress to the Committee on the Rights of the Child. The Committee urges governments to use the convention when developing policies and provision for children. UNICEF (United Nations Children's Fund) is the agency with responsibility for supporting and assisting governments in the implementation of children's rights through advocacy, co-operation and technical assistance. UNICEF works with governments assisting in policy and legislation and direct services of critical need (UNICEF, 2005). Although 192 countries have ratified the convention it does not mean that children's rights are in place throughout. Clearly even from a superficial knowledge and awareness of the state of the world's children we can see great shortfalls in fulfilment of children's rights. The most recent report from UNICEF focuses on children in urban areas (UNICEF, 2012a). UNICEF recognises that urbanisation is spreading across the world and conditions for children within these environments can be harsh. Over half the world's population now live in towns and cities, with over a billion children experiencing the rewards or deficiencies of urban life. For some, urban living provides access to education, healthcare and prosperity but for others it can mean homelessness, inadequate shelter and economic exploitation. Major problems exist for poor and disadvantaged children everywhere. For example, in rural communities in many parts of Africa water for drinking may be a great distance from their homes and children are required to spend time collecting it which affects their participation in education (WHO and UNICEF, 2006).

Welfare rights

There are wide discrepancies in relation to many of the welfare rights covered by the UNCRC. These include survival and development, health and health services, standard of living and access to education. Table 4.1 provides some indication of the differentials in welfare across

Table 4.1 Differentials in welfare across the nations of the world

Category	Specific examples	Industrialised	Developing	Least developed
Survival and development	Infant mortality per 1000 live births (under one year of age)	5	44	71
	Neonatal mortality per 1000 live births (less than 28 days old)	3	25	35
	Life expectancy years	80	68	59
Health and health services	% of population using improved drinking water	100	84	62
	% of population using improved sanitation	99	52	36
	number of children (aged 0–14) living with HIV	2,000	3,400,000	1,600,000
	Children (aged 0–17) orphaned by AIDS, 2009	110,000	16,900,000	7,400,000
Standard of living	Gross National Income per capita (US$)	38,009	5,805	1,374
	% of population below international poverty line of US$1.25 per day	Not known	26	50
	Average annual rate of inflation (%)	2	16	52
Access to education	% gross enrolment ratio of pre-primary school participation	80	41	13
	% gross enrolment ratio of primary school participation	96(m)/97(f)	90(m)/88(f)	81(m)/78(f)

Source: UNICEF (2012a).

the nations of the world. These are only a few selected items categorised into groups of welfare rights and clusters of nations. To gain greater insight into what this means for children across the world we must look at the real life experiences of the children behind the statistics.

The welfare rights of children are inextricably linked to the economic and social policy of states. As discussed in detail in Chapter 6, *Poverty as part of the early years experience*, stunting is a direct consequence of malnutrition during pregnancy and infancy. Therefore, adequate standards of living for families are essential so that mothers and children can avoid health problems. Cultural perspectives also have an impact on the welfare of children. The proportion of women contracting HIV is often linked to the low status attributed to women in some communities and societies and their lack of rights and the dismissive machismo attitude of men towards simple protection measures. Women's rights and children's rights are symbiotic. For example, it is self-evident that for a child to be healthy and thrive its mother must have appropriate nutrition and care through pregnancy otherwise mortality, ill-health or developmental delay will be the result. A clean and safe environment is also essential for good health and evidence demonstrates that many children lack the basics of adequate shelter, clean drinking water and satisfactory sanitation. In urban slums this is compounded by overcrowding, poor lighting and ventilation and results in chronic health conditions for children (UNICEF, 2012a). As the World Health Organization and UNICEF pointed out in 2006:

> *Every year, unsafe water, coupled with a lack of basic sanitation, kills at least 1.6 million children under the age of five years – more than eight times the number of people who died in the Asian tsunami of 2004.*
>
> (WHO and UNICEF, 2006)

WHO and UNICEF recognise the strides made in terms of sanitation and clean water access, with over 1.2 billion people gaining this between 1990 and 2004. But to meet the millennium development goals (MDG) of halving the proportion of people without *sustainable access to safe drinking water and basic sanitation* over 1 billion people still need to acquire these basic requirements for health and welfare (WHO and UNICEF, 2006).

Family incomes and economic conditions affect children's right to education. In communities where wages are low and families struggle to meet their basic needs, a child can be an important economic asset, expected to work from a very young age. Such children do not gain education at any level and even those accessing primary education often do not go on to secondary learning. Figures for primary participation in developing countries of 90 per cent for boys and 88 per cent for girls drop for secondary participation to 61 per cent and 49 per cent respectively, and in least developed countries the comparable figures are 81 per cent and 78 per cent primary participation dropping to 31 per cent and 25 per cent secondary. The Second Millennium Goal is that by 2015 all children, with special emphasis on girls and children in difficult circumstances, should have access to, and be able to complete, free and compulsory primary education of good quality. UNESCO's assessment in 2000 indicated over 500 million children under six with no access to early childhood education and 113 million children, 60 per cent girls, with no access to primary education (UNESCO, 2000). A United Nations review of progress in 2010 clarified that the goal is unlikely to be met (UN, 2010).

Such dire statistics overall show how far we have to go to achieve Article 28 of the UNCRC that *Secondary education must be available to every child*. The data also highlight the impact of gender on access to education with girls having significantly less access to secondary education than boys. There are wide gaps in many countries between education in the wealthiest families and those in the poorest. For example, in Venezuela children in the richest families have an average of eight more years in education than the poorest and in Pakistan the differential is six years (UNICEF, 2009).

There are examples of successful initiatives to overcome educational deficits. Bangladesh set up the 'Basic Education for Hard-to-Reach Urban Working Children' project which provided literacy training across six cities that reached over 200,000 children. Nepal offers an out of school programme for working and disadvantaged children to catch up on their education. And Brazil's Sobral Municipality focused on enhancing education by renovating schools and supporting the development of teachers. Its efforts have been successful with improved results in National Tests (UNICEF, 2009). However, such initiatives, while valuable within the communities they serve, are no substitute for national political will and policy for comprehensive, free and compulsory education with resources to facilitate quality provision and access for all.

Critical question

» *Urban living provides benefits and disadvantages for young children. The UK is a highly urban society. Critically analyse the benefits or disadvantages for early childhood education and care in industrial urban societies. How would you seek to enhance the benefits and reduce the disadvantages through political and economic means and what constraints might you face?*

Protection rights

The UNCRC encompasses a wide range of protection rights, covering exploitation of all kinds and justice issues related to children. Rights of protection for children cover a variety of situations:

- violence or abuse by parents or people who look after them;
- harmful labour;
- drug abuse and sexual exploitation;
- abduction, kidnapping or trafficking;
- war and armed conflict;
- rehabilitation, justice and detention. (UNICEF, 2012)

Although many of these activities are perpetrated by individuals and criminal gangs it is governments that must act to prevent and remedy if children are to be protected. But as we have seen in the UK (Chapter 3, *Cultural and social aspects of the health and well-being of young children*), even with a panoply of legislation, extensive policy development and implementation and a national network of professional support we cannot thoroughly protect children from exploitation and abuse. Incidences of physical abuse and neglect within the home, sexual exploitation of children by organised gangs and abuse of power by those with authority and credentials are frequent items in the news: this exposure is often only realised long after the abuse has taken place, affording little respite and support during childhood and often no recourse to justice as adults.

CASE STUDY

Anna and Melissa

Anna and Melissa were twin girls of my acquaintance, the children of friends. They were lively, bright and engaging children: confident from a very young age and comfortable in adult company. Their parents were interested in music and enabling the children to access a choir. The girls auditioned and were accepted into a prestigious girls' choir and continued as members throughout their primary school years. It was only in their teenage years that they dug their heels in and refused to continue, rather to the surprise of their family. It was also at this time that troublesome behaviour began to occur. Some 20 years later these now mature women disclosed years of sexual abuse. The experience has had disastrous effects on their mental health and well-being. With hindsight there were signs which could have been picked up by those who cared, for example a series of 'accidental' mishaps that could have resulted in physical harm. When talking to them in later life about the experience they say they thought *everyone knew but didn't care*. The police took their eventual disclosure seriously but could do little about it as there was insufficient evidence to support the accusations. For Anna and Melissa the situation has been difficult to bear and for one has led to serious mental breakdown and self-harm.

Critical question

» *Historical cases of abuse have been prominent over recent years, for example those perpetrated by some celebrities of the 1960s and 1970s, endemic abuse across institutions such as children's homes and sexual abuse within the Catholic Church. There are those who excuse some of the allegations, suggesting they are in the past and should remain so or that reinterpretations in later years overstate the abusive nature of the accusation. There are others who want to right the wrongs of yesteryear. What do you see as the issues in such cases? Critically evaluate what this tells us about societal attitudes to the rights of children and vulnerable adults over the past 50 years.*

Domestic child abuse

Protection rights raise high ethical expectations of governance by governments and are challenging for the United Nations in its attempts to ensure that ratification means compliance with the UNCRC. This is particularly the case in intervention within the family and yet this is where parents and other family members can, and do, exploit or abuse their children. Across the world the view that parents know best for their children and that family life is private prevails. State intervention is unwanted for the most part, reflecting the view that it should only take place when there are clear demonstrated grounds to do so. The Children Act 1989 that came into force in the UK in 1991 reflects this perspective when it suggests that state intervention can cause harm to children by affecting family life (DH, 1989). Within the rhetoric of public discourse within the UK we see volatile reactions to state intervention in family life, with derogatory remarks on a so-called 'nanny state' interfering where it is not wanted or needed. This presumes parents know best and ensure the best interests of their children in their child-rearing practice. The statistics, however, suggest a rather different story. If we take an industrialised country such as the USA we can see the extent of abuse of children within the family, which forms the majority of cases for children between 0 and 7 years of age (Tables 4.2, 4.3).

Table 4.2 shows that the younger the children the greater the incidence of abuse. This reflects the increased level of vulnerability and powerlessness of children when they are very young.

The study found that 81.2 per cent of perpetrators are parents and of these some 36.8 per cent are mothers operating alone and 19 per cent are fathers in the same circumstances (Children's Bureau, 2011). The data further demonstrate a recurring theme of very young children disproportionately suffering in areas of both welfare and protection rights.

Table 4.2 *Child abuse within the family (USA)*

Age of victim (years)	Percentage of total children abused
Less than 3	27.1
3–5	19.6
0–7	56.2

Source: Children's Bureau (2011).

Table 4.3 *Type of child abuse (USA)*

Type of abuse	Percentage
Neglect	78.6
Physical	17.6
Sexual	19.1

Source: Children's Bureau (2011).

Critical question

> » *Early childhood education and care professionals often have close contact with young children and their families and may be the first to perceive child neglect or abuse. How would you seek to ensure children's right to protection is supported through professional practice? What are the implications for professional training and practice of this approach?*

War and conflict

Government structures and operations are often chaotic and ineffective during unrest and social and health policy becomes fractured. Families may be torn apart and directly embattled in the conflict. It is clear that the effects of war on civilians are significantly higher than in the past. In the First World War the percentage of civilian casualties was approximately 10 per cent. In the Second World War, with technical developments of weaponry, this rose to 48 per cent. By 2011 it was estimated that some 70 per cent of war casualties were civilians (Mollins, 2012). The organisation Action on Armed Violence (AOAV) identifies extensive detrimental effects on children including personal injury, loss of family members, homelessness and displacement, disrupted education and poor health provision. Very young children continue to be maimed by cluster munitions as they go about their daily activities. Whether at play or doing chores children are vulnerable.

Refugee and displaced children

Children may become stateless and displaced through conflict. In 2006 the Office of the United Nations High Commissioner for Refugees (UNHCR), the Internal Displacement Monitoring Centre of the Norwegian Refugee Council, and the US Committee for Refugees and Immigrants determined that some 40 per cent of refugees (those who seek refuge beyond their national border) and 36 per cent of displaced persons were children. Many are very young accompanying their families (Olusoga in Jones et al, 2008). Such situations have a direct impact on professionals throughout the world as traumatised and damaged children are faced with coming to terms with new environments and cultures. However, Rutter (2006) argues that the impact on these children is not homogeneous and that to assume this is to the detriment of the individual child. She suggests that the pre-migratory and post-migratory experiences of children are diverse and that the impact can be highly varied. Yet we continue to focus on pre-migratory experiences producing trauma rather than taking an inclusive approach considering post-migratory experiences and current circumstances. For example in August 2006, a Darfur camp for displaced people was attacked by Sudanese government troops on the premise that it housed armed rebels. This camp is the size of a small town and people have been living there for years. They cannot go back to their villages and are not safe in the camp. The internally displaced 'people of concern' as they have come to be known by UNHCR are estimated to be in the region of 25 million compared to those with refugee status of 9.2 million and asylum seekers at 680,000 (UNHCR, 2006). Statistics for young children are difficult to obtain but it is safe to assume at least 10 per cent of the total numbers of people of concern are children under five, and that rates vary in particular regions of the world and at different times. For example in some African and Asian countries it can be as high as 24 per cent.

For refugee children, life in the host country is often a hostile experience. Most of them, irrespective of their previous social and economic status, will be housed in some of the poorest housing and neighbourhoods, living in poverty and are likely to suffer from negative behaviour and language on the part of others. In addition they face personal trauma from the events that led to their refugee status and a family in crisis trying to manage the transitions enforced upon them. Host countries are not always sensitive and sympathetic to refugee needs. Inside the UK there is popular belief that we are a nation of tolerant and caring people enjoying and praising the benefits of multiethnic diversity. The reality for many refugees is far from this halcyon perspective. UK policy restricts the ability of almost all asylum seekers to work which means families live in poverty and are dependent on meagre public handouts while often being perceived as idle and scroungers by conservative elements of the press and public. Asylum seekers do not 'jump' housing queues. They cannot decide where they live and are often transported to parts of the UK where they may be further isolated from empathetic community support, often in substandard housing where local people do not wish to live. Provision of early education and care for young children in these circumstances is often reactive with little or no understanding of how to support, alleviate and remedy the effects of the pre- and post-migratory experiences. Incredibly, many refugee children make good progress due to their own determination and family support (Olusoga in Jones et al, 2008; Ofsted, 2003). Research by the Equality and Human Rights Commission found that:

> The right to education is enshrined in a wide range of international and national conventions and laws. In practice, asylum-seeking and refugee children's right to education in the UK is hindered as a result of dispersal, residential instability, financial difficulties and inadequate support in schools.
>
> (Aspinall and Watters, 2010, p vii)

In 2009, the Royal College of Paediatrics and Child Health found that around 1,000 children seeking asylum with their families were detained by the Home Office each year. This number was significantly reduced in 2012 and reflects government commitment, in December 2010, to ending the detention of children for immigration purposes (Home Office, 2012).

Harmful labour, abduction, kidnapping or trafficking

Slavery is illegal across the world but it exists in many parts. Its existence is largely unacknowledged by western industrialised societies and yet it forms part of the global economy. It is not known as slavery in the modern world but bonded labour and human trafficking and encompasses all the elements of slavery without bearing its name. The International Labour Organization estimates there are 215 million child labourers aged between 5 and 17 (ILO, 2010). Some forms of work can create positive benefits for children, developing skills and attributes that aid their development and contribution to society in later life. My own experience clearly demonstrates the creative and playful learning that can be gained.

CASE STUDY

The author's experience

When I was a very young child I lived above a shop. My parents ran a hardware and decorating business. My father was out all day decorating people's homes and my mother managed the shop. For me it was an Aladdin's Cave: full of colourful paints and wallpapers and a multitude of decorating materials and household goods. I could not wait to help and did so with gusto from about three years old: weighing handfuls of sticky putty for customers and bringing goods to the counter for my mother. I met lots of different people and could undertake a simple sale on my own before I started school. When I was five, as a 'Saturday job' I was asked to refill the chewing gum machines belonging to the sweetshop next door. I had to stand on a chair to reach and I loved it – especially the reward of ice cream. By the age of eight I had graduated to counting coinage and recording it on an adding machine for the local postmaster, who as payment opened up a bank account in my name and proceeded to deposit regular savings for me.

These experiences developed my literacy and numeracy skills, boosted confidence in language and communication with people from many and varied backgrounds and helped me develop an interest in new experiences and independence that has stood me in good stead throughout my life.

My experience is a far cry from the harmful child labour that exploits and enslaves children, prevents them from obtaining education and inhibits a healthy life. Such labour often involves some or all of the following elements:

- full-time work;
- excessive hours;
- dangerous work environments and activities;
- compulsion and enforcement;
- little or no pay;

- abusive circumstances, such as prostitution;

- abduction and trafficking.

Anti-Slavery International is an organisation that undertakes research and advocacy in child labour across the world. Its work demonstrates the appalling conditions of young children involved in harmful labour.

CASE STUDY

Ahmed's experience

When Ahmed was five years old he was trafficked from Bangladesh to the United Arab Emirates to be a camel jockey. He was forced to train and race camels in Dubai for three years.

I was scared … If I made a mistake I was beaten with a stick. When I said I wanted to go home I was told I never would. I didn't enjoy camel racing, I was really afraid. I fell off many times. When I won prizes several times, such as money and a car, the camel owner took everything. I never got anything, no money, nothing; my family also got nothing.

Ahmed was only returned home after a Bangladesh official identified him during a visit to Dubai in November 2002.

Source: Anti-Slavery International (2013).

Not only was Ahmed forced into inappropriate and harmful labour but abducted from his home and family. He is one of the lucky ones; others do not fare so well. The International Labour Organization estimates some 1.2 million children are trafficked every year (ILO, 2002). UNICEF identified child trafficking as the

> *recruitment, transportation, transfer, harbouring or receipt of children for the purpose of exploitation. It is a violation of their rights, their well-being and denies them the opportunity to reach their full potential.*
>
> (UNICEF, 2013)

Critical question

»   *Critically compare and contrast the issues raised by the two case studies in relation to young children's rights and needs. From your analysis determine your ethical stance on these issues and the implications for professional practice.*

Children are trafficked in many ways. Some are stolen, some are sold by families and others are taken without coercion with the promise of a better life. They may be trafficked for forced work, drug trading and petty crime or for sexual exploitation and domestic service. The research shows that boys are more likely to be trafficked for work, drugs and crime while girls are more likely to trafficked for sexual or domestic deeds (ILO, 2002).

In any event, the consequences are dire and the remedies few. Clearly prevention is the best form of government and international action, and UNICEF works with partners across the world to support the development and strengthening of legislation and policing to prevent these criminal acts. However, welfare policy and provision are also required to minimise the need and demand for child labour along with cultural change that exacerbates the vulnerability of children to trafficking and exploitation. As was pointed out by the Director-General in the ILO's Global Report on child labour in 2006:

> there has in recent years been a sea change in attitudes towards child labour. The sense of hopelessness and resignation that previously prevailed on the subject; the feeling that, regrettable though it is, there is little that can be done to prevent or eliminate child labour as it is so deeply rooted in poverty and cultural attitudes: these have been replaced by a worldwide consciousness that it is today not only possible but also urgently necessary to eradicate at least the most unacceptable forms of child labour.
>
> (ILO 2008 report cited in Smith, 2008)

It is clear that the extent and diversity of protection rights and the complex issues surrounding them test communities, governments and international agencies in their endeavours to protect children. The fact that many unscrupulous adults seek to exploit children less powerful and with less status than themselves is shocking to those who promote children's rights and status. Authoritative figures in government and non-government agencies across the world have made various attempts to stem the tide. However, it would still seem that the notion of the 'best interests' of the child is overwhelmed by the 'vested interests' of the adults.

Care rights

The main premise of the range of care rights in UNCRC is that children require the support and guidance of parents wherever possible and that parents have a responsibility to their children to assure their best interests. The UNCRC also puts a responsibility on the state to assist parents to enable them to meet this responsibility. How parents raise their children is, in industrialised societies, a matter of choice. It is deemed a private experience in the main, accountable to no outsider in general and only by exception if parental behaviour is outside the law. (This is true in most other countries too, although there are communities where children and child-rearing are perceived as the responsibility of the collective. The Kibbutz approach in Israel is arguably the most well known (Aviezer et al, 1994).) In the UK it is illegal for parents not to send children to school from the age of five, unless other approved arrangements have been made, such as home schooling. It is against the law to neglect or abuse a child, although as we have seen in Chapter 3, *Cultural and social aspects of the health and well-being of young children*, this can happen without the authorities ever being aware or deciding there is insufficient need to intervene. However, it is not against the law in this country, nor is it against any specific UNCRC article to chastise children through physical punishment. This is a strange anomaly in terms of children's rights given the value placed on safety and protection from harm and the presumption that parents are the primary source of such care.

Physical punishment of children

Any discussion on the use of physical punishment by parents, or close extended family, always raises strong feelings and fierce advocates on both sides of the debate. I am of a generation whose parents viewed smacking as a relatively normal part of child-rearing and condoned physical punishment by teachers. My parents did not smack often but enough to frighten me, although I cannot ever remember it stopping me repeating the behaviour if I wanted to do so.

I remember getting up to mischief on many occasions realising I was likely to be physically punished for it but carrying on regardless. On one occasion, when I was about 10 years old, I had been discovered by a neighbour playing in a forbidden area, namely my father's storage premises, and had run off when threatened by my mother. My fear of the 'smack' was such that I stayed out late hoping my father would have gone out and my mother calmed down sufficiently that I could sneak off to bed. Of course worse was in store: not only was I in trouble for the first thing but doubly naughty due to staying out. In both instances the concern of my parents was my safety but strangely their way of dealing with it was punishment not explanation and education.

My story is not unusual. I see many instances where a parent's reaction to a child doing something they have been told not to is to shout and smack. The recurrent joke about '*Why do parents take their children to supermarkets? To smack them*' is an old one but holds an element of truth. Unsettled children in shopping expeditions with parents are a fairly common sight and aggressive reactions often result. There are many explanations for such behaviour that are not part of the discussion here but what we can examine is the concept of physical punishment of children by parents and what this tells us about a society that condones the activity while promoting the UNCRC.

In 1999 physical punishment was highly newsworthy in the UK as a result of the European Court of Human Rights ruling that a child should have the same rights as an adult when it came to physical assault. A British boy had taken his case to Strasbourg when a British court cleared his stepfather of causing actual bodily harm. The stepfather had used a cane to punish the boy. The government was called on to ban physical punishment of children by parents and others but it refused to do so. The government of the day, while banning the use of caning, was inclined to let parents use 'reasonable' physical punishment. A survey at the time indicated some 70 per cent of parents agreed with the government's decision (BBC, 1999).

In 2012 we were still debating the issue and seeking to define what is reasonable. In October 2012 a judge freed a mother sentenced for smacking her children, indicating that while she had overstepped the mark in reasonableness it did not warrant the custodial sentence originally given (Turk, 2012). The Children Act 2004 allows physical discipline as long as it does not cause 'actual bodily harm'. For example, a reddening of the skin but not a scratch is deemed acceptable. Use of a cane is not acceptable but perhaps a kick or a pinch is if it doesn't bruise or break the skin. Writing it down makes me realise how cold and calculating such a law is and how difficult to it is to define 'reasonable'. Are we to believe that an adult weighing 60–80 kilos really understands the power his or her 'smack' conveys, or the fear someone twice as tall creates in the young child when imposing physical discipline? UK politicians have debated the issue on a number of occasions in recent times. In 2004 a three-line whip was imposed by the Labour government on Labour Members of Parliament when a challenge was brought to retaining the 'reasonable chastisement' clause in the Children's Bill. Governing parties in the UK have fought shy of challenging public opinion on this matter for many years. Although surveys and polls of parents and other adults have been undertaken and results have influenced government policy, no policy-makers have surveyed what children think. The recipients of these measures have little say: a clear demonstration of the differential political influence of the franchiseless child and the vote-holding parent. Not only is the continuance of physical punishment by parents against the spirit of the UNCRC, it is damaging to children's healthy development.

A wide range of research shows that experiencing aggressive treatment as a child can lead to aggressive behaviour and potential repetition in adulthood. Studies show how emotional development and well-being can be harmed by physical punishment. Elliman and Lynch (2000) consider that research tends to show that the presence of physical chastisement creates more negative outcomes than positive and that while physical punishment may alter and bring about desired behaviour in the short term it does not change behaviour in the long term.

While the UK holds on to the right to reasonable chastisement other countries have seized the initiative and banned all forms of physical punishment of children. These include Sweden in 1975, which was the first country to do so, and South Sudan in 2011. Alongside its legislation Sweden ran a comprehensive education campaign, with information to every household. Today the legislation is not challenged and recourse to law is rare; persuasion and the existence of a ban seems to have created a zeitgeist that accepts it is wrong to physically punish children in the home or elsewhere.

Critical question

» *Where do you stand in the 'smacking' debate and what is the rationale for your opinion? Critically review your rationale to evaluate whether it is based on informed evidence or speculative anecdote. You might want to explore more case studies and research into the effects of physical punishment and reflect on your opinion.*

Looked-after and adopted children

UNCRC makes special mention of children who may be separated from parents, in care of the authorities and others and those who are adopted. UNICEF emphasises the importance of children in care being able to access the UNCRC welfare and protection rights including access to education and healthcare and freedom from abuse. It also highlights the importance of non-discrimination of children and inheritance rights. It works with governments to facilitate legislation, policy and services that enable communities to care for their orphans and other vulnerable children. For example, in Malawi, UNICEF advocacy helped to gain political commitment and resources to deal with the crisis of children without parental care. UNICEF also set up over 600 locally based childcare centres for over 50,000 children under five (UNICEF, 2006).

Within the UK, in England children in care relates to all children being looked after by the local authority. On 31 March 2011, 65,520 children under 18 were looked after by local authorities. Table 4.4 provides a breakdown by age.

Children are in care for many reasons ranging from abuse to short-term support for families in acute stress. There are three ways in which children can become looked after. These are:

1. care orders;
2. voluntary arrangements;
3. police protection or involvement.

The reasons for being looked after and the numbers and percentage of children involved are shown in Table 4.5. These proportions reflect the trend over the past five years.

Table 4.4 Children in care (2011)

Age at 31 March 2011 (years)	Numbers	Percentage
Under 1	3,660	6
1–4	12,020	18
5–9	11,830	18
10–15	24,160	37
16 and over	13,860	21

Source: Department for Education (2012).

Table 4.5 Categories of need for looked-after children

Category of need	Numbers	Percentage
Abuse or neglect	40,410	62
Child's disability	2,150	3
Parent illness or disability	2,720	4
Family in acute stress	5,880	9
Family dysfunction	8,930	14
Socially unacceptable behaviour	1,230	2
Absent parenting	4,050	6

Source: Department for Education (2012).

Most children are placed with foster carers. This has increased from 70 per cent in 2007 to 74 per cent in 2011. Over the same period there has been a 22 per cent decrease in the number of looked-after children placed with parents (5,110 in 2007 compared with 3,970 in 2011). The reasons for this are not clear. The number of children placed for adoption has fallen by 10 per cent between 2007 and 2011, from 2,720 to 2,450. It is thought that some of the reduction in the numbers placed for adoption may be explained by an increase in the use of special guardianship orders in recent years (Department for Education, 2012).

The predominance of abuse and neglect as the reason for being looked after reinforces the importance of children's protection rights and the need for government legislation and policy in this area. Of course, being looked after presents its own issues as we can see from the statistics given in Table 4.6. Looked-after children do not fare as well as the general populace in terms of educational achievement and progress.

The difficulties looked-after children experience at all stages of their educational experience demonstrate the importance of welfare rights and resources to remedy the circumstances and conditions that help create such an anomaly.

For looked-after children, one of the biggest concerns is the lack of consistent, high quality relationships with those responsible for their care. Munro (2001) highlights the importance

Table 4.6 Educational achievement of looked-after children

Children	Reading		Writing		Mathematics	
	Looked after	All	Looked after	All	Looked after	All
Year 2 (ages 6–7) percentage achieving target for age group	65	85	57	81	71	90
Year 6 (ages 10–11) percentage achieving target for age group	53	81	52	80	43	74

Children	Looked after	All
Year 11 (age 16) percentage achieving A*–C English and maths	13.9	58.6

Source: Department for Education (2012).

children place on continuity and affection in relationships and how this is so often lacking. High turnovers of social work staff, and team responsibility rather than individual all help militate against good relationships. Children want a confidante to share their thoughts with and the conflict between professional accountability and liability is not always conducive to such relationships. I remember a particularly harrowing situation where a child was parted from the caring confidante she had in her 'best interests', largely due to rules and regulations developed and implemented without sensitive understanding of the implications for individual children.

CASE STUDY

Chloe's story

Chloe was a severely abused child residing with a long term foster carer. She had emotional and behavioural problems largely as a result of sustained sexual abuse from a young age. Chloe was estranged from her family and was not allowed to see her younger sibling. He was a baby during the period of abuse and deemed to have been largely unaffected by the environment. The authorities decided he would be able to be adopted, and proceedings went ahead. Chloe was not deemed suitable for adoption as a result of her experience. Her sibling's new parents did not wish contact between their son and his sister. Chloe was distraught by this but had no recourse to change the situation. She was also repeatedly asked by the social worker in charge of her case if she would be willing to meet with her mother who continuously made this request. Chloe's mother had been part of and colluded with the abuse she experienced but because Chloe's evidence was not seen as reliable, due to her age, neither her mother nor her father, the perpetrator, were ever convicted, although all parties concerned were assured this abuse had taken place. Chloe adamantly refused to communicate with her mother.

It is difficult to imagine the emotional situation of Chloe who had achieved no justice and was penalised for the effects of the abuse. She had had a number of foster carers since the age of four all of whom had found her difficult to live with. She was fostered by a family with simple backgrounds and achievement who had a lot of love to give. They had an adolescent son. Chloe adopted all of her usual negative behaviour pushing the boundaries more and more but the foster carers tolerated and supported her without exception. They also fought hard with the authorities to receive play therapy with a renowned expert in the field and Chloe began slowly to trust. After five years, as Chloe reached readiness for secondary school her behaviour had improved and her suspicion of anyone who showed her affection had reduced. Suddenly a furore broke out in the household when the, now older, teenage son was found to have accessed pornographic material on the internet. The police became involved but accepted it was largely a mistake and not predatory and no further action was taken. However, for Chloe that was the end of family life as she had come to know and trust it. She was taken from her home without notice and relocated to another foster carer and not allowed any access to her previous contacts including those at school as well as home.

Critical question

» *Identify the critical path of issues that impact on Chloe's situation and evaluate the rights and wrongs of each aspect. What might be the impact on Chloe of the outcome? How do you think the professionals involved handled the situation and what would you have done differently and why?*

If Chloe had been in a parental home this would not have happened. The family would no doubt have been concerned and shocked by their son's behaviour but would have dealt with the issue as a family. For Chloe that was never an option. The case study shows how the best intentions of protection protocols and procedures can be so damaging to the children they are intended to protect. Munro argues in her recent review for government (Munro, 2011) that social work needs to be more fine-grained, flexible enough to respond and react to individual needs and circumstances and sustained enough to build good relationships that respect the child's opinion. Munro also states that social workers need high quality and comprehensive training, especially in child development. In her research article, 'Empowering Looked After Children' suggests that:

> *we cannot assume that all professionals are beyond criticism in their work with vulnerable children and will always act in their best interest ... Acting in the child's best interest is not just a question of good intention but also of knowledge: what is in the best interest of the child in a particular circumstance?*
>
> (Munro, 2001, p 15)

Looked-after children have little flexibility to make mistakes and foster carers are also constrained. In most parental families children develop at their own rate; they are allowed to make mistakes, and while they may be criticised by parents will still be part of the family. In most parental families problems are overcome and short-term superficial mistakes are quickly forgotten. Not so with looked-after children: in an effort to ensure a suitable lifestyle authorities are highly prescriptive, determining standards and goals that leave little opportunity for children to determine their own pace and path.

Status and participation rights

As we have seen in earlier discussion, children's rights are not realised equally. This inequality is multiplied for those children who have no official identity. A birth certificate is essential for legal and inheritance status within families and for state identity and nationality. Without a formal identity children are vulnerable to all forms of exploitation, such as abduction and trafficking; they may also experience miscarriage of justice and be barred from receiving health and education services. In 2010 there were 51 million children unregistered at birth (UNICEF, 2010). Unregistered children are often those on the margins of society, in areas where social security networks are slight or non-existent. For example children in urban areas where the social infrastructure is most developed and actively administered are twice as likely to be registered as children living in rural communities. One of the biggest stumbling blocks to registration is the low priority it is often given by families and the state. When other pressures are more immediate, such as welfare needs, families do not see the urgency of registration: nations in turmoil through war, pestilence or weak administrative systems tend to be challenged with more immediate problems than nationhood status. For some countries it can be a predetermined policy to avoid growth of specific cultural communities. For others it may be a cultural context in relation to marital status or recognition of fatherhood. In any event the outcomes have severe consequences for the children directly affected (Innocenti Report Card, 2002).

The notion of participation rights is for many children unrealised. Freedom to choose how to live their lives is not a concept that sits well with most adults, especially parents. Adult society tends towards determining policy and services on behalf of children not in response to their personally articulated needs and wants. Families are often ruled by the choices of adults within them. We see this through all strata of society and across all aspects of daily life. If we revisit Munro's findings in her research with looked-after children (Munro, 2001) we see that one of the biggest complaints from children in care was lack of privacy. As children, friendship networks may be chosen for us and woe betide the child who takes up with 'bad company' as perceived by the parent. For many children freedom of association is hardly the reality. There are counter-arguments, usually formed by adults, to this in relation to guidance and protection of children but on delving deeper, restrictions are more often to serve adult wishes and choice rather than for the protection of the child. Parents choose friends for their children, they choose activities for them to engage in and they determine where they go and when. This is often done for the benefit of the child and enjoyed by him or her but it gives little recognition to the autonomy of the child and lacks any recognition of the child as a rational being capable of making decisions and choices.

CASE STUDY

Friendships

I was nine years old when Penelope and her parents moved into the neighbourhood. Her siblings were considerably older than her and already living away from home. Her mother, a business woman too, got talking to my mother about Penelope being lonely and not knowing anyone. Without so much as a backward glance I was offered as the prospective friend and told to call on her the next day.

Penelope and I rubbed along okay but neither of us was really interested in the other and I found her home and family rather off-putting. My mother never heeded my concerns but continued sending me to Penelope's to play until the family moved a couple of years later. There was never a thought given to our views or choices by either mother.

Critical question

» *Critically appraise your own and other families that you know to evaluate the extent of personal freedom and choice young children have. As an advocate of children's participation rights how would you seek to achieve autonomy for young children and what parameters, if any, would you place on freedom and choice?*

The debate on participation has raged for many years and is highlighted by Franklin (2002) in his consideration of two distinct forms of children's rights as articulated by Archard (1993): caretaker rights and liberty rights. Caretaker rights are largely the groups of welfare and protection rights of the UNCRC. Advocates of caretaker rights tend towards a view of the child as needing care and protection but not participation, in the belief that since children will make mistakes that could influence their future lives they are not experienced enough to make informed decisions. Such advocates work on the basis that children need adults to guide, support and direct them as they are not yet fully rational beings. Proponents of liberty rights challenge the caretaker perspective arguing that children should have the same status as adults, and while acknowledging developmental aspects, do not see these as a sufficient constraint to limit participation rights of children (Franklin, 2002). Welch (in Jones et al, 2008) puts the argument for liberty rights, making a number of simple but pertinent observations.

* Children are able to make rational decisions and need to gain experience of decision-making.

* Mistakes are part of learning for both children and adults and adults are not denied the right to make decisions because they might make mistakes.

* Age requirements for rights are inconsistent and arbitrary and competence is not a requisite for participation rights.

* Children can do nothing to change their status if they do not have access to decision-making.

Welch provides credible examples and reasons for liberty rights for children and articulates clearly the inability of many adults to avoid mistakes and make credible decisions. Adults made bad economic and financial decisions for many years, which resulted in a severe and long-lasting recession but no one has suggested taking away their right to participation in decisions affecting their lives.

Young children do not create the world they live in. They play no active part in determining how it is run or deciding the social, cultural and economic circumstances of their lives. It is easy to see them as victims of forces beyond their control. However, this is not because of lack of competence or capability to affect their lives but largely due to being powerless to do so. If children as young as three can work the buses of Argentina (UNICEF, 2013) and at six work in factories and at 10 become soldiers, they are capable of making informed decisions about their lives given the right to do so.

The Convention on the Rights of the Child recognises that children should have increasing autonomy, in line with their evolving capacities and that parents, communities and governments must give children the support and status they need to enable them to use it effectively in influencing their life experiences and circumstances.

Critical reflections

Children's rights, rhetoric or reality?

All bar two nations of the world have ratified the UNCRC. This means they have made a commitment to enshrining these rights into their government laws, policies and services. UNICEF considers that *The Convention has inspired a process of national implementation and social change in all regions of the* world (UNICEF, 2005).

The political rhetoric is strong: in Addis Ababa in January 2013 health ministers of African nations held a conference to consider how to improve child survival. The outcome was a pledge to end preventable deaths of children under five by 2035 and reduce infant mortality rates to fewer than 20 per 1,000 live births across all African nations. It was, as UNICEF suggests, *a promise renewed* (Westerbeek, 2013). Progress is slow in many African nations where governments are unstable and internal unrest creates difficulties in building the administrative infrastructure for pledges to become policy and provision. Simply renewing a promise is not sufficient for children now; what is required is immediate and positive action. Governments are taking positive steps but in large countries with extensive rural communities and entrenched poverty, welfare reform and services are thin on the ground.

The protection of children is high on the agenda of most nations, yet extensive incidences of trafficking, abuse and exploitation of children continue. Often perpetrated on the poorest and most vulnerable of communities, those lacking education and welfare support provide rich pickings for criminals involved in bonded labour. To remedy and stop such practices is a complex matter and requires co-ordinated and diverse action and resources. Simply legislating and policing is not sufficient as it does not move families out of the conditions leading to the activity. It requires 'joined up' thinking by governments and a commitment to alleviating the poor economic circumstances of those vulnerable to such exploitation.

Almost half of the world's forcibly displaced people are children. Many of them spend their entire childhood far from home. Children displaced from their homes who may also be estranged from their families are more vulnerable to abuse and exploitation. It makes little difference whether they are internally displaced, refugees or asylum seekers in other countries or even stateless, their lives are at risk of harm. Such children often find little solace in their new environments where harsh treatment, inadequate facilities and racial abuse may prevail. Governments around the world are not always sympathetic to the plight of such children, sometimes drawing up legislation and policy that is at odds with the UNCRC.

War-torn countries such as the Democratic Republic of Congo have extensive displacement of the population with all the concomitant issues of health, education and nutrition. Even when government and rebel forces are talking, the general lawlessness in parts of the country displaces settled communities. For others, such as in Darfur, refugee camps become home for years yet remain inadequately served by clean water and good sanitation. In the UK children of asylum seekers are not given the same rights as other children. Their families cannot choose where they live and schooling is often inadequate. It seems governments and communities may be selective in the children that they care for.

In 2008 the four children's commissioners identified participation and civil rights and freedoms as falling short of UNCRC expectations (Marshall et al, 2008). Their report shows that participation rights lack government endorsement and policy that would enable comprehensive requirements and implementation. There is also a lack of will to make enforceable the civil rights of children comparable to those of adults, for example by making physical punishment of children illegal. The commissioners also found that younger children had fewer participation rights than older children and that their input was rarely sought when determining decisions and actions that have an impact on their lives whether in a familial or governmental context.

We cannot underestimate the importance of children's rights throughout the world. The critical discussion in this chapter continuously demonstrates the parlous state of many of the world's children and the importance of collectively seeking to remedy this. The attitude towards and treatment of children by communities and nations reflect the values they hold and the collective conscience. If we are to turn rights rhetoric into reality, action at all levels of policy-making and international collaboration must be strengthened. Cultural norms that discriminate against children must be challenged and children must have the same status and civil rights as human beings.

Further reading

B. Franklin (ed.) (2002) *The New Handbook of Children's Rights*. Abingdon: Routledge.

> A definitive text on children's rights offering theoretic perspectives and challenging common perspectives. It covers the range of debates on children's rights, critically examines the impact of UK actions and the UNCRC and Human Rights Declaration and the implications for children. It also discusses ways in which children may become participants in policy-making.

Laura Lundy, Ursula Kilkelly, Bronagh Byrne and Jason Kang (2012) *The UN Convention on the Rights of the Child: A Study of Legal Implementation in 12 Countries*. UNICEF, UK and Queen's University, Belfast.

> A research team from Queen's University, Belfast undertook research into the implementation of UNCRC at the request of UNICEF UK. The team studied 12 countries to demonstrate the variety of ways in which countries with common or civil law legal systems have provided for children's rights at national level by taking steps to implement the UNCRC. This study provides an international context to compare the current status across the United Kingdom.

Peter Aspinall and Charles Watters (2010) *Refugees and Asylum Seekers: A Review from an Equality and Human Rights Perspective* (Research report 52). London: Equality and Human Rights Commission.

> This report examines the situation of asylum seekers and refugees from an equality and human rights perspective and places the evidence within its legislative context but without going into the detail of case law. Due to a lack of official data available on the group and few large-scale quantitative studies, the report draws strongly on qualitative and more localised studies to examine the situation with regard to a number of issues including, among others, health, education and employment.

5 Education and care for early learning and development

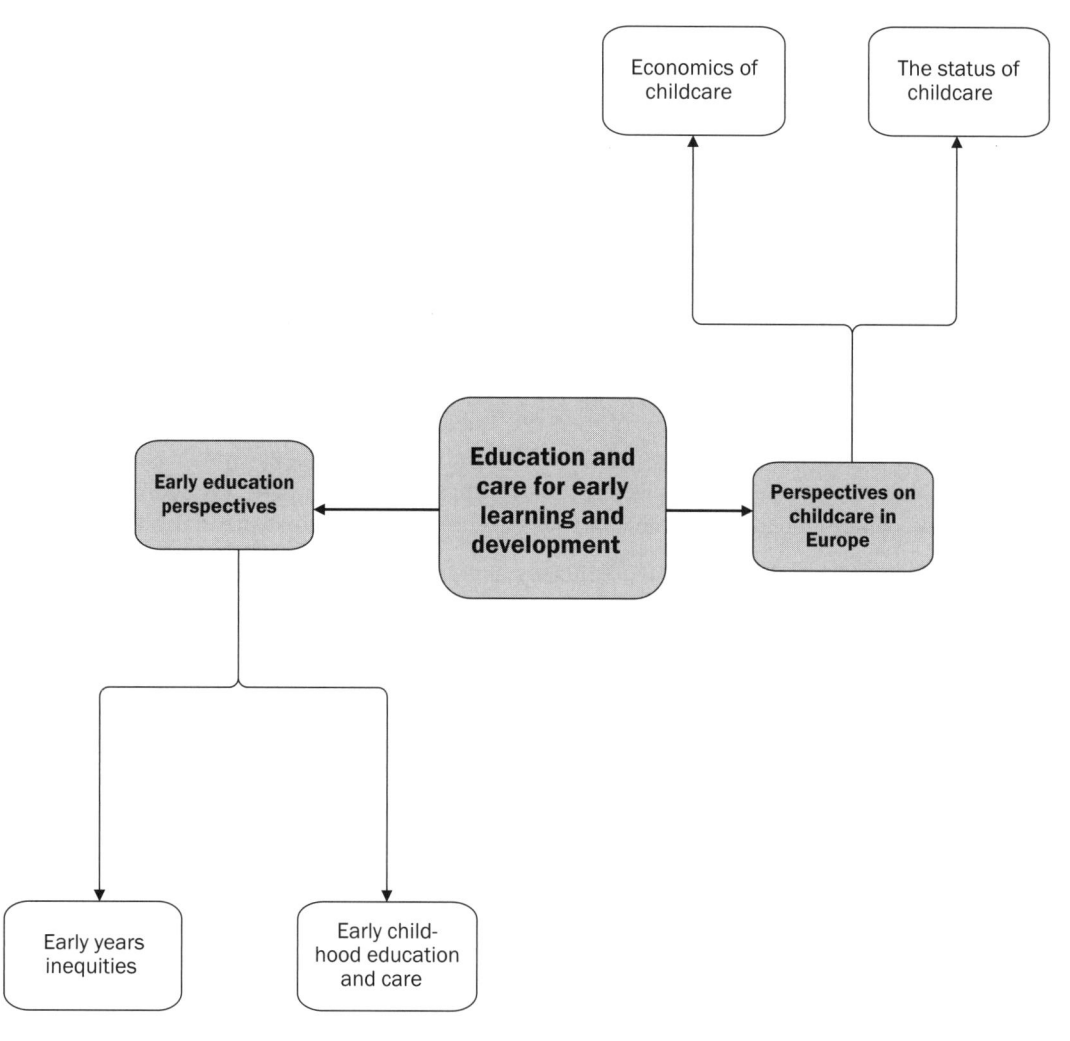

Economics of childcare

The status of childcare

Education and care for early learning and development

Early education perspectives

Perspectives on childcare in Europe

Early years inequities

Early childhood education and care

Introduction

This chapter examines and evaluates educational and care policies within Europe and in particular the United Kingdom. The economics and status of childcare have dominated the public debate and influenced the nature of provision and services for the last few decades. In the voluntary sector in the 1980s at least four different departments of government launched early years initiatives. These ranged from the Home Office with a view to early intervention to alleviate crime and disorder, to the Department of the Environment supporting local neighbourhood play and care projects. The Labour administration between 1997 and 2010 made attempts to co-ordinate child and family policy with a lead department. However, segregation of functions is still prevalent as in Scotland where Westminster controls elements of childcare funding such as tax credits, the government of Scotland determines entitlement, and local authorities decide levels of subsidy for low income families. The split continues in government with education located in a different directorate to early years provision (Children in Scotland, 2011). Whatever the structure of decision-making and policy responsibility the two factors, economics and status, pervade childcare decisions. These issues form a substantial part of the discussion in the chapter and raise a range of questions for you to consider. There is comparative discussion drawing on international childcare case studies to exemplify diverse approaches and examine cultural influences on provision. The chapter explores the issues and policy debates on early education. This debate is not separate from childcare but has distinct features within the context of education policy. In summary the chapter considers the politics of early learning and care in UK society and the impact for a range of relevant professionals.

Perspectives on childcare

Provision of education and care for very young children was a contentious debate for most of the twentieth century and continues to be so today. From pundits to politicians and academics to practitioners, views are diverse and opinions can be polarised. While none dispute the value of early learning and the influence on life chances of the early years experience, what is argued is the best ways to go about it. There are advocates of care of very young children exclusively within and determined by the home and family, alongside those who view state childcare as the epitome of best practice. Such broad perspectives provide argument for political manifestos and policy decisions.

Many societies view childcare and nurturing as an individual family responsibility, one that should only be interfered with by exception. There is a widely accepted view that parents know best how to raise their children. Concepts of child-rearing, such as discipline, are strongly aligned to individual family perspectives and the state only intervenes in extremis when a child is at risk of harm. By adopting an individual perspective on children's issues, society tends to expect parents to take responsibility for the needs and behaviours of children and consequently focuses policy on parental responsibilities rather than children's needs. Truancy legislation, where parents are legally responsible for their child's school attendance, demonstrates this perspective. Policy related to children is often subsumed under greater manifesto priorities, such as employability and economic regeneration. Childcare beyond the home, be it private or public, can be seen as an economic necessity and not an enhancer of early years potential. Even when children take centre-stage, as with education policy,

Early years issues are not given the same status as other matters (Bostrum, 2002). Indeed, Bostrum's analysis showed that while a majority of participants favoured early years education (52 per cent) it was the lowest priority on the list of tested priorities. This is reflected in UK policy where compulsory early education in the maintained sector requires graduate professionals but early learning pre-school provision outside the maintained sector does not. There are changes afoot to address this anomaly in the latest government policy, which appears to provide a halfway house between a graduate profession and a graduate-led profession (DfE, 2013).

Economics of childcare

Alongside developmental debates run economic ones. Economic strategies entwine with family and employment policy to create a complex set of circumstances surrounding how young children are educated and cared for. For example, anti-poverty strategies of recent years in the UK have viewed employment as one of the best routes out of poverty and subsequently used childcare support as part of enabling parents into work. However, it is important that policy-makers take a broader perspective on childcare. As the Early Years Stakeholder Group advised ministers in 2008 when reviewing the 10-year childcare strategy:

> *Policy should avoid casting childcare as simply a route to higher parental income – it needs to be balanced by a vision of childcare as a valuable nurturing environment for children.*

> (Early Years Stakeholder Group, 2008, p 7)

Recent policy briefings by the Organisation for Economic Co-operation and Development (OECD) (2008) have extended the debate, looking at demographic trends in relation to childcare issues. The OECD suggests that personal desires for career and income needs, alongside childcare quality and costs, mean many people are choosing to start a family later or not at all. Some parents wish to take temporary or permanent leave from work to care for children but many are forced to in order to provide the level of care and nurturing they desire for their children. As OECD highlights:

> *children whose parents are not in paid work are more likely to be poor, while mothers who have interrupted their careers to care for their children are at higher risk of poverty in later life.*

> (OECD, 2008, p 1)

The briefing goes on to demonstrate the importance of providing not only a reasonable work/life balance for parents to enable satisfactory child-rearing but also affordable and quality childcare.

The dominant political issue on childcare in the UK is an economic one. The government spends almost £5 billion a year on early education and childcare with around £2 billion a year on funded early education. All three- and four-year-olds can receive 15 hours of early education and care for 38 weeks of the year. Around 260,000 two-year-olds from low income families will also be eligible from September 2014. Tax credits and benefits disregards account for £1.5 billion a year plus an additional £200 million a year under Universal Credit. Depending on their income, some working parents can claim up to 70 per cent of the costs of childcare up to a maximum of £175 a week for one child and £300 a week for two or more children (DfE, 2013). Recent media and public debate has centred on childcare costs, with emphasis on the high cost of childcare in Britain. UK childcare funding is complex due to the variety of elements involved. When estimating the costs account must be taken of universal benefits such as free childcare places for all for three- to five-year-olds, means-tested benefits such as Working Tax Credit which applies only to those on low incomes, and tax relief such as on employer-supported childcare benefits which support mainly those on middle incomes.

This, together with a lower compulsory education commencement age than in many other European countries, makes it difficult to make simple comparisons across countries. For the UK it has been estimated that a 'typical' family with two parents both on average wage with children of two and three years will pay approximately 27 per cent of the family income on childcare. This is not an undisputed figure. There are suggestions that this is an overly high calculation and the 2005 Families and Children Study (Conolly and Lyon, 2007) showed families spend an average of 11 per cent of their income on childcare, with lone parents and low income families spending higher proportions (16 per cent and 20 per cent respectively). However, the ongoing recession resulting in frozen or low wage settlements and higher inflation may all have contributed to raise the 2005 findings.

In a number of Nordic countries there are limited benefits related to childcare costs as childcare is subsidised at the supply side. For a Danish family the cost of childcare would be more like 10–15 per cent of the family wage. In the Netherlands, since the demand-led reforms of 2005, the cost is approximately 10 per cent of the family wage. However, this figure does not take account of the requirement of employers to contribute a third of the childcare fees which, if taken into account, would put the Netherlands in the highest cost range (Cooke and Henehan, 2012).

As a back-bench MP the Parliamentary Under Secretary of State (education and childcare), Elizabeth Truss, questioned the cost of childcare and the demise of the child-minder. She suggested raising the ratio of children to child-minders as a means of cutting costs with little comment on the implications for quality. The thrust of the paper (Truss, 2012) is that the delivery of childcare across the UK is fragmented and diverse and that the costs are high due to the type of provision and heavy regulatory requirements. Funding is complex with a diverse range of subsidy, tax credit and vouchers in the mix. Truss's paper proposes a move towards the Dutch approach to childcare implemented since 2005.

Demand-led funding

The demand-led approach puts the purchasing power in the hands of parents which reflects the UK coalition government's ideology of localism and individual choice. In the Netherlands this approach is not without problems as it requires parents to pay up front for childcare and then reclaim. Demand-led funding has a varying impact on quality and availability of provision with low income and disadvantaged areas having fewer childcare services, and of questionable quality. In the Netherlands the reduced regulation also resulted in a stream of childcare claims for previously informal childcare arrangements, such as those with grandparents and family friends.

It is apparent that the intricacies of funding for childcare in the UK could be more efficient and clearer, but to suggest that demand-led funding is the way to reduce costs is not supported through the Dutch experience and that of others. In Australia the move to demand-led funding increased the supply of services as public expenditure inflated and childcare costs rose by over 100 per cent (Cooke and Henehen, 2012). The experience indicates that demand-led provision does not necessarily reduce unit costs of childcare and may militate against quality provision where it is most needed.

CASE STUDY

Child-minding the Dutch way

Child-minder regulation and funding was introduced by the Dutch government following the 2005 Dutch Childcare Act. The Act deregulated childcare beyond a requirement on childcare business operators *to provide responsible childcare*. In its place the Dutch government set up a system of self-regulation comprising an annually renewable national 'covenant' between provider and practitioner organisations and oversight of each group setting by a parent committee. Apart from complying with health and safety rules, Dutch childcare businesses are required only to produce a 'pedagogical plan'. There was no national regulatory regime.

Compared with a similar representative sample of childcare settings studied in 2005, a significant worsening of the quality of the physical environment as well as much-impaired sensitivity and responsiveness in staff/child interactions were evident in 2008. The study identified increased pressures on staff due to the industry's rapid growth, an insufficient focus in training on working with very young children, and the limited childcare setting choice open to parents. As a result the Dutch government has now also decided to reverse its earlier deregulation policy. Current childcare policy guidance is being converted into a set of enforceable regulations, with a view to protecting children's well-being and longer-term outcomes.

With the advent of reform the number of registered child-minders increased by over 200 per cent within four years, largely due to the number of informal childcare arrangements, usually among grandparents, seizing the opportunity to receive payment as formal child-minders. As a result the Dutch authorities launched an investigation into possible fraudulent use of the childcare tax credit system, mostly in relation to relative-based care, which informed the 2010 amendments to the 2005 Childcare Act. This includes the requirement that child-minding grandparents had to be prepared to care for children other than just their own grandchildren and during regular business hours. Childcare tax credit contributions were frozen at that point and were reduced for child-minding compared to other types of childcare provision. Child-minding as a form of formal childcare was downgraded in respect of the amount of fiscal support it could attract. Subsequently, between 2009 and 2010 the number of parents in receipt of a childcare subsidy for child-minding provision reduced by 25 per cent. Between 2006 and 2008 there was a 68 per cent increase in the number of child-minder brokerage agencies and in the 2010 amendment to the Childcare Act the role was curtailed. The Dutch government recognised that brokerage companies played a significant role in 'formalising' informal care.

Even though claims for tax credits rose by 40 per cent following the changes, there has been no substantial increase in the number of mothers taking up full-time, as opposed to part-time,

Table 5.1 *Child-minder ratios in England*

Age of child	0	1	2	3	4	5	6
England (current)	1:1	1:3	1:3	1:3	1:3	1:3	1:6
England (proposed)	1:2	1:4	1:4	1:4	1:4	1:4	1:6

Source: Adapted from DfE (2013b, p 10).

work. The official statistics body in the Netherlands calculated that the increased childcare offer accounted for at most 26 per cent of the increase in female labour market participation in the period 2005–2009. It cost the Exchequer some 100,000 euros per additional job taken up, out of a total of 30,000 additional women entering employment. In fact childcare related costs to the Dutch Exchequer had risen by 3 billion euros compared to 2005. Rough estimates suggest that 80 per cent of the childcare system funding is accounted for by public subsidies. (Lloyd and Penn, 2010; Daycare Trust, 2012).

The Dutch childcare reforms in 2005 adopted a demand-led approach focusing on an extensive child-minding network managed by regional agencies responsible for training, quality and local regulation, sitting alongside nursery provision. The regional agency and nurseries are regulated by an overarching regulator (Truss, 2012). Truss talks extensively about structure of services providing a simpler and more local management and regulatory regime but the primary driver for the proposal is economic. Truss suggests that by moving to a less regulated, higher child/minder ratio the numbers of child-minders would increase and costs be reduced for consumers (see Table 5.1). Cooke and Henehen (2012) in their critique of the Truss paper suggest that while some simplification would not go amiss, differences in structure and levels of regulation are not of great import. Their report is concerned about the recommendation to adopt higher ratios of children to child-minders and move payment to a demand-led approach. The question of ratios is one of quality, particularly given the relatively low level qualification required for child-minders in the UK. The ratio formula is convoluted and could be simplified. The proposal for England in the government's latest early years policy, *More Great Childcare: Raising Quality and Giving Parents More Choice* (DfE, 2013b) increases the numbers of children per child-minder for babies and pre-schoolers, but maintains the maximum limit of six children in total. The aim is to provide greater flexibility for child-minders across the age range of children in their care. Cooke and Henehen argue that for ratios to be increased training and qualifications should be higher, as is largely the case in the Netherlands. Truss also argues for improved training and suggests that a simplification of the structure of provision, regulation and funding would enable a more cost-effective service. However as Parliamentary Under Secretary of State (education and childcare), Truss does not require any change in qualification and training for child-minders in the 2013 policy.

There is no evidence showing higher levels of qualification and training to be synonymous with reduced regulation or costs. Indeed, in the Netherlands the incidence of unsatisfactory childcare provision has risen from 6 per cent in 2006 to 49 per cent in 2010 (Lloyd and Penn, 2010). The policy of the UK government appears to be to promote the formation of child-minding agencies with a view to reducing the numbers of child-minders to be inspected and rerouting the regulatory process, provided by Ofsted, through these agencies on a sampling basis. On the face of it a collective of child-minders working through an agency can create a dynamic learning environment. But, as was found to be the case in many agencies throughout the Netherlands, the arrangement can allow poor practice to hide. It is proposed that these agencies would provide training and quality assurance alongside organisational services and marketing. However, there is no surety that such providers will put quality before profit, which happened in some instances in the Dutch experience.

Critical question

» *What do you view as the issues for early childhood education and care in the UK if demand-led funding becomes the norm? You might consider a critical appraisal of the 'More great childcare' policy, in particular the implications for types of provision and availability of services and status and salaries of ECEC professionals.*

Supply-led funding

A number of northern European countries adopt a supply-led approach for funding childcare. The usual formula sets a maximum percentage of unit costs that parents can pay irrespective of income combined with decreasing costs for those on low incomes. Denmark operates such a system with around a 25 per cent maximum unit cost cut-off. This equates to around 10–15 per cent of the average family wage (Cooke and Henehen, 2012). Supply-led funding can enable diverse demographic childcare distribution. Provision can be linked to other elements of public policy such as anti-poverty strategies and equality issues. Childcare policies of this type tend to focus on the value of childcare services and put the emphasis on availability and standards.

CASE STUDY

Denmark pedagogy in the early years

In Denmark childcare is offered to all children from age one to starting school at age six. The strategy reflects the Danish culture of working parents, supported through child-friendly employment patterns and parental leave. Public spending on children and families is less complex than in the UK. Beyond a similar level of child benefit Denmark's primary spending is on direct subsidy of childcare services. Half the total amount spent on families is devoted to childcare and there is no tax credit. Compared to the UK, Denmark offers high quality childcare at lower cost for only slightly more overall expenditure on families (an additional 0.1 per cent of GDP).

This model of supply-led differentiated subsidy is reflected across other European countries too. In France a family with a taxable income of €3,000 a month pays around €1.80 an hour, while those with an income of €1,500 per month and three children may pay as little as €0.60 an hour for childcare. In Sweden the maximum payment is equivalent to £114 per month for children from one to six years (Rock, 2012).

Supply-led models allow for a range of childcare provision and devolved regulation. The model offers sustainability for the provider across diverse demographic neighbourhoods, therefore enabling access to good provision for low income families. It caps costs for parents who because of a sliding scale of contribution can be assured that changing circumstances do not impact on affordability of childcare.

Critical question

» *What do you see as the key social and economic imperatives influencing the move towards either of these models in the UK and what impact would they have on current UK provision?*

The status of childcare

There is an ongoing debate about the comparative requirements and value of childcare and early education, which largely focuses around the level of qualification required for professionals in the childcare sector and the standards expected of the provision across the sector. In the UK the debate is frequently clouded by vested interests and political expediency rather than sound developmental and pedagogic understanding. Policy developments in these areas have been some of the most fragmented and difficult to sustain, in particular the thorny issue of qualifications for childcare workers, where attempts to implement a baseline qualification level have led to challenges from providers and users alike.

Qualification issues

Underpinning the debate about the level of qualifications and skill set required for childcare workers is the nature and ethos of the work. This broadly falls into three categories, which are professional, vocational and what I have called 'instinctive'. Childcare has different roots according to social class. From the seventeenth century children of the elite had nannies. This live-in carer of other people's children took responsibility for managing the lives of young children such as washing and feeding them and maintaining the nursery in good order. Anecdotal evidence also shows nannies involved in social and emotional development as well as informal learning.

Among the working classes childcare has its roots in informal extended family and neighbourhood networks, when older relatives or siblings cared for young children while parents were otherwise occupied at work or with other demands. This extended to friendship networks in small communities. At its best it provided a nurturing environment for young children. From the 1500s women looked after children for payment. History tells some horrific stories of these settings where children were neglected and went hungry, with records highlighting the infamous 'baby farms' of the 1800s. The advent of industrialisation required more women for work leading to an increased demand for childcare and public opinion demanded regulation of these child carers. The Infant Life Protection Bill of 1872 required the registration and supervision of baby farms and others looking after children in manufacturing areas (www. childminding-success.co.uk). These surrogate family perceptions of childcare continue today largely based around the notion of child-rearing as an instinctive set of human skills. This tends to perpetuate the notion of childcare as modest work to be carried out by lowly qualified but 'caring' people, usually women. Despite challenges to this perspective for hundreds of years by thinkers such as Froebel and reformers like McMillan in the nineteenth century (see Chapter 1) and research by established academics in the twenty-first, this view still persists in many quarters. This 'instinctive' view undermines the status of childcare, which can result in provision of questionable quality, staff with low expectations and standards and perpetuation of low wage employment. It does not serve children to reach their potential and can in some instances be detrimental.

Childcare as a vocation – the UK context

Although the 'instinctive' notion of childcare still persists, it is consistently losing ground to the current discussion about childcare as a vocation or profession. Childcare as a vocation is strongly reflected in the concept of the nursery nurse. Traditionally tied to earlier notions of nursing as caring work subordinate to professional concepts of medicine, nursery nurses were seen as subordinate to professional pedagogy. In 1945 the National Nursery Examination Board (NNEB) was established as the awarding body for qualifications for the nursery and child-minding workforce. The dominant qualification for the childcare workforce has been post-16 level 3 qualifications. Heads of maintained nurseries are qualified teachers not experienced nursery nurses. The NNEB and subsequent courses are firmly positioned within further education and care work and largely attract school leavers and women. As a result wages are low and career progression severely limited. There is little cohesiveness across the workforce who tend to work in small units of provision, thus limiting potential for building a collective movement to promote and support the status of the work. This situation still prevails with a level 3 qualification (equivalent to GCE A level) being the most usual highest level of qualification of child carers, with 50 per cent of the workforce holding a maximum level 3 qualification in 2010 (Nutbrown, 2012). The desire of professionals and the expectations of providers have led to a growth in level 3 qualified childcare workers. This has been reflected in regulatory expectations as Ofsted requires ratios of staff to hold 'full and relevant' qualifications at, or equivalent to, level 3. However, the childcare qualification landscape is very confusing. There is a plethora of awarding bodies with qualifications in abundance. There is no coherent structure to compare and contrast qualifications effectively, although attempts to do so were made by the Children's Workforce Development Council (CWDC). Within this environment, policy-makers fought shy of determining minimum statutory qualifications in childcare. Governments with strong commitment to early education and childcare backed away from statutory requirements. Qualification levels influence salary and work status within most societies. The advent of minimum level qualifications has implications for costs of provision. The private sector in childcare forms a strong lobby in raising concerns over costs for businesses and as 80 per cent of childcare is provided by the private, voluntary and independent sectors, with commercial businesses making up two thirds of this provision, viability and profit margins are high on the agenda. The fall into recession in 2008 reduced public sector finance and the high cost of childcare to parents on diminishing incomes added to the mix and resulted in further distancing of government from statutory minimum qualifications. Thus the vocational nature of childcare is predominant across the service, whether in maintained day-care or private child-minding services and is vulnerable to diminution as recession continues. The vocational status of childcare is reinforced by the earlier discussion about moves towards reduced regulation and increased ratios of children to staff across provision.

Professionalising childcare in the UK

There are moves to create a professional workforce in early years work. The Labour administration (1997–2010) took a bold step in this direction in response to its consultation regarding a 10-year strategy for childcare. The summary report (2005) highlighted *strong support from a majority of respondents for radical reform of the childcare workforce. Raising the qualifications levels of the workforce was seen as the key to raising the quality of childcare. Local authorities and representative groups highlighted the low pay of the childcare sector as a key constraint. There was strong support from representatives from the academic and research community for the continental model of Early Years Professional such as the pedagogue.*

(HM Treasury, 2005, p 6)

As a result, the Labour government aimed to provide *high quality provision with a high skilled childcare and early years workforce, among the best in the world* (HM Treasury, 2005, p 9). The main thrust was reform of the workforce providing professional leadership for settings and building a career structure. CWDC, a non-departmental public body with a remit for reform across the children's workforce, excluding the teaching profession (CWDC, 2009), was charged with undertaking the task. In 2006 it launched the Early Years Professional Status (EYPS) programme which purported to confer graduate professional status for those working in the early years sector. By 2010 the Labour government had given a commitment in its statutory guidance for local authorities (DCSF, 2010) to all day-care settings across the private, voluntary and independent (PVI) sector being graduate-led by 2015.

The demand for higher learning and qualifications started well before CWDC commenced the graduate professional programme. From the early 1990s early childhood studies degrees were being validated in higher education institutions and demand for them has steadily grown. Undergraduate programmes were developed further when foundation degrees were launched in 2000. Early childhood studies foundation degrees were seen as a way of improving the quality of the workforce. Over 35 institutions across the UK validate early childhood studies degrees and foundation degrees (UCAS, 2012). These programmes provided education and training for new professional roles emerging across early childhood education and care (QAA, 2007). Foundation degrees were promoted and subsidised by the Labour government. In many vocational academic areas foundation degrees were not well received but professionals and academics in the early childhood sector welcomed them as a means of providing a stepping stone into higher education for early childhood professionals. When the Sector Skills Council for Care and Development, through the auspices of CWDC, endorsed these foundation degrees it further reinforced the qualification as a bona fide vocational qualification at a higher level. The advent of the Labour government's Transformation Fund (2006–8), later to become the Graduate Leader Fund (GLF) (2008–11), ring-fenced monies for improvement in the quality of early years provision in the PVI sector. The ability to study part-time with subsidy for settings and participants created a win–win situation that led to increased demand for foundation degrees and higher qualifications. The concurrent development of EYPS required entrants to the programme to hold a degree and offered a pathway for foundation degree graduates to undertake a degree top-up followed by professional status.

The programme was funded directly by government and was the first professional endorsement of early years practice at degree level. The GLF specifically funded existing staff to become graduate professionals, the recruitment of graduates into the sector and a premium to settings that had an Early Years Professional (CWDC, 2011).

CASE STUDY

The making of a graduate professional

Early Years Professional Status (EYPS) was devised by CWDC as a means of conferring an early years graduate professional status without being a higher education award and qualification. The aim was to fast-track mainly existing experienced members of the early years workforce to become senior graduate professionals. It also provided routes to the status for graduates who wished to enter the profession of early years. Its aim was to raise the level of qualification and practice of the early years workforce. EYPS was contentious from the start with much debate as to its equivalence to qualified teacher status (QTS). It was seen as a threat by some representatives of qualified teachers as potentially undermining their professional status and, most importantly, wage levels. Many early years private providers were concerned that graduate professional status would mean graduate levels of pay, and professionals had concerns about impact for entry to the work and job prospects. Government fought shy of making statutory requirements for professional status. Thus EYPS did not have the same authority of statutory requirement for practice as QTS and was subject to the vagaries of non-statutory funding and operated in a low wage, highly commercial sector of the economy. However, what became clear over its relatively short existence was a demand and appetite for higher level education and training and graduate professional status within the sector. Participants had high praise for the experience and its impact on the quality of practice. Settings with EYPS highlighted improvements in provision and recognition by parents and other users. The 10,000th graduate, Nafeesah Rafiq, was hailed by the Minister for Children and Families, as being one of the *talented and passionate* professionals now working in our nurseries and pre-school facilities who have the potential to *make a particular impact on those who are among the most disadvantaged* (Hanson, 2012) Some 10,400 childcare workers achieved graduate professional status between 2006 and 2012 and but for funding limits many more would have done so (Teaching Agency, 2012b).

The support for foundation degrees in early years, EYPS combined with GLF and the commitment of government to graduate leaders in PVI settings were a powerful example of cohesive policy-making leading to desired outcomes. Research has shown that early years graduate professionals do make a difference, improving practice and raising standards within settings. The final report on the GLF (Mathers et al, 2011) for the Department for Education identifies that:

> Settings which gained a graduate leader with EYPS made significant improvements in quality for pre-school children (aged 30 months to 5 years) as compared with settings which did not. Gains were seen in overall quality and in a number of individual dimensions of practice, including: positive staff–child interactions; support for communication, language and literacy; reasoning/thinking skills and scientific understanding; provision of a developmentally appropriate schedule; and providing for individual needs and diversity.
>
> (Mathers et al, 2011, p 60)

The EYPS case study is an example of a highly centralised approach to policy implementation. Although local authorities were charged with managing the GLF it was largely prescribed by central government, with monies ring-fenced for supporting the increase in graduate professionals in early years settings. The coalition government has adopted a different approach concentrating on its principle of devolution and advocating decision-making at a local level. Thus out went the GLF and in came the Early Intervention Grant (EIG). The grant is not ring-fenced and local authorities can allocate it based on local determinants of services. Together with public sector cuts the change in funding has had an impact on the steady march of professionalisation in early years. From April 2011 local authorities have been funding support for Early Years Professionals in PVI settings through the Early Intervention Grant. Central funding for EYPS continues although it is under discussion as part of the Nutbrown review of early years qualifications and is seen as vulnerable in view of the changing perspective of the coalition administration towards early education rather than childcare, which is discussed later in the chapter. The picture is now more mixed with some local authorities continuing to make a substantial commitment to supporting graduate professional status, while others have severely cut back this area of expenditure.

The coalition administration stated in its early years evidence pack: *Staff characteristics, especially qualifications and training are the key driver of high quality provision* (DfE, 2011, slide 12). In doing so it referred to earlier research by Siraj-Blatchford et al (2002) that highlights the value of qualified teachers in the pre-school settings as they raised the performance of less qualified colleagues and were able to provide high quality, appropriate curricula to enhance young children's learning and social development. This research took place before the graduation of the first Early Years Foundation degree cohorts and the development and implementation of EYPS in 2006. There has been, as discussed earlier, subsequent research looking at the impact of early years graduate professionals, showing a positive and similar impact on practitioners and children (Mathers et al, 2011).

Critical question

» *The coalition government has chosen only to refer to research linked to qualified teachers in its evidence pack when identifying high level qualifications influencing quality of pre-school provision. Do you view this as a careless omission or an indication of recognition of QTS over EYPS? What is the basis and evidence for your opinion?*

Early education perspectives

Research consistently shows that the experience of babyhood and infancy has arguably the most significant impact on child and adult achievement and well-being. Early learning experiences together with nurturing practice have a direct impact on physical, social, emotional and intellectual development. The research studies of Peisner-Feinberg (2007) and Sylva et al (2008) among others show that good quality pre-school provision, whatever its nomenclature, has an impact on social and intellectual development.

The wealth of evidence generated has raised public and political interest in early years activity and its quality and increased expectations of professionals in the sector. As identified in the previous section childcare debates about quality and levels and types of qualification have occupied the political agenda of all parties in the UK. As a result discussion has become centred on the nature of provision and professionals role. The challenge is how childcare relates to schooling and the early years workforce to teachers. The UK is not alone in engaging in this exercise. The Centre for Economic Research and the Institute of Economic Research at the University of Munich (CESifo Group) recognised a similar situation emerging across Europe, noting that:

> *Beside the availability of childcare services, policy has become more and more concerned with the quality of childcare services. Different developments have led to this increasing interest. Firstly, the tasks of the staff have become more complex and demanding from a pedagogical, social and societal point of view. Secondly, the increasing impact of research on early education has also contributed to more interest ... A big challenge for almost all countries is to bring the profession of childcare workers more in line with that of other teachers. A higher level of training would enhance their status. Several countries are trying to raise the qualification levels.*

(CESifo, 2010, p 70)

Early childhood education and care

The growing focus on education and teaching tends towards the notion of instruction and tutoring for acquisition of knowledge and skills. It suggests a directive approach to early years provision. Such an approach does not find favour with the promoters of childcare which has become synonymous with a child-centred developmental approach to learning largely through play and non-directive activity. This is reflected in OECD's research into childhood education and care (OECD, 2006a, 2006b). However, the term 'early education and care' has been adopted throughout the European Union with member states endorsing commitment to a number of approaches to raise quality of provision and equitable access (Official Journal of the European Union, 2011). The concept underpinning the terminology requires integration of education and care across provision whether it is provided by the public or private sector. It adheres to a holistic approach to meeting young children's welfare and developmental needs. Early childhood education and care has been successfully developed by a number of European countries. These tend to be ones with strong pedagogy and informal learning approaches to early years provision. The Finnish case study provides an example of how this has been achieved.

CASE STUDY

Finland

Finland's approach to early years provision has adopted the concept of early childhood education and care (ECEC). It provides integrated day- care, education and instruction with play as the primary tool for learning. In Finland all forms of early years provision, whatever the age of the children or setting, are part of the ECEC. All services from 0 to 6, including specific pre-school provision for those entering formal schooling, are embraced by the concept of ECEC. Most provision is through local day- care centres, which are regulated by legislation. Legislation was revised to include education as part of the Children's Day Care Act in 1983. The quality of ECEC is high and costs to parents are low. Staff are well qualified and multidisciplinary. Finnish day- care offers child welfare and social as well as educational services. ECEC has high parent satisfaction levels (Taguma et al, 2012a).

For other countries, such as France and the UK, a more school readiness approach has prevailed with cognitive development and knowledge and skill acquisition being the primary driver. The problem with this approach is that it is not suited to the inherent learning methods of very young children and almost precludes babies. This can lead to a differential in status of work with children under two or three. OECD in its Starting Strong series highlights this issue, drawing attention to lack of regulation of services for under-threes in many countries contrasted to those of the 'pre-school' years (OECD, 2006a, 2006b). In the UK the Labour administration (1997–2010) began moves towards ECEC, although tending to use the term 'learning' rather than 'education'. The Labour government highlighted the development of Children's Centres incorporating a holistic service of welfare, social, learning and care needs for young children and their families. The aim was to provide an integrated and universal service easily accessible by children and their families that was reinforced by a statutory duty on local authorities to provide sufficient Children's Centres to meet local need (DCSF, 2010). Children's Centres, when fully functional, provided integrated early learning and care for children from birth to age five; a range of family support and health services including antenatal and postnatal advice; employment and training advice for parents; and support for families with special needs. The model reflects those essentials highlighted in the *Lancet* by the International Child Development Steering Group (2007) and was acknowledged by OECD (2006a, 2006b).

> *Since 1998, ECEC provision in the United Kingdom has significantly developed, having begun from a low base relative to other European countries … In all areas reviewed by the OECD review team in 2000 – funding; policy coordination; expansion of access; staff recruitment and training; quality assurance and inspection regimes; work-family supports – significant progress has been made.*
>
> (2006, pp 417, 423)

The UK coalition government has maintained a Sure Start Children's Centre strategy albeit with a less centralised approach to operational implementation. Since 2010 the coalition has set up a range of reviews linked to early years, in particular the Early Years Foundation Stage (EYFS) and early years workforce qualifications. Both of these reviews have been driven by a strong focus on early education and its links to formal education led by the Secretary of State for Education, Michael Gove.

Critical question

» *Across Europe different principles and beliefs influence policy for provision for babies and young children. Finland adopts an ECEC ethos while the UK tends towards a school preparation approach. Compare and contrast these models, especially in relation to work with babies and very young children under three. What costs and benefits prevail in each approach? What ethos underpins your rationale for being a professional early years practitioner?*

EYFS is the statutory framework setting the expectations and standards for early years settings. It set out a series of Early Learning Goals for children in settings and guidance on how and what settings should provide. EYFS is used by professionals, providers, trainers and inspection regimes as the basis for good practice and achievement. EYFS developed in 2008 focused on four principles:

1.   a unique child;

2.   positive relationships;

3.   enabling environments;

4.   learning and development.

(DCFS, 2008, p 8)

While the principles have remained relatively unchanged in the review undertaken by Dame Clare Tickell, we can see a change of emphasis in the purpose of the EYFS. The emphasis in 2008 was on health and well-being and enjoyment and achievement enabling economic and community happiness. In 2012 the stress is on teaching and learning to build knowledge and skills; a shift from nurturing development in young children to a more functional approach of preparation for school (DCSF, 2008; Tickell, 2012). This is reflected in the review of EYPS standards, which had as its brief to

> *test how the standards can support the concept of teaching in early years and help to spread leadership practice; streamline the standards where possible ensuring that they link with other standards; and ensure that the standards properly reflect outcomes of developments since 2007.*

(CWDC, 2012, p 3)

Throughout the standards' review consultations involved much discussion of the notion of school-readiness and teaching. Cognitive development was viewed as important but no more so than other developmental areas such as emotional and social. These views raised concerns over the use of 'education' rather than 'learning' in the early years. For others the use of the term education did not cause concern, although the ethos behind the term reflected the wider and informal concept described above.

The focus on education and teaching in government conversation suggests a move away from the ethos of ECEC as articulated in the Finnish case study and reflected in Labour policies in the first decade of the twenty-first century. However, the coalition's policy document on early years, *Supporting Families in the Foundation Years* (DfE and DH, 2011b) counters this notion with its stated focus on child development:

> *so that by the age of five children are ready to take full advantage of the next stage of learning and have laid down foundations for good health in adult life.*

(DfE and DH, 2011b, p 4)

The policy goes on to detail its expectations for the EYFS as

> *offering a universal framework for integrated, play-based learning and care from birth to five.*

(DfE and DH, 2011b, p 17)

Such statements echo the character of ECEC.

Early years inequities

The differing concepts of early education and childcare create disconnect between childcare and education policy-makers and professionals. This results in inequitable early years

Table 5.2 *Average annual salaries (GBP £) (DfE, 2013, p 18)*

European country	Child-minders	Childcare workers in formal settings	Supervisors / managers of formal settings	Primary school teacher
Denmark	£21,500	£20,350	£32,800	£38,050
Finland	£14,800	£18,800	£22,300	£28,100
France	£13,250	£16,300	£23,950	£25,400
Germany	£14,600	£19,150	£28,250	–
Netherlands	£22,500	£22,100	£34,400	£34,000
Sweden	£20,150	£22,450	£29,250	£23,250
England	£11,400	£13,300	£16,850	£33,250

provision for young children and their families and undermines the idea of universal standards and access. There is inequity in funding between early years childcare provision and primary schooling. It is evident in the nature of provision with childcare being largely provided within the PVI sector and early education as a public service. It is conspicuous in differentials in statutory requirements for workforce qualifications and rates of pay (see Table 5.2).

Primary education and ECEC

Primary education in the UK is an entitlement of all children, fully funded through public finance and free at the point of delivery, whereas childcare is subsidised through a mix of public funding and entitlements are prescribed. Current policy entitles three- to five-year-olds up to 570 hours of free early education per annum, roughly equating to 15 hours a week over 38 weeks (the notional school year). Providers of this entitlement must be settings delivering EYFS and with an Ofsted rating of satisfactory or better. (There are some caveats to this for legislative purposes but the basic requirement remains.) Free entitlement to two-year-olds will be rolled out in phases from September 2013 with the emphasis on availability to disadvantaged children (DfE, 2012). For working families, additional childcare is inevitable and as we have shown earlier in the chapter the cost of UK childcare for parents is one of the highest in Europe. For mothers, inequity is compounded, as they are still the primary provider of childcare in the home. Their need for time out from employment or reduction in working hours results in lower potential career prospects and incomes over time and higher risk of poverty (OECD, 2008). To achieve parity with primary education, entitlement to ECEC would need to be available 'full time' and at low direct cost to parents.

Publicly funded primary education is provided in local communities, irrespective of the economic and social status of families. It is prescribed in terms of staff and curriculum and as such all primary schools provide a benchmark of provision regardless of location. This is not true for early years settings. There is no requirement for the PVI sector, the main provider of early years provision, to render full geographical cover. Thus, distribution may be sparse in areas of greatest need as ability to pay may be a primary driver for locating an early years business. While primary education is viewed as an entitlement, childcare may be seen as a commodity for parents to purchase. As with any business endeavour the market influences supply. Affluent communities attract more and high quality services, whereas low wage economies attract a narrower range of low budget services. This is as true for ECEC as it is for retail outlets. Without statutory intervention the quality of provision in such localities is likely to be low. While all registered provision is Ofsted inspected and required to work within fixed child to staff ratios and EYFS requirements there is a wide variation in quality of provision. Low budget providers will need to trim costs and consequently staff will be at a minimum both in number and level of qualification and setting environments may lack enrichment. For many families choice is limited by supply, access and affordability. The growth in public sector provision, such as Sure Start and Children's Centres, which set high standards of ECEC and focused on areas of disadvantage, seems to have alleviated some of these limitations from 2000 to 2010 but cutbacks in funding since 2011 and a lengthy recession are likely to result in less supply and increased costs relative to income for many families requiring childcare.

Workforce qualifications

One of the greatest inequities between childcare and primary education is staff education and qualification, professional development and pay and conditions. In the UK all classroom teachers in primary education must have Qualified Teacher Status (QTS). This is a graduate qualification, usually achieved as a first entry to teaching in schools and largely delivered through a university undergraduate or postgraduate programme. QTS courses have highly prescribed curricula and placement requirements overseen directly by the Department for Education, through its executive arm, the Teaching Agency. Teachers have a national pay scale and significant representative bodies. The starting salary for a Newly Qualified Teacher (NQT) is over £21,000 and all NQTs serve a statutory induction period.

There is no statutory minimum qualification for childcare staff, although moves have been made to make a post-secondary qualification at level 3 the minimum level and Ofsted requires that at least half of the staff in a childcare setting have a minimum level 2 qualification in a relevant area and the manager holds a relevant qualification at level 3 or above. In any event, there is a significant difference in terms of education and qualification for entry into work with early years compared to that of teaching. It begs the question as to how that is reconciled with the emphasis placed on the importance of the early years experience to health, well-being and positive development throughout our lives. It seems a step too far to expect childcare workers educated to level 2, equivalent to GCSE, to provide the range of expertise required for delivery of effective ECEC.

The move towards the graduate professional in early years, as discussed earlier, has not met with the same status as QTS and it is not interchangeable with QTS and it is still the case that nurseries in the maintained sector must have a qualified teacher leading provision. Research evaluating the impact of the Graduate Leader Fund (Mathers et al, 2011) summarised the impact of EYPS graduates on settings:

> *In summary, gaining a graduate leader with EYPS was associated with gains in quality for children aged 30 months to 5 years, as compared with settings that did not change their graduate leader status at all. Gains were seen in overall quality, and in a number of individual dimensions of practice, including support for learning*

and communication, positive relationships and meeting individual needs ... The fact that these dimensions relate very strongly to direct work with children rather than to setting management may be an accurate reflection of the role of EYPs as 'leaders of practice'.

(Mathers et al, 2011, p 47)

From 2013 the coalition administration is introducing the status of 'Early Years Teachers'. The government recognises that the status of ECEC staff is low and is converting the early years graduate professionals to teacher status.

Early Years Teachers will specialise in early childhood development and meet the same entry requirements and pass the same skills tests as trainee school teachers.

(DfE, 2013, p 7)

Training starts from September 2013 and the EYPS standards will be reviewed to bring them in line with those of a classroom teacher. From 2014, early years teachers will have the same entry requirements as primary trainee teachers, including GCSE grade C in English, maths and science and for PGCE entry a 2.1 honours degree (see Figure 1.5). There are attempts to bring the professional areas of teaching and ECEC closer together. It is not the intention that all ECEC staff will be teachers and alongside this development the policy proposes an 'Early Years Educator', who will be a level 3 qualified practitioner, requiring GCSE grade C English and maths on entry who will provide assistance to early years teachers. There is still no statutory directive in relation to workforce qualifications – more a hope and expectation that these changes will engender a desire by practitioners and providers for a well-qualified workforce.

In her review of early education and childcare qualifications Professor Cathy Nutbrown (2012) suggested that level 3 qualifications were not robust enough for practitioners to guarantee quality practice and recommends extensive revision to the syllabus to include learning and practice of greater breadth and depth. She clearly states that a level 2 qualification is insufficient for practitioners and recommends the move to minimum level 3 across all types of provision. She advises that entrants to relevant courses at level 3 should also hold level 2 mathematics and English awards. Government has accepted these recommendations apart from the most contentious, yet important in raising standards, which is the recommendation for a minimum statutory requirement for a level 3 qualification.

The review goes on to highlight the significance of graduate leadership in ECEC and while acknowledging the achievements of EYPS suggests a new early years specialist QTS route building on the best of EYPS. Nutbrown recommends as a priority a transition arrangement for current EYPS to become early years specialist qualified teachers. These recommendations reflect growing practice in Europe, especially Nordic countries, where ECEC has a long established practice of graduate pedagogues. Government has taken the accepted basic premise of these recommendations by developing the early years teacher equivalent to teachers in other sectors currently holding QTS.

There are serious implications for take-up of these recommendations, not least the cost of childcare – whether to the public purse, the private provider or the individual user – which would inevitably increase as salaries better reflected graduate expectations and professional parity. The cost of training would also increase for many as courses would be of longer duration and at higher levels of learning. There could be repercussions from the existing teaching workforce as indicated earlier in relation to pay, with a typically low paid and largely private sector becoming involved with professional recruitment and employment. Alongside these and other concerns there is the potential for highly qualified professionals providing improved quality provision across the sector. Government has grasped at least part of the nettle by developing policy to create an early years teacher programme and award and provide transitional arrangements for existing and current EYPs. Many more details have still to be reviewed and confirmed and there is no indication of commitment to make this the baseline entry requirement for the profession. However, there is the prospect of offering ECEC for all children and improved developmental and well-being outcomes. The vocational and professional workforce could anticipate improvements in pay and conditions and recognition of the important work it does. And over time, UK society would reap the benefits, economically, technically and socially of early education and childcare.

Critical question

» *Government has taken steps towards Nutbrown's recommendation for a specific teacher qualification for early years work. Many aspects of the EYPS programme are now under review as this new award is taken forward. The requirement for GCSE science is new. Why do you think government has done this and what added value does it bring to early years work? Other key elements of the programme have yet to be finalised, such as placement and assessment. What do you think are essential requirements for early years teachers?*

Critical reflections

ECEC: commodity or pedagogy?

The case for investing in early years has been made and universally adopted across developed countries. The issues of how much and in what way are still being debated. Few would dispute the idea that learning and care are interwoven from birth.

However, there is still a divide between those who see the process as instinctive, requiring only a caring mentality and liking of children and therefore a workforce with only low-grade qualifications. This is challenged by those who view the experience of working with very young children as demanding high-level knowledge and skills. This broadly reflects common concepts of care and education, where education is seen as a 'good' thing, which we all benefit from experiencing, and care is viewed as a commodity that parents purchase to enable them to work. The discussion in the chapter has shown that this a reductionist view of the needs of young children in either capacity and that early childhood education and care (ECEC) is a much more holistic concept that encompasses the best notions of learning and nurturing. Children in Scotland is the national agency in Scotland for statutory, voluntary and professional organisations and individuals working with children and families. Its special report in September 2011 states:

> *We believe this split works against the best interests of both young children and their families ... The conceptual divide between 'care' and 'education' is not merely a problem of terminology. Rather, it adversely pervades policy and practice in very*

practical and consequential ways; made manifest through differences in funding, regulation and inspection, data collection, curriculum and planning, as well as staff education, professional development, pay and conditions. It is deeply ingrained in our early years thinking and the current system, and will not be easy to change.
(Children in Scotland, 2011, p 6)

Through case studies from Finland and Denmark we see that the integrated approach of ECEC produces economic, technical and social benefits and lower levels of inequality and poverty.

There is diversity in early years services across important areas of the provision. There is inequality in access, quality and nature of provision. Economic, fiscal and political perspectives and policies have a direct impact. Where universal services are the norm and supply-led policies are in place we find better distribution and availability of ECEC and accessibility for families whatever their incomes. Supply-led services tend to adopt high level qualifications across the workforce, with pedagogues being routinely engaged in ECEC in Nordic countries. Where eligibility is restricted and subsidy demand-led, distribution and choice are limited, often resulting in already disadvantaged areas suffering from a lack of provision or lower quality, as indicated in the Netherlands case study.

There are two major challenges for policy-makers. The first is whether to transform early years provision into a universal service based on the model of universal education and the second is to raise the quality and status of the workforce. Transformation will meet resistance from many stakeholder groups as well as acclaim from others. Indeed, there are different perspectives within interest groups and settings. It is not unusual to hear contradictory comments from owners and staff that express a desire for quality while opposing high-level qualification across the workforce. The Nutbrown review (2012) has resisted the educational model of qualified teachers as the majority workforce and suggested a strengthened level 3 in this capacity with specialist early years teachers as leaders within settings. This is a significant proposal but stops short of the universal model. Government is taking two approaches that lack cohesiveness. On the one hand it is proposing the adoption of a demand-led approach following a similar model to that of the Netherlands, focusing on increased ratios of young children in nurseries and with child-minders and seeking to increase the child-minding workforce, arguably the cheapest and lowest qualified sector of childcare, and providing tax relief on childcare costs for working parents. At the same time it is adopting one of Nutbrown's recommendations by providing a new teacher qualification in early years, which is more reflective of the Danish pedagogy approach. Whatever the outcomes of these proposals it is evident that the current qualification requirement for childcare settings is inadequate to meet the widespread endorsement of high quality ECEC. The private sector is a strong lobby and has consistently challenged a move towards statutory requirement for minimum level 3, never mind a graduate profession, and awarding bodies have resisted a common curriculum benchmark for awards in the further education sector.

In such a climate policy-makers have consistently fought shy of making transformational change of this nature and it will take a bold government to take this on in a period of economic decline. However, if we seriously want to transform the lives of children and adults in the UK then early childhood education and care are good places to start.

Further reading

Graeme Cooke and Kathleen Henehan (2012) *Double Dutch: The Case against Deregulation and Demand-Led Funding in Childcare*. London: Institute for Public Policy Research.

> A detailed and thoughtful critique of demand-led childcare as promoted by the Parliamentary Under Secretary of State (education and childcare) and alternative proposals. It provides insight into the complexity of funding and regulatory requirements and challenges some commonly held views.

Sandra Mathers et al (2011) *Evaluation of the Graduate Leader Fund Final Report, Research Report DFE-RR144*. London: Department for Education.

> This report considers the impact of early years graduate professional on settings and children. It is presented in the context of other research on early years. A highly credible research group take a rigorous analysis of the evidence on the effectiveness of graduate Early Years Professionals in practice.

Miho Taguma, Ineke Litjens and Kelly Makowiecki (2012) *Quality Matters in Early Childhood Education and Care: United Kingdom (England)*. Paris: OECD.

> I recommend the complete series of *Quality Matters in ECEC* as a sound and interesting analysis of the status of ECEC across European countries. The series enables comparisons across countries and gives insight into the impact of different approaches. It relates policy measures to impact on a range of social and economic indicators and in doing so enables us to see the links between policy implementation and societal outcomes.

6 Poverty as part of the early years experience

Why poverty matters to pre-birth and young children

Poverty as part of the early years experience

Policies of poverty

Definitions of poverty and critical debate

Introduction

Poverty is not an abstract concept; you can see and feel it even if you are not personally experiencing it. Throughout my life I have met examples of poverty. As a child I saw it in my grandmother's eyes and her purse. I remember vividly times when the latter was empty – not a penny piece to be had. This meant she was not able to catch a bus to work but had to walk over five miles before starting a low paid cleaning job for a travel agent. At times, particularly the days before payday, my grandparents could not afford a local paper or much needed groceries. But for the practice of small shopkeeper credit and my parent's continuous shoring up of their lives through hand-outs of various kinds my grandparents would have been destitute.

When working for a local play scheme on a post-war housing estate I was involved in a desperate situation with a young boy, Darren, who longed to go on an outing but consistently 'forgot' the payment and parental consent letter required to secure a place. When I visited the house in an attempt to obtain parental agreement no one answered the door and as I was about to go a small voice, Darren's, came through the letterbox, begging me to wait so that he could get his mother to sign the consent and provide payment. Eventually the door was opened to a home with inadequate heating, insufficient furniture and undernourished children and adults; a home where poverty was pervasive. The family was forlorn and neglected and could not seem to scrape even the smallest amount of loose change together for the trip or a pen to sign the form. Darren became desperately resigned to not going on the trip.

I felt it in India, when as wealthy western tourists we met Anil, a fantastically optimistic child of about 8 or 9. He was the epitome of entrepreneurial Mumbai. He worked the markets with his parents who collected and sold spices. His poverty meant living in inadequate housing with limited access to welfare and education and poor sanitation. His environment was mean yet his spirit was abundant and aspirations high. He was going to set up his own business, make money and move up in his world.

I saw it in Kenya when visiting a Maasai village. Life was tough, drought was affecting grazing and the men of the village had gone far away with their goat herds to try and find food for the animals. The government was doing little to alleviate the plight of the Maasai in spite of continuous drought over a number of years. There was no public health system and the consensus among the Maasai community was that what little public education was available was of poor quality and intermittent.

The presence and manifestation of poverty is diverse and extends throughout the world. Its causes are many and varied as can be surmised from the examples above. What is clear is that it detrimentally affects people's lives and prospects and has a direct effect on young children's experiences.

This chapter explores some of the 'big picture' issues of poverty, the impact of political and economic perspectives and actions and the direct implications for young children, from pre-birth through the early years. It discusses the effects of poverty and describes current definitions and goes on to examine the reasons for and challenges to these definitions. The chapter proceeds to a critical analysis and evaluation of recent poverty policies on the national and international stage. It considers the costs and benefits of a range of social and fiscal strategies through case studies and evaluates these examples in relation to impact, effectiveness and sustainability for early years.

Critical question

» *How have you reacted to poverty? Have you experienced it at close proximity, in your district, in school or at work? Have you seen it at a distance through media reports or the stories of others? What did you feel about these different experiences and how did you react? What impact has it had on your experience and professional outlook?*

Why poverty matters to pre-birth and young children

Poverty can destroy the lives of young children. It can, in extremis, lead to premature death, seriously affect development and achievement and impose deleterious effects on personal lifestyle. Its impact is affected by the circumstances of poverty. Such circumstances include the demographic and cultural situation of the child, the political and economic context that prevails and the dynamics of her or his environment. Poverty may be chronic, that is, entrenched within the family and community of the child and may lead to intergenerational poverty and sustained impediment of development and personal prospects. However, it can also be acute and short-term, such as through environmental or personal disaster.

Some experiences can happen on a massive scale, such as the flooding of New Orleans in 2005, and can exacerbate an already precipitous situation.

CASE STUDY

Hurricane Katrina

Levels of poverty and disadvantage among young children in New Orleans were already high when Hurricane Katrina struck in 2005. The infrastructure of support for deprivation and dis-advantage was already stretched. Some 17,000 children under six lived below the Federal poverty level. Poverty was high among young children as many parents were not in work or in low paid jobs. There was little investment, nationally or locally in early years; what initiatives existed were very limited and often covered emergency action only. Childcare was sporadic and frequently inadequate with no mandatory licensing of facilities (Golden, 2006).

The devastation Katrina caused compounded the situation for many of these children who often experienced the worst of the problems, being unable to evacuate with ease due to lack of family transport and awareness and access to evacuation plans and disaster advice. Children in poor families often ended up in shelters, and experienced distressing rescue and delayed return if separated from their families.

Such traumatic experiences can be ameliorated if parents are able to recover quickly from catastrophic disaster, perhaps by avoiding it in the first place and/or having assets and resources to tide them over in the short term and stabilise home and work in the longer term. If parents remain in limbo, experiencing stress and depression, as was the case for many in New Orleans, then young children are likely to face greater risks to their development, which may already be heightened due to existing poverty (Shonkoff and Phillips, 2000).

For some, traumatic personal change can create dire effects pushing individuals further into poverty despite their best endeavours to manage and control the situation.

CASE STUDY

Working mother Sophia

Sophia was a working mother living in London. She was passionate about her work as a healthcare assistant at a hospital. During one of her antenatal check-ups and routine blood tests she discovered she was HIV positive. Her life then turned upside down. Her husband had been unfaithful and was the carrier of the disease. Fearful of her condition she had to stop work and divorced her husband. She became dependent on state benefits but returned to college to study. This affected her income detrimentally, losing housing benefit. With a student loan supplementing her disability living allowance she has managed to maintain her family but as she says,

> *Money to eat is always a problem ... It's very, very hard meeting the daily needs. I can't go in the streets and start begging.*
> (London poverty profile, posted on 11 October 2010)

Sophia has gone on to university but is now concerned that in the prevailing economic conditions she may not be able to obtain work.

Many of the circumstances of Sophia's experience are beyond her sphere of influence. Government reviews of benefit entitlements, changes to student finance and an economic recession all impact directly on the lifestyle and opportunities for her and her family. You might feel this is exceptionally cruel for a seriously ill lone parent who is trying hard to ameliorate her position.

Critical question

» *Consider the potential impact of Sophia's experience on her children, one of whom was unborn when she was first diagnosed as HIV positive, and critically evaluate how early years intervention would support the family. You might want to explore the impact of the recently introduced Universal Credit on young children with single mothers with health problems.*

Understanding the dynamics of poverty matters if we are to alleviate, or eradicate it. The strategies required in one set of circumstances will be different from those required in another. Indeed a 'one size fits all' approach could further exacerbate problems, as in Sophia's case. Bradbury et al (2001) discuss in depth the significance of understanding *children's movement into and out of poverty in addition to their poverty at a point in time* (p 1). They suggest a number of reasons for poverty, which lead to greater insight and enable better potential solutions. For example, the longer the experience of poverty, either continuously or repeated periods for the child, the greater the impact on future development and prospects. Understanding the changing demographics of poverty for children can support political and fiscal policy approaches. For governments desirous of alleviating poverty such data can make the difference between effective or ineffective policy solutions.

Attainment and poverty

Studies consistently show that poverty has detrimental effects on the growth and intellectual development of young children. These include a range of risks, such as:

- low birth weight and growth inadequacies;

- essential mineral deficiencies and toxic exposure;

- low cognitive ability measures;

- increased detrimental behaviours such as anxiety and depression.

Pre-birth and early years children are especially vulnerable due to factors indicative of poverty such as inadequate nutrition, maternal deficiencies of physical and mental health, environmental dangers such as trauma and the quality of childcare (National Center for Children in Poverty, 1999; International Child Development Steering Group, 2007).

Cognitive and social development

The review of research literature by Johnson and Kossykh (2008) shows a direct correlation between poverty and cognitive and social development in the early years. Studies show a clear relationship between cognitive ability of three- to five-year-olds and highest educational achievement at ten and income at age 30. The development of positive social skills such as co-operation, openness and self-regulation also impact on educational attainment. Research indicates an association between positive social skills and post-16 education. Cognitive and social skills are mutually important in relation to educational success; evidence indicates that a marginal improvement in cognitive ability has little impact on school achievement if social skills are low but a significant impact if social skills are high. The common deprivations of poverty on health, nurture and environment affect and diminish cognitive and social development and restrict accomplishment throughout life.

A primary factor in cognitive development in the early years is the socio-economic status of parents. Sylva et al (2007) show the impact on reading and mathematics ability of ten-year-olds in families of different socio-economic circumstances. Children from unskilled and unemployed households, typically low income, are at least ten points lower in reading and mathematics attainment at age ten than those from professional households, typically high income.

Sylva et al also demonstrate how the quality of the home learning environment (HLE) in the early years effects cognitive achievement later in life. The research highlights the importance of the condition of the HLE for three- and four-year-olds in developing good cognitive and social abilities. The report goes on to indicate the relevance of early years childcare as a means of reducing the negative impact of a poor HLE on young children.

Poverty matters because it affects the quality and achievement of people throughout their lives. It matters especially *in utero* and to very young children as the consequences influence what happens for the rest of their lives. The dynamics of poverty are multidimensional and the effects are most intense when poverty is chronic but also when experienced in the early years of life (Brooks-Gunn and Duncan, 1997).

Definitions of poverty and critical debate

There is no single definition of poverty and certainly no universally accepted one. On a simple level poverty is defined by income which, until recently, was the prevailing perspective. The large and emotive international appeals by UNICEF and a number of NGOs of the late twentieth century epitomised by swathes of the population across whole continents existing on less than two dollars a day have been superseded by more sophisticated concepts of poverty.

Absolute poverty

However, the notion of absolute poverty is hard to dispute. It has dire consequences for very young children, often resulting in infant mortality or chronic disease and disability. It leaves children vulnerable to the vagaries of decisions and actions way beyond family influence due to natural strife, corporate and political indifference or corruption and national and international conflict. It puts pressures on families that undermine their ability to feed, clothe, shelter and care for their offspring. It is often endemic, for example stunting, or stunted growth, and results in chronic nutritional deficiencies during pre-birth and the first two years of life. Stunting results in limited bone growth and impaired brain development and is irreversible. It affects some 180 million children across 21 countries (Lake, 2012).

For the growing numbers of urban poor, as previously rural populations move to expanding cities and towns, the deprivations of poverty are immense. UNICEF estimates that the world's urban population increases by 60 million every year. While for some children the move brings benefits, for many it results in cramped conditions with no sanitation or clean drinking water, a lack of secure and satisfactory shelter and non-existent or overstretched healthcare. These children's environments make them vulnerable to disease, disaster and exploitation (UNICEF, 2012c).

Such are the ruinous effects of absolute poverty.

Relative poverty

The European Union uses an income based relative definition of poverty which is based on the share of persons with a disposable income below 60 per cent of the national median (Lelkes and Gasior, 2011). The UK adopts this measure of child poverty. Relative poverty reflects a relationship with an average level of income whereby falling below it reduces the opportunity to participate fully in the expected norms of daily living and acquire the resources that support this. There are flaws to such a definition as levels of relativity are not discerned and the deprivations might be subtle or blurred. You may consider whether a family £1 above the poverty threshold and so defined as out of poverty is suddenly able to access all the expected lifestyles and opportunities not afforded to the family with £1 less than the poverty threshold. You might also question the meaning of resource acquisition and how it is assessed. For example, during the early part of the twenty-first century acquisition of material goods was made easy due to accessible and largely unrestricted credit availability. At times households might be rich in material goods but poor in assets. Such households could slide into deeper poverty as debt grew and ability to pay reduced while continuing to acquire goods. This has led to serious economic deprivation during the recent (2008) recession and a debt crisis for many low income households.

Another phenomenon of relative poverty measures is that changing national statistics can create 'false' measures. For example in 2011 the mean figure for income in the UK dropped from £432 to £412 a week, thus the income level defining poverty fell, raising some 300,000 children out of poverty. However, there was no change to their life circumstances (Department for Work and Pensions/Department for Education, 2012). In his speech at the Abbey Centre on 14 June 2012 in response to the above report the Rt Hon Iain Duncan Smith MP, Secretary of State for Work and Pensions highlighted the anomaly by saying:

> In 2010/11 the economic downturn brought with it the largest drop in median income since 1980, dragging the relative poverty threshold down with it. But even as relative poverty fell, absolute poverty remained flat at 11%. So these figures make the powerful point that while some families may have crossed an arbitrary threshold, real incomes did not rise and the lives of the poorest did not change. How perverse that the simplest way of reducing child poverty is to collapse the economy.

Social exclusion

Frequently linked to the notion of poverty is the relatively new concept of 'social exclusion'. The term is often used to indicate a series of situations and status that together create disadvantage. Social exclusion within UK policy was adopted by the Labour government in 1997 with the establishment of the Social Exclusion Unit. It claimed that certain members and groups within society were excluded from the social, cultural, political and economic benefits afforded to and expected by the majority of British citizens. The Social Exclusion Unit in 2010 highlighted:

> Social exclusion is a short-hand term for what can happen when people or areas have a combination of problems, such as unemployment, discrimination, poor skills, low incomes, poor housing, high crime and family breakdown. These problems are linked and mutually reinforcing. Social exclusion is an extreme consequence of what happens when people do not get a fair deal throughout their lives and find themselves in difficult situations. This pattern of disadvantage can be transmitted from one generation to the next.
>
> (http://webarchive.nationalarchives.gov.uk and www.cabinetoffice.gov.uk/social_exclusion_task_force/context.aspx)

Remedial policy related to social exclusion tends to focus on functional elements such as education, health, wealth and shelter. How it is measured and assessed is determined by prevailing preferences and priorities. The Field Report (2010) suggests that the greatest risk of social exclusion is in the early years, through developmental disadvantage that impacts later on life chances. In Frank Field's report for government, the main recommendations cover improving parenting strategies, increasing awareness of exclusion and policy to counter the main causes of exclusion, through the use of local life chances indicators (p 6) and improved status and provision of early years care and education.

Social exclusion in policy terms looks at groups in particular circumstances and does not differentiate between individual states. It tends to make assumptions about people's preferences of lifestyle as reflecting a set of societal norms and that those not aspiring to or achieving these norms are dissatisfied or ashamed. Policies related to social exclusion are generally perceived as positive moves to alleviate the bad situation for people in particular circumstances. Such approaches may take little account of individual preferences and differences and subsequently cause hardship. On 25 June 2012 the Prime Minister, David Cameron, delivered a speech at Bluewater in Kent that suggested that families with parents who were not employed should restrict their number of children or face the consequences by not receiving welfare for more than three children,

> *Quite simply, we have been encouraging working-age people to have children and not work, when we should be enabling working-age people to work and have children.*

> (Cameron, 2012)

Such ideas prescribe personal choice and exacerbate inequality within society. For some, a large family may be a personal, cultural or religious aspiration. If the family in question is not on benefit, although not in employment due to personal wealth, then the size of the family is of no consequence. This suggests that social exclusion definitions based on lifestyle norms can be unfair and unequal. For those expecting a fourth child who fall on hard times such a policy could push families into poverty and dependency and thus run counter to the general assumptions of social exclusion policy as the alleviation of disadvantage.

The concept of social exclusion can be wide and diverse. There is a danger that all of society's wrongs are lumped under this phrase and thus result in many definitions of social exclusion and its component parts. I have mentioned important functional elements above but what about concepts of gender and ethnic equality and justice and fairness? Such notions allow us to see more clearly the tensions in using social exclusion as a poverty definition and measure. A woman with a good education, high income and comfortable lifestyle might experience social exclusion due to gender inequality but does not experience poverty. A black family may experience social exclusion in accessing housing or jobs not because of poverty but prejudice. Social exclusion is a multifaceted and complex concept. By implication it is a counterpart to social inclusion and any definition used to guide the exclusion agenda must have a notion of inclusion. It must also consider the moral purpose underpinning the concept if it is to prevent negative impact on those already excluded and take account of personal choice. Peace (2001) in his extensive discussion searching for a definition concludes:

> *a desire for social inclusion could be interpreted, in a policy context, as an agenda to facilitate, enrich and enhance individual and group capacity for at least three things: opportunity, reciprocity and participation.*

> (Peace, 2001, p 33)

Peace (2001) and Percy-Smith (2000) among others argue that for social exclusion policy to be effective it needs to engage with the multidimensional aspects, including structural policies identified earlier such as health, education, housing, policies to protect and manage risk and policies that provide opportunities and access to them.

The House of Commons Scottish Affairs Committee stated in 2000 that,

There are basically three current definitions of poverty in common usage: absolute poverty, relative poverty and social exclusion.

(Section 2, para 14)

It is true that such concepts are common and universally used by governments and institutions, but within these concepts definitions are not fixed, as we have seen. You might want to reflect on the difference between surviving on 2 or 5 dollars a day as a measure for absolute poverty and how such knowledge informs poverty policy. You might deliberate whether an extra pound or two in the pocket through fiscal policy alleviates relative poverty and its impact on children's growth and development. And you may cogitate on the opacity of social exclusion. In doing so a prevailing thought might be the inadequacy of these definitions in evaluating how poverty is experienced.

Critical question

» *The context and complexity of social exclusion policy can have the opposite of the intended effect. In relation to young children's poverty, critically evaluate what you would include in your definition of social exclusion to determine its potential effect.*

What poor people say

Definitions and measures of poverty have generally been devised by politicians, economists, researchers and academics of many persuasions, so in the main by those with little, if any, experience of poverty other than at third hand. As such, they tend to reflect the desires and expectations of policy-makers, influencers and advisers. As we have discussed earlier, the circumstances of those in poverty largely prohibit opportunity and access to such professions or status.

However, there is a body of research and inquiry that is seeking to ascertain the *voices of the poor* (Narayan, 2000) and reflect it in analysis and policy discussion. Participatory Poverty Assessment (Robb, 2001) is a method to include poor people in influencing poverty policy and informing definitions. It uses three main approaches:

1. drawing on field research;
2. engaging with policy-makers and influencers;
3. taking account of demographic and other data of the relevant area.

Synthesis of these components provides insightful and relevant discussion and development of strategies in the fight against poverty.

The poor in Narayan's (2000) field research indicated five main areas of importance to poor people.

1. Lack of material necessities.
2. Low status and powerlessness.
3. Absence of social participation and cultural identity.
4. Lack of infrastructure.
5. Focus on assets rather than income.

Lack of material necessities

Some elements reflect components of poverty definitions already identified such as a lack of necessities for material well-being, particularly food, but also other assets including housing and land. These physical privations mean the difference between life and death for some and health or disease for others. This has been a dominant focus of appeals and campaigns over many years. It is often linked to conflict and displacement as well as natural disaster.

In Rakhine State in Myanmar, ethnic tensions exploded into conflict and within months had displaced an estimated 110,000 people according to UNICEF. This graphic tale shows how children often experience some of the worst privations during conflict.

CASE STUDY

Mahmoud's story

Mahmoud was ten years old and one of nine children. He was going into Third Grade at school. He was living with his family in the Thet Kay Pyin internally displaced persons' camp. His father was a fisherman before the conflict started in Rahkine State, Myanmar in June, 2012, and his mother looked after the family. His father was forced to stop work and move the family to the camp due to the violence taking place around their home.

Mahmoud's home was set on fire and as they escaped the family became separated and his youngest sister was burned. His father was out fishing and Mahmoud also got separated from the family and hid. The family attempted to move back home but there was little food available and due to lack of medical resources his youngest sister died as a result of her injuries in the fire.

The camp is not a suitable place to live; there is not a lot to eat and nowhere to play. Mahmoud wants to go back to his life before the conflict, to have enough food to eat and go to school.

Source: www.unicef.org/infobycountry/myanmar_66426.html

Mahmoud has suffered loss of home and bereavement. He cannot continue with his schooling and is confined to the camp. Food is not sufficient and his family are unable to adequately provide for him and his siblings. Thus a self-sufficient thriving family is forced into poverty with all the concomitant detrimental effects it can have on children's lives.

Low status and powerlessness

Poor people are acutely aware of their lack of status and influence. They are often *vulnerable to rudeness, humiliation, and inhumane treatment* (Narayan, 2000, p 31) when seeking help from officials and agencies. I saw this often when I worked at a local benefits office in the early part of my working life. Colleagues who were kind and considerate to work with became obstructive and uncaring with those on the other side of the counter. In many instances they did not listen to claimants' explanations, being unwilling to sympathise and unable to empathise with their situations. As a young and raw recruit I was shocked by the disdain in which clients were held.

Critical question

» *Reflect on your own reactions when confronted with poverty, for example homeless people on the streets, families struggling to adequately feed and clothe their children. Critically appraise your reactions and the impact for your professional practice.*

The poor are often powerless against financial exploitation, sometimes paying excessively high rates of interest on loans. Indeed, a recent advertisement on British television showed, in the small print, an interest rate of over 2000 per cent. Such loans may be the only option for poor families who have no assets or bank account. Poor children in many parts of the world are subject to exploitation, working for a pittance in unsatisfactory environments, used as soldiers in conflicts and manipulated by the sex trade. Such situations graphically demonstrate the low status and powerlessness of children in poverty.

Absence of social participation and cultural identity

Poor people are often unable to contribute and engage in community life. They have not the wherewithal to access social gatherings and play a part in the activities of others. Consider one of my experiences of poverty recalled at the start of the chapter. The young boy who was unable to go on the outing was full of despair and disappointment, which was potentially damaging to his social development. Poverty also inhibits fulfilment of cultural identity. Poor people are often unable to participate in cultural events that bind communities, and can be ostracised when unable to do so.

Lack of infrastructure

For poor people, roads, transport, water and health are important resources to enable their well-being, participation and wider family support and income generation. Surprisingly, many of the participants in Narayan's study were not so concerned with education. Most viewed literacy as highly important but otherwise there were mixed views and for many it seemed irrelevant to their lives. Within most poverty strategies education is given high priority. It is perceived as a means of getting out of poverty. Given that the study comprised 40,000 people from 50 countries across Europe, Africa, Asia and South America, perhaps a revisit to our priorities for poverty is in order.

Focus on assets rather than income

Poor people focus on assets rather than income when considering poverty. They *link their lack of physical, human, social, and environmental assets to their vulnerability and exposure to risk* (Narayan, 2000, p 31). What poor people demonstrate is that poverty is not only about enabling the fundamentals of human existence, food, water and shelter; it is also about maintaining social and human investment. In Britain in the 1980s there developed the notion of an underclass (Murray et al 1996). Generally used in a derogatory manner, the underclass was epitomised as disenfranchised often homeless people with little investment in society (indeed the Prime Minister of the time, Margaret Thatcher, publicly decreed that there was no such thing as society in an interview for *Woman's Own* on 23 September 1987). However, many structural factors were at play that contributed to a swathe of the population feeling divorced from the social and civil norms of society.

During the 1980s and early 1990s, Britain had below average economic growth and very high inflation and suffered two deep and long lasting recessions (Bradshaw et al, 2004). Bradshaw's report highlights that,

> *The return of 'mass unemployment' cast a dark shadow over many aspects of social policy and contributed to the increasing concern about social exclusion.*
>
> (p 25)

Homelessness increased due a number of factors including housing shortage and rising prices, the sale of council houses and decline of private rented accommodation, alongside rising unemployment, reductions in welfare benefits and the closure of mental health institutions. Such people had no social assets and were unable to participate in day-to-day social functions. Their cultural identity was diminished as communities based around failing traditional industries were decimated. Alongside a loss of livelihood, loss of social solidarity and cultural identity left communities in limbo and intergenerational worklessness and benefit dependency was the outcome for many.

Poor people are disproportionately affected by diminution of environmental assets. Planning and development can have a severe effect on those living at subsistence level. Alterations to habitat may put already vulnerable people at greater risk. For example, population density and climate change affect subsistence farmers through diminishing yields, availability of supply and reduction of natural resources.

The Labour government (1997–2010) made a foray into asset-based strategy, largely focused on finance through the Child Trust Fund. The initiative sought to invest in children by building a fund of savings for each child. The Fund was kick-started from public finance with each new child having a savings account set up of £250 which could be increased by family and friends and provide a fund for the young person on reaching adulthood. The fund started in 2002 and was closed by the coalition government in 2011. The Fund was available across the population, within eligibility conditions, and was only a small amount of cash, but it did suggest a different approach to poverty based on having assets to fall back on and support social inclusion (www.gov.uk/child-trust-funds/overview).

Whatever the approach, the formula is straightforward. The more and diverse the range of assets within the purview of the poor, the less their vulnerability. The fewer and narrower the range of assets, the more defenceless they become.

Critical question

»   *There is a challenge to the traditional income-based approach to poverty alleviation towards asset-based strategies. Analyse and appraise the issues for early childhood education and care of such an approach. You might wish to employ a SWOT analysis to assist your appraisal. (See Chapter 8,* International issues in the early years, *for a description of a SWOT analysis.)*

Policies of poverty

> *Some may wonder why babies matter in public policy. Surely they are the province of their parents or caregivers. Yet, public policies often affect very young children,*

policies that are sometimes created with little thought as to their consequences for this age group. In addition, many policies focus on the effects of ignoring the needs of infants and toddlers, for example, by having to address the cognitive gaps between low-income preschoolers and their more affluent peers or providing intensive special education services for problems that may have begun as much milder developmental delays left untreated in a young baby. Mr. Chairman, my message to you is that babies can't wait.

This was the opening statement of a submission by Matthew E. Melmed, J.D., executive director of Zero to Three to the Committee on Ways and Means, US House of Representatives in 2007. As true today as then, babies cannot wait. Pre-birth and the early years are potentially only a short period in the life span, which can be cruelly curtailed if poverty pervades the experience. As identified earlier in the chapter, what happens during pregnancy and the first few years of life sets the scene for potential growth and development and life chances.

As we know, social and fiscal policies are crucial to the well-being of young children. There is clear evidence through years of research and data analysis that economic and social hardship compromises a child's development and life chances. It is acknowledged by UK policy-makers, from Hadow in 1933 to Field in 2010, that the experiences in the early years of life are vital to well-being. At all levels of policy making, child poverty and social and economic strategies to alleviate it are prolific with reports and recommendations.

Policy operates at many levels through huge global initiatives such as those launched by UNICEF, some of which are worldwide and some targeted on particular regions and localities. UNICEF works with state politicians and officials as well as NGOs to undertake its campaigns and projects. Most policy initiatives, however, are determined, developed and implemented through state administrations and legislature and tend to reflect political ideology and interests. When initiatives are external they often need governmental endorsement and support to be effective and sustained. There are sometimes configurations of a transnational nature such as the European Union that have the capacity to develop and implement poverty policies. The next three sections provide illustrations of poverty initiatives at these levels.

Global initiatives

Since 1946, UNICEF has been working to alleviate hunger and disease for children. Over the years its brief has widened to include the education and well-being of children and alleviation of poverty and disadvantage. As an arm of the United Nations it has the capacity to lobby, influence and intervene on policy issues in relation to the health and welfare of children. Its 'Baby Friendly Initiative' is a worldwide programme. Launched in 1992 with the World Health Organization (WHO) to encourage successful breast-feeding and ethical marketing of breast milk substitutes this programme has two primary goals, both of which seek to influence social and economic policy.

1. Within a social context the initiative works with health services and governments to support education and training for midwives and other professionals working with expectant and new mothers in successful breast-feeding programmes.

2. At the same time, UNICEF engages with business, for example its recent referral spurious claims of a breast milk alternative supplier's inappropriate advertising to the Advertising Standards Authority.

UNICEF claims that over one million child deaths could be prevented if governments promoted breast-feeding. UNICEF Director Anthony Lake asserts:

> *If breastfeeding were promoted more effectively and women were protected from aggressive marketing of breast milk substitutes, we would see more children survive and thrive, with lower rates of disease and lower rates of malnutrition and stunting.*
>
> (www.unicef.org.uk/BabyFriendly/News-andresearch/News/
> Take-action-on-child-stunting, 1 August 2012)

The focus of global initiatives tends towards a specified subject such as the example above. The eradication of polio is a topical example, given a high profile in the media largely due to the extensive involvement of the Melinda and Bill Gates Foundation. The Foundation works directly with the Global Polio Eradication Initiative (GPEI) and has used its wealth and status to speed up the work in achieving the goal. Since 1988, about 2.5 billion children around the globe have been vaccinated against polio, and the number of polio cases per year has decreased by 99 per cent (Gates Foundation, 2009). The Foundation demonstrates the inter-relationships and partnerships needed for success.

International poverty intervention is not always global. In many instances it is a mobilisation of international concern and action to alleviate the effects of poverty in specific countries or regions of the world. The case study about the situation in Rakhine State, Myanmar highlighted in the earlier section on poverty definitions shows how, through UNICEF, the problem is brought to the world stage. In Myanmar, the dire situation for children is not caused by a single factor and the resolution cannot be achieved by a single issue methodology. It requires a diversified approach. In this instance, UNICEF launched an appeal, sent in volunteers to alleviate the immediate devastation and worked to bring about a 'basic co-operation agreement' with the government.

European initiatives

The European Commission set up a working group (Social Protection Committee, 2012a, 2012b) to advise it on its intention to make a recommendation on child poverty in 2012. The ad hoc group had a remit to provide a report encompassing:

- a set of common principles;

- a portfolio of child specific indicators;

- recommendations to the Commission and Member States regarding monitoring and implementation of the Recommendation (Social Protection Committee, 2012a, p 2).

The EU has been involved in policy development concerned directly with child poverty and children's well-being for many years. Indeed, earlier in the chapter we discussed the EU's definition of relative poverty. It is now reviewing existing policies in light of greater understanding of the causes, impact and effects of child poverty and is looking for strategies that facilitate and extend the impact of intervention. There is also a pragmatic aspect to this review, which is to energise members during the economic recession affecting all party states. The EU sees child poverty alleviation and improved child well-being as important in its own right but also as a *direct contribution to the Europe 2020 objectives of smart, sustainable and inclusive growth* (Social Protection Committee, 2012b, p 6). Pragmatism rather than altruism is an essential factor of the European Union's review of the poverty strategy. Many political and economic entities have such a perspective.

Critical question

» *In a recession that bites hard into nation states how would you seek to persuade policy influencers of the importance of a poverty intervention and alleviation strategy to support young children?*

National initiatives

In the UK, policy-makers and influencers are also discussing the changing understanding of child poverty and seeking different policy solutions. The Labour government of 1997–2010 made a policy declaration in 1999 to eradicate child poverty in Britain within a generation. Prior to Labour's election in 1997 child poverty had had little acknowledgement from the Conservative government (1979–1997) with no formally adopted definition or concession to it in direct policy terms. This, then, was a bold intent and was followed by a series of social and fiscal initiatives. The focus of these initiatives was income based and used relative poverty measures.

Income based strategies

The common measurement of poverty in families was *half average income after housing costs*. As Piachaud and Sutherland (2000) summarised, policies fell into three main areas.

1. *Policies to alter income levels directly through the tax and benefit system. The aim is to provide direct financial support to all families, recognising the extra costs of children, while targeting extra resources on those who need it most.*

2. *Policies to promote paid work. The aim is to ensure that parents have the help and incentives they need to find work. Paid work is seen as the best long-term route to financial independence for families. The Government aims to reduce the number of working age people in families claiming Income Support or income-based Job-Seekers' Allowance for long periods of time.*

3. *Measures to tackle long-term disadvantage.*

(Piachaud and Sutherland, 2000, p 10)

The main initiatives to promote paid work were about supporting working income, ie 'making work pay' largely through working families' tax credit and supporting families into work through the 'New Deal'. The New Deal (renamed Flexible New Deal from October 2009) was a programme of active labour market policies introduced in the United Kingdom by the Labour government in 1998. The stated purpose was to reduce unemployment by providing training, subsidised employment and voluntary work to the unemployed. The dominant focus was on income-based strategies and intervention with the long-term disadvantaged. The coalition government formed in May 2010 is taking a different approach. In its report *A New Approach to Child Poverty: Tackling the Causes of Disadvantage and Transforming Families' Lives* published in 2011 the coalition takes to task the previous government for focusing on welfare benefits; as Ian Duncan Smith puts it in the foreword, *work not welfare*. You might think that this is not significantly different from 'making work pay', both of which are popular catchphrases but say little about actual policy and process. The main principles of the coalition strategy are work, fairness, responsibility and support for the most vulnerable. Again, these are not very different from those of the Labour administration, which identified the tax and benefits system as a means of creating greater fairness, work as the primary means of getting out of poverty and intervention for long-term disadvantage (most vulnerable in other words). The rhetoric between the administrations is somewhat different, with the focus of the coalition on rewarding an individual who finds and takes work and of the Labour government on helping and incentivising parents into employment. Both administrations see income improvement through work and taking personal responsibility for it as cornerstones of their strategies.

Employment focus

The employment circumstances of parents are often used as a major determinant of child poverty and creating employment opportunities and access is often a cornerstone of fiscal policy. However, there are a substantial number of children within the EU, (13 per cent) whose parents work but fail to bring in enough income to keep children out of poverty. In some EU countries – Spain, Poland and Portugal – this increases to 20 per cent. In such circumstances, job creation or entry to employment may not be the only fiscal approach needed. Legislation for a minimum wage may be seen as part of the solution and was introduced, as such, by the Labour government in Britain in 1999 as part of its child poverty strategy. The policy was and remains contentious with opposers suggesting it stifles business development and growth thus inhibiting job creation, while many advocates want a living not a minimum wage. At the time the Labour government said it was a key step in combating poverty, while the trade union leader of UNISON, which represents many low paid workers in the public sector, said it would *perpetuate poverty* and that his union would be pressing for a living wage. This policy debate in the United Kingdom has moved on in 2012 with politicians and businesses as well as employee representatives seeing the minimum wage as a step in the fight against poverty but not a guarantee of escape from it for working parents. Thus the notion of a living wage has come to the fore in policy debate. The Living Wage Foundation encourages employers to sign up to paying employees a living wage and advocates the notion by lobbying influential agencies and government. Boris Johnson, Mayor of London, backs the campaign, saying at the launch of new rates on 5 November 2012:

> *By building motivated, dedicated workforces, the living wage helps businesses to boost the bottom line and ensures that hard-working people who contribute to London's success can enjoy a decent standard of living.*
>
> (www.livingwage.org.uk/home)

The wage debate continues but in any event income does correlate with child poverty. Levels of income affect the ability of the family to meet obvious basic needs such as food and shelter but also influence social and cultural experiences for the child.

Social exclusion strategies

Both Labour and coalition strategies regard intervention as important for those at the extremes of poverty. The coalition uses the concept of 'vulnerability' and Labour launched its notion of 'social exclusion'.

Sure Start and Children's Centres

A major policy of the Labour government for tackling the effects of poverty was the Sure Start scheme. This was launched in 1998 with the aim of giving young children the best start in life. It supported childcare, early education and health and parenting issues. Initially it operated in areas identified as most disadvantaged but was later rolled out to include the 30 per cent poorest children under four. It was primarily about alleviating the impact of income poverty but soon became a means of supporting income generation through working families by providing childcare and other services and as such became a major tool to raise children out of poverty. The government viewed the early years as crucial in breaking the cycle of disadvantage and Sure Start offered this opportunity. Its focus was young families, improved antenatal and parenting skills and childcare. The scheme had drawbacks, such as inadequate reach to encompass those disadvantaged living outside of the designated areas, and accessibility by those who were not disadvantaged who lived within the designated areas. To address the issue the government of the day took a decisive step in supporting Children's Centres across all areas. The core purpose of Sure Start Children's Centres is to improve outcomes for young children and their families, with a particular focus on the most disadvantaged, so children are equipped for life and ready for school, no matter what their background or family circumstances (DfE, 2012).

CASE STUDY

Clifton Street Children's Centre

The Clifton Children's Centre in my locality reflects the range of services offered within one setting. Its services include physical activity sessions for young children, antenatal check-ups, health visitor drop-ins, links to Jobcentre Plus for training, afterschool and holiday sessions for children up to eight, a child-minding network, family support workers, health service clinics and childcare for children from six weeks to five years old.

It has now formed a federation with another Children's Centre in the area and shares good practice, ideas and staff to enable the widest variety of activities it can to support its aim of providing *the very best for children and families*.

Source: www.clifton-childrens-centre.co.uk/services

The Centres were not established and welcomed overnight. It sometimes took years to build service networks and input, and the low status of early years childcare workers compounded the difficulties. This led to the development of the Early Years Professional Status programme to increase the body of graduate early years childcare staff and moves to require a minimum level 3 qualification to practise and supervise in a setting (Hadfield et al, 2012). The National Qualifications Framework (NQF) illustrates the level and category of the qualifications that have been accredited by the Qualifications and Curriculum Authority (QCA), which enable recognition of candidates' achievements and which facilitate career progression. There are eight levels, level 8 being the equivalent of a doctorate and level 6 a degree. (See Chapter 5, *Education and care for early learning and development*, for further information on qualifications and accreditation.)

The experience of Children's Centres reinforces the importance of focusing on social assets rather than just income, and inclusion rather than exclusion as important aspects of poverty alleviation. Naomi Eisenstadt concludes:

> *We have learned important lessons from the early work on Sure Start. In particular, we learned that a service meant for everyone must reach out to those least likely to use it, while remaining welcoming to all.*
>
> (Eisenstadt, 2012, p 49)

This questions the coherence of the coalition's approach to Sure Start of taking it back to a premise it never had, as a service restricted to those especially vulnerable and disadvantaged rather than as an open service for the benefit all of young children and families. The coalition's programme for government (2010) states,

> *We will take Sure Start back to its original purpose of early intervention, increase its focus on the neediest families, and better involve organisations with a track record of supporting families.*
>
> (Cabinet Office, 2010a, p 19)

Poverty targets

Earlier in the chapter we raised questions about relative poverty as a definition and measure and identified recent challenges by the coalition government of its validity. The Secretary of State for Work and Pensions, Rt Hon Ian Duncan Smith, in *New Approach to Child Poverty* presented to Parliament in 2011 commented:

> *We seek to learn the lessons of the previous decade, where prosperity bypassed the worst-off and welfare dependency took root across the country. Good intentions failed to translate into effective policies. The previous Government attempted to hit child poverty targets by paying out record amounts in welfare payments – £150 billion alone was spent on tax credits between 2004 and 2010, with the majority spent on families with children. Yet by 2009 progress on child poverty had completely stalled. And between 1998 and 2009 poverty for working-age adults actually increased by 800,000 and social mobility showed little sign of improving.*
>
> (HM Government, 2011, p 2)

However, drawing on data from the Institute of Fiscal Studies analysis shows that child poverty did decline and that for any measure used income improved for families with children, with income rising most for the lower half of the distribution (Joyce, 2009). If we go on to peruse the qualitative data related to income we have evidence that shows increased spending on fresh food and children's clothes and books, and the share of the population who always worried about money falling from 45 to 29 per cent. While there is no room for complacency this does show that income policy can make a difference (Brewer et al, 2011). However, the Institute has predicted a surge in child poverty upwards of 100,000 a year under coalition government policies. It suggests the main reasons are substantial cuts in welfare, weak back to work initiatives and continued recession (CPAG, 2012).

Governments are not always at odds in their policy proposals. Some important elements of the Labour administration related to early years provision have been maintained by the coalition government. We now have in the UK universal entitlement to 15 hours per week of childcare for all three- and four-year-olds, extended and increasingly flexible parental leave, and the requirement that local authorities ensure adequate provision of childcare for parents who want to work. The coalition is in the process of rolling out funding for free childcare for two-year-olds. 150,000 children in England will be entitled to 15 hours a week from September 2013 and some 260,000 as the policy extends in September 2014.

Agencies not often associated with social welfare can be highly active in social as well as economic strategies for poverty alleviation. The World Bank has sponsored a plethora of research in this area and produced some of the most insightful works on poverty, including Narayan's 'Voices of the Poor' series referenced earlier in the chapter. The Confederation of British Industry (CBI) launched its proposals for pre-school age children as part of its report, *First Steps: A New Approach for our Schools*, on 19 November 2012 at its annual conference. In its press release it states that:

> *Research shows that children failing to achieve adequate standards in primary education disproportionately come from disadvantaged backgrounds.*

The CBI may have economic and business motives underlying its interest in raising educational attainment, suggesting a clear relationship with economic growth. However, the CBI is calling for two main thrusts of poverty policy based on social exclusion:

- *the Government to target structured childcare provision in areas where educational performance is low, as this is one of the best ways to raise attainment;*

- *raising the quality of pre-schools by aspiring to having at least one person with Qualified Teacher Status.* (CBI, 2012)

Critical question

» *As a professional working with young children, what argument and evidence would you use to seek to persuade and influence the development of policy among powerful bodies that have the ear of government, such as the CBI?*

This selection of contemporary initiatives identifies evidence of child poverty policies largely based on income strategies but with a significant regard for asset strategies for young children and their families. The deployment of both fiscal and social policy as a means of alleviating poverty and its effects has gained ground.

Critical reflections

Impact, effectiveness and sustainability of child poverty programmes

We can take much from the child poverty discussion throughout the chapter to inform and understand the important facets of child poverty policy. In summary these include:

- a clear and consistent contemporary message that child poverty is multifarious and strategies to alleviate it must reflect this;

- the imperative to listen to the poor in determining any strategy and working with them not just for them in implementing action;

- that diverse assets matter to the poor;

- that new thinking ought not to dismiss existing or more traditional approaches but combine, enhance and reconstruct them;

- that political and economic ideology should not get in the way of the goal and purpose but facilitate its achievement and success;

- that small scale and locally based initiatives can make a difference;

- that collective action at macro and micro levels can add value and increase the pace of improvement.

The case studies highlighted throughout the chapter demonstrate these tenets in a number of ways.

The children of the Maasai Mara have their environmental difficulties compounded through lack of interest of national government and lack of infrastructure. The way of life and community bonds are breaking down as urbanisation and environmental change take their toll. The Maasai have a strong sense of social and cultural identity, which is at risk of being undermined by world economic effects. In parts of Kenya local joint initiatives between Maasai communities and tourism, supported by European Union education programmes, have resulted in land maintenance, leasing and ecological tourism that bring income to cover lean periods and make living on their land sustainable for future generations of Maasai families. As Kakuta Ole Maimai, Managing Director of the Maasai Association states:

> We would like to be agents of our change rather than victims of change.
>
> (www.maasai-association.org/mission.html)

The poor children and families of New Orleans suffered disproportionately as a result of Hurricane Katrina largely due to years of inequality in the accessibility of local and national resources. Government failure, inequality and corruption are frequently mentioned as reasons for inadequate policy. These families had no social assets and their infrastructure was weak, so that when the hurricane hit their poor housing, lack of transport and media access and low demographic status left them vulnerable.

Darren's experience was multifarious. A simple income strategy was not going to alleviate his poverty, although it might have enabled his day out. He was already suffering the effects through poor growth and development. His cognitive and social skills were weak and his environment lacked stimulation, warmth and care. Income might have increased physical comfort and better nutrition but the long-term effects of poverty were already entrenched. His home learning environment, as described by Sylva (2007) lacked almost everything required for good social and cognitive development. For Darren and his young siblings there were diverse needs that required an array of professional support and improved infrastructure over a lengthy period of time to have impact. Children's Centres could have helped if available when Darren was a baby and very young child. Such provision requires intensive resources and long-term commitment. Unfortunately, such projects are subject to the vagaries of political and economic policies and can lack sustainability as a result.

It is imperative that policy sees beyond ideology and into process. Sophia should to all intents and purposes be a shining example of endeavour. Her effort to improve her income through education and training, despite serious personal circumstances, was undermined because of a blinkered perspective that focused on cutting the welfare bill at all costs. At a national and international level such measures are impersonal and lack direct consequence but on a local and personal plane the effects are sorely felt and can rebound on policy-makers with negative results.

There is only one thing most agencies, experts, individuals and governments agree on about child poverty: that it is a huge problem. Beyond this, different entities sign up to different views on how it is being tackled, the level of success or otherwise and who should be involved in what ways. Clearly top-down emergency aid approaches have only limited effect as we see every day in the media. The intentions are good but the impact and endurance are questionable. And, in any event, the greatest threat to poor people across the world is entrenched, intergenerational poverty. Action that has the potential for long-term success and sustainability is that determined and managed by the poor themselves with the support of experts and policy-makers along the way, epitomised by the 'Trickle Up' project that supports some of the poorest people across the world to build sustainable livelihoods. It provides *training and seed capital grants to launch or expand a microenterprise and savings support to build assets* (www.trickleup.org/about/About-Trickle-Up.cfm). It is a twenty-first century approach to child poverty reduction.

Further reading

Peter Antonioni and Sean Masaki Flynn (2010) *Economics for Dummies: UK Edition*. Chichester: John Wiley.

> This easy to understand guide takes you through the world of economics from micro- and macroeconomics to demystifying complex topics such as capitalism and recession. It provides a straightforward guide to all the terminology you have heard but not fully understood: for example what is monetary policy and fiscal policy? It gives an insight into how economics impacts on our everyday lives.

Abhijit Banerjee and Esther Duflo (2012) *Poor Economics: A Radical Rethinking of the Way to Fight Global Poverty*. New York: PublicAffairs.

> A highly informative read demonstrating the complex economics of poor people's lives. The discussion draws on field experiences across five continents. By working with poor communities the authors have been able to analyse and understand the specifics of poverty and some interesting solutions. It examines the reasons why poor people do not always value and take up top-down policies and resources. The authors argue that most anti-poverty policy to date has failed and that for it to succeed in the future it must learn from the evidence and be developed through a direct relationship with the poor.

Deepa Narayan (2000) *Voices of the Poor*, Volume 1: *Can Anyone Hear Us?* Oxford: Oxford University Press for the World Bank.

This and the other two books in the series listen to the poor and reflect their different and diverse voices. It is research on a massive scale – some 60,000 women, men and families across 60 countries. The participants tell their own stories and articulate their views on government and society. They define poverty and well-being in their terms. The book identifies challenges for policy-makers and influencers in relation to poverty alleviation strategies.

7 The landscape of rural and urban living

Global and national perspectives

The landscape of rural and urban living

Housing

Planning the environment

Introduction

Young children's lives are affected by their physical environment: the landscape in which they live, the housing that provides their shelter and the patterns of life that surround them. Children may live in rural idylls or rustic nightmares. They may enjoy the benefits of urban life or suffer the deprivations of city living. The circumstances of their condition are influenced by the social, economic and environmental policies of the state. Earlier chapters have looked at many aspects of social and economic policy in relation to family, rights, welfare and care; this chapter considers the impact of environmental policies, such as planning, infrastructure development and resource access and availability. Such policies and outcomes may be determined on the international stage and at a governmental level or be devolved to regional and community decision-making, but in any event, directly and indirectly, they affect the lives of young children. For example, greenhouse gas emissions contributing to global warming and consequently more air pollutants, can result in respiratory symptoms and aggravate asthma that is especially harmful to children, while housing policy can leave a child homeless or in inadequate accommodation.

The World Health Organization (WHO) has already determined that the effects of climate change since the mid-1970s are likely to have caused 150,000 additional deaths in 2000. The organisation reckons this may be an underestimate given the limited range of health impacts measured in the study. As in so many areas of environmental health and well-being, the greatest risks are to children in the poorest communities, the group that contributes least to greenhouse gas emissions (WHO, 2010).

Land-use policies and infrastructure design can impede children's healthy development and may be at odds with young children's needs and wants. This chapter debates the benefits and costs of some of these high level developments and presents a critical analysis of the effect on young children's lives. It discusses the importance of housing and local planning policies in supporting the welfare of young children by examining important elements such as play space, access to health and welfare facilities and housing to enhance children's lives. The focus is on recent United Kingdom policies but draws on international case studies and trends that add depth and breadth to the debate.

Some global and national perspectives

WHO has developed a tool to enable policy-makers and other interested parties to determine the existence of health inequities and aid in correcting them. The process evaluates the socio-economic factors prevailing in countries and communities and how effective or otherwise policies may be in perpetuating or stopping undesirable outcomes. The tool is the Urban Health Equity Assessment and Response Tool (Urban HEART). It is designed *to tackle avoidable differences in health that are socially produced rather than biologically determined* (UNICEF, 2012, p 52). The tool takes account of three components.

1. *Sound evidence: reliable, representative and comparable data, disaggregated by sex, age, socio-economic status, major geographical or administrative region, and ethnicity, as appropriate.*

2. *Intersectoral action for health: building relationships beyond the health sector in order to influence a broad range of health determinants – in particular, working with other government sectors (e.g., education, transport and public works), community groups and non-governmental organizations.*

3. *Community participation: involving community members in all aspects of the process, from planning, designing and implementing interventions to helping ensure that these efforts are learned from and sustained beyond the initial phase.*

(UNICEF, 2012, p 52)

The tool revolves around the planning and implementation of policy. It is intended to augment existing state and community planning for a healthy population. The programme has been piloted in Brazil, Indonesia, Islamic Republic of Iran, Kenya, Malaysia, Mexico, Mongolia, Philippines, Sri Lanka and Vietnam since its launch in 2008.

CASE STUDY

Urban HEART in Nakuru, Kenya

Nakura is the fourth largest town in Kenya and has witnessed a tremendous increase in its population over the past three decades. The population includes migrants from rural areas who tend to settle in already overcrowded informal settlements in Rhoda Ward. Population growth is expected to continue with an annual growth rate per year of 3.8 per cent. The current population of Nakura is estimated at 500,000, 54 per cent being under 18 years of age and 16 per cent children under five years. This has led to an increase in demand for basic services and infrastructure such as housing, water and sanitation and roads, among many others. It puts a strain on the available resources, and increases the challenges for the local council. It also endangers the environment as the last rows of houses in Rhoda are literally leaning against the electrified fence surrounding the Lake Nakuru National Park. Urban HEART helped the local council to analyse the health situation and prioritise action. It found problems and inequalities with clean water access, human waste disposal, refuse collections and access to electricity. Traffic was a growing problem with large numbers of accidents throughout the town. Health services were well distributed among most of the town but severely lacking in the Rhoda district. Literacy levels were good but unemployment was high. By using the Urban HEART tool the town council has been able to draw up a plan and prioritise action as shown in Table 7.1.

From the analysis the town council identified the following priorities:

- the provision of land, shelter, physical infrastructure and services (water, roads, solid waste management, etc.), and social infrastructure facilities (schools, hospitals, etc.), for the urban population and especially in low-income neighbourhoods and in the new settlements;

- effort to increase the number and variety of economic activities with the aim of creating employment opportunities.

- a comprehensive municipal urban land-use policy to regulate the supply of land for urban development.

Table 7.1 Naruka Action Plan

Domain	Indicator	District and %	
		Ward 1	**Ward 2**
Physical environment and infrastructure	Access to safe water	75	**4**
	Access to improved sanitation	98	90
	Households with waste collection services	90	**27**
	Households using LPG or electric energy	**42**	**8**
Social and human environment	Literacy rate	96	85
	Births attended by skilled personnel		
	Proportion of one-year-olds immunised against measles		
	Prevalence of children on road to health		
Economics	Employment	**29**	**15**
	Percentage of women earning an income	**48**	**35**
	Proportion of households with income-generating activities	**40**	**27**
Governance	Percentage of government spending dedicated to health and education	**12.8**	
	Voter participation rate	77	

Bold denotes priority area
Source: Adapted from Urban HEART assessment matrix, Naruka, Kenya (UNICEF, 2012).

Each priority has produced more detailed plans and data requirements and identified key stakeholders for implementation (Nyasani, 2009).

Critical question

» *Investigate the potential for use of the Urban HEART assessment matrix in your area of professional practice with young children and families. In particular, critically appraise the value of assessment using the four domains to help identify relevant issues and priorities and determine action plans.*

Urban living and young children

UNICEF (2012), estimates that by 2030 children will make up the majority of city dwellers, with approximately 60 per cent under the age of 18. Children in developing and expanding urban communities may experience deprivation as severe as their rural counterparts, such as lack of access to safe drinking water and sanitation. The close proximity of living in urban areas can worsen the effects by increasing the occurrence and intensity of related diseases such as diarrhoea, causing death in very young and vulnerable children. However, other facets of urban living put children at risk, including inadequate housing enclaves, unsafe streets, traffic hazards and inaccessible health and education facilities.

Roads and highways

Road traffic injuries among children are of significant concern in urban areas. Lack of consideration to children in urban and transport planning contributes to the problem.

> *In 2004, the last year for which comprehensive data is available, road traffic injuries killed more 5- to 14-year-olds than malaria, diarrhoea and HIV and Aids.*
>
> (Kelly, 2012)

Annually, 260,000 children die and another 10 million are injured in road traffic accidents (World Health Organization, 2008). Children have extensive interaction with road networks in neighbourhoods and beyond, yet transport and highway planning does little to involve children or prioritise them as users or recipients of planning outcomes. Children live near to roads, play on them, navigate them on the way to school and, in some instances, even work on them. Such proximity, together with the level of cognitive and spatial development of children, creates high risk of injury on the roads. Children are also susceptible to the vagaries of drivers whether they are passengers, pedestrians or cyclists. Many developed countries have worked towards reducing death and injuries in recent years. In the UK, for instance, there has been a downward trend in the numbers of road traffic deaths and injuries over the last two decades (Table 7.2).

Globally, though, the outlook is more disturbing. By the year 2030, road traffic injuries are predicted to be the fifth leading cause of death worldwide. For example in Bangladesh, road traffic injuries were the second most common cause of injury deaths in children aged 1–9 years and in children aged between 10 and 14 years they were the leading cause, accounting for 38 per cent of all child deaths. The impact of road traffic accidents goes further, with approximately 1,250 mothers and 2,850 fathers dying from traffic injuries in Bangladesh each year, resulting in thousands of children experiencing the loss of a parent and primary carer (Peden et al, 2008).

Both children and adults share some of the vulnerabilities that contribute to the chance of a road accident but others are particular to children and present added risk for them. For example:

- roads and vehicles are constructed with the adult in mind;

- diminutive children find it more difficult to see traffic hazards and it is harder for traffic to see them;

- young children's spatial awareness and cognitive judgement are not fully formed, which affects their capability when assessing traffic conditions;

- children's physique is not fully formed and therefore is more susceptible to collision with a vehicle.

Table 7.2 *Road casualties killed or seriously injured by road user type and age (Great Britain number of casualties)*

Type of user	Age	1994–98 average	2003	2006	2009	2011
Pedestrians	0–4	571	271	239	214	229
	5–7	831	392	308	253	279
	8–11	1,350	753	557	475	497
Cyclists	0–4	19	13	6	4	9
	5–7	146	53	48	45	30
	8–11	377	216	159	129	120

Source: Adapted from table in *Reported Road Accident Statistics* (Keep, 2013).

The growth in car ownership and use and the trend towards motorised rather than railway transportation of goods leads to increased road building and traffic. Within urban areas traffic pollution in all its forms is a risk to children. Planners and policy-makers need to pay heed to this important sector of its population. Peden et al (2008) identify extensive road traffic and planning factors that increase risk of injury and ill-health for children, which municipal and state politicians and providers ought to consider. In summary these include:

- high volume of traffic exceeding 15,000 motor vehicles per day;

- poor planning of land use and road networks, such as:

  - long, straight through-roads that encourage high vehicle speeds, together with mixed land use made up of residential housing, schools and commercial outlets;

- lack of playgrounds, resulting in children playing in the road;

- lack of facilities to separate road users – such as lanes for cyclists and pavements for child pedestrians;

- the location of street vendor businesses, in which children may work;

- lack of safe, efficient public transportation systems;

- inappropriate speed, particularly in residential areas where children play or walk to and from school.

Poor families are more often exposed to the hazards of road traffic. In many places they work on the streets and in some instances live there. Disadvantaged children are especially susceptible to the injury and health risks of traffic focused planning, vehicle speed, and air and noise pollution generated by urban traffic.

CASE STUDY

Living beside the fast lane

In Mumbai there are families with young children living in the space between highway lanes beneath flyovers. These families are often immigrants from poor parts of India who flock to the city of Mumbai to earn a living and seek a better life. The fast growth of Mumbai's population and discrimination against immigrant groups means that families are unable to find work that generates sufficient income to access the already stretched housing demand. Whole families have and rear children in the streets and communities evolve under flyovers and the like. Children learn to walk among urban traffic flows and eat and sleep amidst the fumes of vehicles. When old enough, for many children in such circumstances, school is not a realistic option and they resort to selling artefacts to queuing drivers and passengers during an almost permanent rush hour. Some families have built structures to live in and semi-permanent residential enclaves have emerged (*Toughest place to be a ... taxi driver*, BBC2, March 2013).

However, the picture does not have to be so bleak. In Sweden's Vision Zero road safety policy (Whitelegg and Haq, 2006), introduced in the late 1990s, the emphasis is on children's safety and ability to use the city environs for pursuance of their business and pleasure. Children take centre stage, not traffic, and where the two mix traffic must give way to the child. Swedish municipalities provide car-free play areas, bicycle and pedestrian lanes, and tunnels and speed limits to protect those road users most at risk. Many cities have followed suit to some extent with speed restrictions in residential areas, cycle lanes and pedestrian-only areas being some of the most common road safety measures.

Critical question

» *The situation for children of the Mumbai flyovers is a tough one with many risks and obstacles to their well-being. What aspects of policy need to be addressed and in what priority to reduce risk and realise opportunities? Use the domains and approach of the Urban HEART tool to analyse and evaluate the policy issues.*

Prevention of injury

Injuries account for a significant number of deaths and acute and chronic health problems among children. As indicated above, road traffic injuries are arguably the most common cause. However, for infants the most prevalent causes of injury death are fires, drowning and falls, and for children between one and four years of age the predominant cause of injury death is drowning followed by road traffic injury. To reduce the incidence and severity of such injuries a comprehensive approach to policy is essential. This might include health and safety legislation and environmental planning to minimise fire incidents, house building regulations and use of smoke alarms alongside education and training for families and children and professionals.

CASE STUDY

Child injury reductions in Sweden

Sweden followed a multifarious approach to tackle child injury, involving policy development and change in:

* environmental planning;

- traffic safety measures;

- measures against drowning;

- safety measures in the home;

- home visits by health professionals;

- improved product safety and standards;

- improved healthcare services for children;

- safety measures at school.

The measures achieved dramatic results from injury death rates of 24 boys per 100,000 and 11 girls per 100,000 in 1969 to 5 per 100,000 boys and 3 per 100,000 girls in 1999 (Peden et al, 2008).

While injury is not the biggest killer of young children, over 160,000 children under five die through injury each year (WHO, 2010). Most are probably preventable if the Swedish case study is representative of what can be done.

Critical question

» *What would you do as a professional working with young children to minimise injury among young children in an ECEC setting and beyond? How would you determine your actions and seek to implement them effectively?*

Planning the environment

Urban planning needs to ensure that children can move safely within their environments. It also needs to ensure that children's planning needs are considered in policy development and implementation. Too often urban, and increasingly rural, development creates hazards for children and barriers to a positive experience of childhood and development. Throughout the UK there is a nostalgic perspective of childhood in the middle part of the twentieth century, one of children free to roam, continuously expanding their range of places and spaces to explore. Nostalgia conjures up happy and mischievous children who get into scrapes with grown-ups that elicit the benevolence of adults and not their wrath. The literature, popular at the time, reinforces this perception with authors such as Richmal Crompton creating the Just William stories (1912–70) and Enid Blyton's Famous Five (1942–62). It is arguable that this was an idealised childhood that bore only tenuous connection to the real situation. Whatever the circumstances of the past, the reality is very different for children in the twenty-first century. Rural environments have turned into factory farms across much of Britain and urban sprawl has put the countryside out of easy independent reach for the majority of children. The freedom to explore one's environment as a child has been seriously curtailed as the urban environment is seen as dangerous and harmful.

CASE STUDY

Pat's world

In the 1950s, Pat's parents lived within a quarter of a mile of the city centre on a busy road that was a transit route from the city centre to the suburbs. The environment was not idyllic, traffic was a hazard and strict instruction to stay away from the main road was the order of the day. The neighbourhood was mixed demographically with low income families in largely rented accommodation on the south side of the main road and large Victorian villas on the brink of transition from the family homes of professionals to multi-occupancy dwellings. The clientele of Pat's family's business included doctors, the coroner, small business owners and office workers alongside factory workers, seafarers and domestic staff. There were aggressive families around the area who were renowned for public arguments and brawling and quiet industrious families who supported and held the community together. Perceptions of danger and risk for children were low. As a consequence, Pat had a high level of freedom as a child, walking to school on her own after the first week, being sent on the bus alone to her grandparents before she reached school age and playing out with friends after school from the age of six or seven. Pat's world was rich and varied as part of a large and diverse community. The local business owners and staff made her welcome and kept an eye out for her. She 'helped' the dry cleaning staff bag the clothes for dispatch to the factory for cleaning, and she walked to the newsagent for her weekly comic. The postmaster, confectioner and butcher all knew her and when her mother was busy often took her in for refreshments. She once got her tricycle stuck when negotiating it out of the back gate and the butcher happened along to help her with it, while she held the newly slaughtered chicken for him. Her father asked her to post letters for him and her mother sent her to the bakers for bread and cakes.

Her play space was the streets of the neighbourhood and the play centre run in the primary school after school finished. Friends gathered in the evenings for games of block, off-ground tag and 'May I'. Sometimes in the summer the men and women would appear on the doorsteps and turn a large rope stretched across a terrace for a game of skipping. Occasionally she would play indoors, making hideaways under the table using sheets or 'performing' impromptu concerts for the adults to watch. But mostly Pat's play was informal and outdoors, determined by the fashions and whims of the children out and about at the time. The play did not generally involve adults and at times was exasperated by them. However, it was largely observed by the neighbourhood. The comings and goings of children tended to be viewed collectively by the community. Adults interfered if things got out of hand. They reported sightings to parents and they admonished or helped as they deemed appropriate. Children were not seen as a nuisance on the streets but as expected participants in the life of the community.

Critical question

» *How does your childhood experience compare with that of Pat? Identify differences and similarities and critically review the reasons for them.*

Participation of children

Being a participant in their settlements is important for children. To be able to use the environment and resources with confidence and comfort enables healthy development and awareness of patterns of living. In Pat's case the interaction with people of different social and cultural backgrounds enabled understanding and appreciation of difference and confidence in communication with others. For many children across the UK such a childhood experience would be deemed unsuitable, viewed with trepidation by middle-class parents who fear for their children's safety and capability to deal with the dangers of the outside world. For others it is an idealised past as communities are no longer cohesive enclaves where housing and services are together in one location and populations interact on a daily basis. For children in the UK Pat's childhood is no longer possible as families travel miles for their weekly shop and adults commute long distances for work and the mix of the population becomes more homogeneous within residential areas. This is somewhat incongruous given the heterogeneous nature of the UK's population. Lindon (2011) and Edgington (2013) suggest that young children who are over-protected from risk and challenge are often unable to make sound judgements about their capability to deal with situations that arise in later life and are likely to be ill-equipped to avoid and manage new or difficult situations. The tension remains that for parents to be able to allow and support their children in this way they must have confidence in the community to engage with children in a positive manner. This includes those responsible for planning the environment as well as those living in it. Unfortunately the prevailing approach to planning our cities and residential areas is not child centred. As urbanisation grows exponentially across the world, the demand for industry, homes and infrastructure to support economic growth expands too. Children often get lost in the ferocious appetite for growth. In such circumstances cities can be places of plenty or deprivation for children. For children in sound economic and social circumstances cities can provide the richness of education, health services and all manner of cultural activities. But for those experiencing economic and social disadvantage cities are places where children are injured, exploited and homeless.

Social capital for children

Children need to have a stake in their communities and a voice in decision-making. The concept of 'social capital' is well known and relates to sociability and social networks and support and engagement with and reciprocity between communities and civic society (Harpham, 2002). UNICEF (2012) views social capital as pivotal to the development of children. The key elements of the concepts of trust, reciprocity and a sense of belonging are crucial to children in all aspects of their lives. The discussion has considered these elements in various ways in other chapters in relation to family and poverty, education and care and health and well-being. However, children's interactions and relationships with the broader environment can have far-reaching effects on children's opportunities, choices and outcomes in life. As UNICEF points out:

> *Just as physical toxicity threatens human survival and well-being, a toxic social environment – for example, one in which violence, deprivation and abuse are common – can hamper the development of children and adolescents. In general, children are less mobile than adults and can exercise only limited control over their external circumstances. When growing up amid social disorder, they are likely to internalize problem behaviours, including aggression and substance abuse.*
>
> (UNICEF, 2012, p 62)

Children achieve social capital by being able to influence and affect their cities and neighbourhoods. Policy-makers and resource providers who view children as an investment and a voice worth listening to get positive pay-back through greater interaction among adults in communities and a growing sense of ownership and shared responsibility for the landscape. In such situations, environments can provide social support, facilitate a sense of self-worth and access to education and health services that meet children's welfare and development needs.

Critical question

» *As a professional working with young children how would you seek to enable young children to achieve social capital? What policies and provision within your professional setting would you want to provide to enable the children to have a stake and voice? What would you do to promote the concept in the wider environment that affects the children in your setting?*

Open and play spaces

Brown (2012), in an interview for the *American Journal of Play*, when asked if there were dangers in the current trend of risk aversion in children's play provision by policy-makers and planners replied:

> *Yes, – obvious ones such as the creation of boring playgrounds for children and the reduction of playtime in schools. However, I think there is one very fundamental consequence that outweighs all others. Children's play is often chaotic and unpredictable. Educational and local authorities do not like that, and instinctively they seek to control it – often under the guise of health and safety. In short, the child's right to play is routinely ignored by local authorities, teachers, the police, and community associations who are overly adverse to risk.*

> (Brown, 2012, p 269)

Theory and research over many years shows how fundamental to healthy development play is for children. Respected writers such as Piaget, Erikson and Vygotsky among others all highlight the importance and value of play for children. When children play, they reap the benefits of physical exercise and develop advanced motor skills and emotional stability. Play also promotes children's cognitive abilities, creativity and social well-being. As Fraser Brown suggests, play is not formal or routine but spontaneous and diverse. Whether play is provided through organised service provision or is impulsive and opportunistic it is essential that it is engineered by the child. It is imperative that urban and rural planners and policy-makers take account of a child's need to play in a spontaneous and free manner.

The outdoors is an important requisite of play, enabling free movement, exploration, engagement with nature and adventure. Even in urban surroundings the outdoors can provide all these elements if planners listen to and take account of children's voices and develop cities that are child-friendly. Too often play space is allocated in housing developments as an afterthought and designed to appease adult perceptions rather than play needs. The end result is frequently flat boring playground spaces with a few ugly pieces of unadventurous equipment. These are usually ignored by children or used in contradiction to the expectations of the designer and adult community.

Critical question

» *Think of a playground you have recently visited or seen. Undertake a brief analysis of use. How many children were at the playground and what were their ages and gender? If they were accompanied who was with them? What were they doing? Think about its fitness for purpose. How welcoming or otherwise was the playground in your view? What features did it have to facilitate the diverse play needs of young children? What would you have changed to make it more attractive to young children?*

UNICEF (2012) makes great claims for urban play spaces, suggesting that they can help mitigate the effects of inadequate housing and sedentary lifestyles and may enable children to play with others from different and diverse social and cultural backgrounds. Children make play spaces anywhere and everywhere given the opportunity. Children play on railway lines, around deep lakes and beside roadways. They play in puddles of dirty water and among the debris of building sites. The essence of play is that it is an intrinsic motivation for children and an essential requirement for development. However, it is important that societies and communities mitigate risk without stifling play opportunities and enable safe but adventurous play provision within an environment that supports children.

Open spaces

Children need access to nature. There is a large body of evidence indicating that exposure to the natural landscape has positive effects on children's physical, mental, social and emotional health. The notion of a 'therapeutic' landscape demonstrates the value to physiological and psychological health of access to green spaces including trees, water and plants (Muñoz, 2009). The landscapes can be manufactured or natural and enclaves in cities or part of the rural environment and need to be accessible to children on a regular and frequent basis. Gardens and parks in their neighbourhoods are important sites for children. A once a year outing to the seaside while exciting and adventurous is not sufficient to sustain a child for the remaining weeks of the year. Therefore, open spaces in towns and cities and access for rural children to a safe outdoors is an essential aspect of policy and planning. The Fields in Trust organisation shows that open spaces are being reduced across cities and towns in the UK as demand for housing grows. Recent slackening by the coalition government of planning rules regarding in-fill and greenfield sites is likely to increase rather than stem this trend. Fields in Trust advise that:

> *Outdoor recreational spaces have been under threat ever since we were founded in 1925 and in difficult economic times selling a playing field to a developer can seem a quick financial fix. Playing fields are often particularly attractive targets as, unlike brown-field sites, they do not involve an extensive clean up before building can begin.*
>
> *There are always peaks and troughs in development trends but a steady rise in planning applications to develop playing fields can clearly be seen – the numbers more than doubled between 1999 and 2009 rising from 625 up to 1322 (DCMS).*
> (www.fieldsintrust.org/Loss_of_Sites.aspx, 2012)

The 2011–15 Business Plan of the Department for Culture, Media and Sport highlights one of its aims as securing the legacy of the Olympic Games and identifies the protection and development of playing fields as part of its action plan (DCMS, 2011). However, the lessening of the requirements for planning approval for housing and business development by the coalition government, allowing development of green spaces in and around urban enclaves seems at odds with the intentions of the DCMS plan. The results of the potential conflict between these two sectors of government policy have yet to be seen.

Planning for child-friendly cities

Neighbourhood play and open spaces can be created with assistance from local policy-makers and planners but need to form part of the bigger picture of planning to avoid being swept away.

CASE STUDY

High-rises elbow children out of play areas

Vertical growth is being seen as the only way out for urban agglomerations – but high rises have little space for children. Children living in and adjacent to high-rises are often banned from playing ball games such as cricket and football. In India adults feel the sense of loss of informal play for children. Surojit Roy, a senior citizen and resident of an apartment at Vijaynagar says. *I feel very sad when I see young children in my apartment not being allowed to play any ball games. Many of them have complained to me saying that they love to go out and play but are unable to do so.* Ball games are banned around his apartment; though some apartment blocks do have play areas, they are restricted to purpose-built play equipment usually for young children or those who are too small for such games.

Sandeep Kadtane, whose apartment complex in Brookefield has insufficient space for games like galli cricket and basketball states, *Due to the lack of open spaces, I was forced to enroll my young son into swimming and tennis coaching so that he can get adequate exercise.*

This 'no ball play zone' is not restricted to apartments alone. Residential enclaves and layouts too often discourage youngsters from playing games like cricket, and the main culprit is the fact that glass dominates building facades. Earlier, crossroads in residential areas were hubs of sports like cricket, football and badminton. But this, too, is slowly dying out. *People tend to make use of every piece of empty land today. In our area, people are even encroaching on roads by extending their boundaries. Where will children find space to play?* asks Joseph Paramel, president of Sri Veerabhadra Nagar Citizens Association.

Source: *The Times of India* (2013).

The case study above highlights the lack of concern for children shown in urban developments and how out of touch policy and planning can be from the communities it is intended to serve.

Planners are key players in shaping and managing the built environment both at state and municipal level. As the Planning Institute of Australia (PIA) suggests, p*lanners are in a unique position to directly impact the creation of child-friendly cities and communities* (PIA, 2013). UNICEF has identified the following set of characteristics that it believes supports child-friendly cities.

- Children should have good access to basic services.

- Policies, resource allocation and governance should be in the best interests of children.

- Safe environments and conditions that nurture the development of children.

- A sustainable future – equitable social and economic conditions and protection from the effects of environmental hazards.

- Children have the right to participate in decision-making that affects their lives.

- Special attention should be given to disadvantaged children.

- Non-discrimination (gender, ethnicity, economic and social).

These are high-level aims, which link directly to the articles of the United Nations Convention on the Rights of the Child (UNCRC). They cover a wide range of resource issues and cross a number of governmental policy areas. In such instances it is likely that responsibility rests with various government departments. This may lead to a lack of focus by all or uncoordinated policy and provision that may be at odds. So high-rise developments become the norm to ease a serious housing shortage without reference to the developmental needs of children for play space and safe access to other services such as education and health.

The PIA suggests that to ensure planners pay attention to the needs of children they must:

- involve and listen to children;

- avoid leaving or excluding children out of the built environment as if they were not participants in it;

- access research and information on children's issues during training and beyond;

- avoid segregated planning where activity is compartmentalised due to departmental structures of working briefs.

The PIA advocates and lobbies for this approach throughout Australia and seeks to influence the planners of the future through research and learning.

CASE STUDY

Melbourne's children's plan

The city of Melbourne has taken seriously the commitment to become a child-friendly city and developed a three-year plan to make this happen. The plan focuses on seven themes that incorporate the characteristics of UNICEF's child-friendly cities.

1. Rights of children.
2. Opportunities to connect and build strong communities.
3. Healthy children.
4. Safer city.
5. Natural and urban environment.
6. Services and infrastructure.
7. Mobility.

The specifics of each theme encompass a holistic approach to urban development and living for children. For example themes 4, 5, 6 and 7 relate directly to planning policy, identifying succinct and clear outcomes relevant to children.

- Theme 4 outcome: *Improve the real and perceived safety of the city for children.*

- Theme 5 outcome: *Children are better able to connect with the natural and urban environment.*

- Theme 5 outcome: *High quality, accessible services and infrastructure are available to meet the needs of children and families.*

- Theme 7 outcome: *Children are able to move around easily, safely and confidently both with their families and independently.*

Each theme has a series of city- and local-based actions to enable the outcome. The city has a family and children's advisory committee that provides a formal link between families with children under 12 and the city council and monitors the progress of the plan. It actively engages in consultations at local level; for example, its urban forest plans enable residents in local areas to help design and determine the location and types of trees for their area.

Countries in different circumstances adopt different priorities for action within the child-friendly cities initiative. High income countries tend towards urban planning, safe and green environments and child participation as in the Melbourne case study. Low income countries have tended to prioritise service delivery in health, nutrition, education and child protection. In some instances individual cities, such as Melbourne, have taken up the remit. In others a national framework prevails, such as in Italy and Brazil. In Brazil, the 'Platforms for Urban Centres' promote collaboration among municipal and state authorities and other stakeholders in order to reduce socio-economic inequalities affecting children in the biggest cities (International Secretariat for Child Friendly Cities, 2013). In Italy, the initiative has received the support of the national and local government as well as other stakeholders. The environment ministry has been encouraging cities to adopt a strategy that allows them to be declared child-friendly (Riggio and Kilbane, 2000).

Critical question

» *What is happening in your locality to promote a child-friendly city? How would you seek to influence or enable such an approach in an area? What might you do to ensure an ECEC or school setting encompasses a child-friendly environment?*

Housing

828 million urban residents live in slum conditions worldwide (UN, 2013). In 2012 over 32 per cent of the developing world's urban population lived in slums and over 60 per cent of those live in sub-Saharan Africa. Such statements, while being appalling, do not give credence to the dire experiences for children living in such conditions. The United Nations (UN–Habitat, 2010) gives five deprivations that define slum settlements.

Access to improved water: An adequate quantity of water that is affordable and available without excessive physical effort and time.

Access to improved sanitation: Access to an excreta disposal system, either in the form of a private toilet or a public toilet shared with a reasonable number of people.

Security of tenure: Evidence or documentation that can be used as proof of secure tenure status or for protection from forced evictions.

Durability of housing: Permanent and adequate structure in a non-hazardous location, protecting its inhabitants from the extremes of climatic conditions such as rain, heat, cold or humidity.

Sufficient living area: Not more than three people sharing the same room.

(Adapted from Table 1.2, UN–Habitat, 2010 p 16)

The images of children in Mumbai living and scrounging among rubbish tips are familiar to many. Indeed Dharavi, slum home to approximately one million people, together with other slums across Mumbai account for more than half of its 12.4 million people. Dharavi has become somewhat infamous and a certain mystique and pride has come to surround it, with film-makers and celebrities using it as a backdrop for media events. For children in such circumstances there is no magic, life is riddled with health problems, dangerous chemicals and waste, inadequate water, sanitation and light and poor roads and transport. Slum conditions are dangerous places for children, with little infrastructure for safety and support. They inhibit developmental potential of children through inadequate housing and limited accessibility to schools. Slum-dwelling children often experience discrimination and disadvantage from the wider communities of the city. In such circumstances children are struggling to survive and are unable to thrive. As cities grow and more people migrate to them, in the hope of a better life, slum enclaves grow and create extensive problems for city authorities as ever growing demands overcome the ability to supply resource needs. The tensions imposed often lead to aggravation of the problem rather than resolution. Slums are not simply created by overcrowded cities and mass migration of the population. Poor governance and political instability create conditions for slum development. For example in Zimbabwe, which at the turn of the twenty-first century had one of the lowest incidence of slum dwellings in the developing world, now has over 17 per cent of the population living in slum dwellings due largely to politically motivated house eviction in 2005 producing overcrowding for many families. A further example, discussed in Chapter 4, *The status and rights of children as political and policy influencers*, are the slums created by overcrowded and beleaguered refugee camps as a result of war and conflict (UN–Habitat, 2012).

From slums to inadequate housing

Slums on such a large scale do not exist in Britain today. A massive house clearance programme through the 1960s and 1970s moved many people from homes lacking amenities and space into newly developed council housing, built to a rapid schedule and on large newly constructed estates. Some of these estates engendered more problems that they solved as houses of poor quality were built to designs that alienated children and families. For example, high-rise living created many psychological stresses for families as children lost traditional play spaces that were close to home and easily accessible by adults. Parents refused to let children play outside when they were living some nine or ten storeys up. Many of these estates lacked the infrastructure of the traditional streets the families had moved from. There were no corner shops open all hours, less public transport at greater distances and configurations of housing that lacked passing neighbours and a chance to meet on the doorstep. By the 1980s in a socially divided Britain many of these estates became sink estates, virtual no-go areas where the demise of manufacturing and traditional industries had left many families with unemployed members on low incomes and few, if any, prospects.

The breakdown of social cohesion led to tranches of people feeling disenfranchised and sectors of society being referred to as an 'underclass' (Lister, 1996).

CASE STUDY

The 'Colditz' estate

In my own locality one such estate had blocks of flats reminiscent of communist bloc buildings. The locals called it Colditz because they could not escape. There were buses in the morning to take those who worked off the estate and a few in the evening to bring them back. The privatisation agenda resulted in public transport cuts for non-profit-making journeys so midday and evening services to outlying estates were severely curtailed. Residents were left without cheap and easy egress or access to the estate. Access around the estate was complicated with confusing street patterns and house numbering and to get anywhere required a very long walk indeed. The population became more and more isolated and services less frequent as local authorities cut back on house and landscape maintenance. The 'right to buy' sale of council housing resulted in the choice parts of the estate being sold off, leaving the inferior housing for council tenants. A myth began to emerge of criminality, aggression and danger by those who lived outside the area. This was soon turned into a reality out of frustration and disenfranchisement of the residents, many of whom felt abandoned by the state and society. Some families took advantage of the breakdown of social order to terrorise residents and form criminal gangs who revelled in the ability to steal and not get caught. Those who wished to be different could not avoid the prevailing situation. They could not afford to move and no one would buy their houses or exchange with them. For the children in such circumstances disadvantage prevailed. Schools lacked sufficient teaching staff and those who had a choice would not work in the area. The few shops and facilities that had existed began to close or encase themselves in armour-plated shutters. Of course the area was ripe for the drug dealers to move in and children were prime targets for addiction. Criminal entrepreneurs saw an opportunity to fill a gap law and order had left behind. The estate became a race track for joy-riders as police resources were allocated elsewhere and crime was left to fester in the area.

The case study does not paint a pretty picture of the UK, often portrayed as a civilised, fair and caring society, but such scenarios were happening across the country. The 1980s was a divisive decade. There were growing differentials between those with wealth and those in poverty. It is difficult to know how many young lives were sacrificed to addiction, criminality and lost opportunities during this period but it will have been many. The Colditz story could be replayed in most cities across the UK. The children on these estates and other enclaves had no choice in where they lived or any impact on the social and economic policies that led to their dire situations; however they suffered the consequences of years of policy-making that was detrimental to their development and future prospects.

Many of the social issues behind the situation of the 1980s have been addressed through anti-poverty and social welfare policies throughout the late twentieth century and the first decade of the twenty-first. Such programmes as Sure Start and Welfare to Work (Labour administration, 1997–2010) and changing police and drug strategies came to the fore. And some of the worst housing has been demolished or refurbished. The 'Colditz' flats have now gone, blown up to great cheers from community residents. Many of the social divisions of the 1980s and early 1990s have healed but bad housing still remains.

Bad housing

There are many types of bad housing which children endure. The concept includes temporary accommodation, often provided for homeless families. Such accommodation is likely to be multi-occupancy housing with shared amenities and limited space or undesirable properties which are rejected by prospective tenants who have a choice. Overcrowding is another form of bad housing, where children and parents have to share bedrooms, or sleeping arrangements involve the use of sitting rooms or kitchens. Unfit housing comes into the 'bad' category and includes poor weather resistant and sub-standard housing that may be structurally unsafe and in need of substantial repair. It may also lack basic expectations of modern facilities such as central heating.

(Rice, 2006)

It is estimated that over one million children in Britain live in bad housing of one form or another. Such children have to deal daily with inadequate facilities and run-down homes. They may be squashed into overcrowded accommodation, unable to play, read or do homework. Other children may be homeless, forced to move often from one temporary facility to the next (Shelter, 2006).

Homelessness

Official records from the UK government's Department of Communities and Local Government show that 53,130 households were in temporary accommodation on 31 December 2012. Of these, 40,860 included dependent children and/or a pregnant woman (within which households there were 76,790 children or expected children). The average number of children in households in temporary accommodation with children is about 1.9. Eighty-nine per cent of households with children were in self-contained accommodation and 1,690 (4 per cent of the total) were in bed and breakfast style accommodation, up from 1,310 (also 4 per cent of the total) at the end of the same quarter in 2011, an increase of 29 per cent. Of these households 850 had been in bed and breakfast style accommodation for six or more weeks, an increase of 92 per cent since the end of the same quarter the previous year, when the number was 450 (Presland, 2013). Research suggests that the effects on children can be devastating, with problems with cognition and emotional and social development continuing long after the period of homelessness is passed (Grant et al, 2007; Harker, 2006). Harker also notes that the effect of homelessness on children begins at birth:

> Children born to mothers who have been in bed and breakfast accommodation for some time are more likely to be of low birth weight.

(Harker, 2006, p 14)

Children's education suffers when they are made homeless. Often temporary accommodation is not in the school catchment area and so creates transport difficulties for the child and family. It may be too far to walk and too expensive to take transport. Shelter highlights the case of a child needing to catch two buses to get to school each day (Rice, 2006). If families and children try to move to a school in the new locality it may be full and in any event involves the stress of adjusting to a new environment and people at the same time as dealing with the trauma of homelessness.

Inadequate housing

Poor housing causes ill-health in children. Children in poor housing are almost twice as likely to develop health problems as other children. Children in inadequate housing are at greater risk of respiratory illnesses, such as asthma, and frequent colds and flu than those in adequate housing. Depression and emotional flare-ups are more common in children in poor housing. Children can become angry at the lack of play space and frustrated with their meagre surroundings. Family pressures of overcrowding can result in tensions and upset in and between families. Children living in bad housing are nearly twice as likely as other children to leave school without any GCSEs. Overcrowding and poor facilities influence children's ability to learn and lack of space for quiet and private study and poor sleep patterns detrimentally affect school performance (Rice, 2006).

Housing improvement policy

The UK government launched the Decent Homes Programme (DHP) in 2000 which was intended to *refurbish all social sector homes to a minimum standard between 2000 and 2010* (Parliamentary Office of Science and Technology, 2011, p 1). The aim was not met and the coalition government is continuing to invest money in the public housing sector. However, the most inadequate properties are in the rented private sector. It is arguable whether public funds should be provided to support private landlords and at the moment residents in this sector may not be eligible for investment from the DHP. The programme is managed by the Department of Communities and Local Government (DCLG). By 2010, total funding of approximately £40 billion was allocated, £38 billion of which was for the social sector and £2 billion to the private. The standards used are given in Table 7.3.

Table 7.3 *The Housing Health and Safety Rating System (HHSRS)*

Accident hazards	Physiological hazards	Psychological hazards	Infection hazards
Falls associated with bathrooms, stairs and steps, on the level and between levels Poor electrical wiring Fire risks Hot surfaces and materials Collision and entrapment risks Explosion risk Poor position and operability of amenities Risk of structural collapse and falling elements	Damp or mould Excessive cold Excessive heat Asbestos and MMF Biocides Carbon monoxide and fuel combustion products Lead Radiation (eg radon) Uncombusted fuel gas Volatile organic compounds	Overcrowding Entry by intruders Poor lighting Excess noise	Poor domestic hygiene and/ or pests Poor facilities for food safety Poor sanitation and drainage Poor water supply for domestic purposes

Source: Adapted from Parliamentary Office of Science and Technology (2011, p 3, box 3).

The policy to improve homes in the public and private sector makes a difference to children's lives. The World Health Organization identified that,

> Interventions that deal with structural aspects of housing – for example, the quality of heating and ventilation systems – have been shown to dramatically improve health outcomes. Renovations and repairs to poor-quality housing reduce illness and death in both children and adults.
>
> (WHO/UN–Habitat, 2010, p 110)

However, the funding supply will not meet the estimated demand, which is expected to be double the allocation. There are also concerns that the standards are too low and subject to the vagaries of property managers. While some may seek only the barest minimum standards for improvements others may aim higher. The main problem is with the private rented sector where maintenance and investment are at the whim of the landlord. Tenancies are often short and tenants may not wish to embark on home improvement unless the landlord is supportive and involved.

Shelter believes that many of the existing social care providers and professionals can support children and families with housing support and advice. It suggests housing advisers as members of the Children's Centre team and ECEC professionals receiving training in housing issues and advice. It recommends extending schools to provide a location for advisory sessions and also a means of supporting children by providing space and sustenance for children in inadequate housing to help ameliorate some of the detrimental effects highlighted above. Shelter sees family support workers as key agents in dealing with or referring housing issues for families and the Common Assessment Framework as an excellent tool for assessing housing conditions and needs. Housing advice and information has tended to be left to housing officers or to voluntary agencies such as the Citizens Advice Bureau when difficulties arise. However, Shelter's suggested approach offers continuity and co-ordination of professionals involved in the education, care and welfare of children (Shelter, 2009).

Critical question

» *Shelter's approach implies a role for ECEC and school professionals and settings in housing advice and support for families of children in their care. What do you feel about this suggestion and why? What would you offer and how would you seek to provide the service?*

Critical reflections

Children seen but not heard

Children are continuously affected by change. Whether it is environmental, demographic or geographic change, throughout the world it affects children's lives. In some instances it is positive, through improvements in health and maternity care and availability or when education becomes accessible. But in others it can be detrimental to children. For example, rapid and massive urbanisation may leave children living in slums or on the streets and greenhouse emissions hit the most vulnerable, often young children, the hardest with increases in chronic health problems such as asthma. Children are frequently powerless recipients of these effects but rarely influential participants.

The world is managed by adults, largely men, who make war and bombs that damage and disrupt children's lives, making them homeless or unsafe. In some instances, as with the Colditz case study, they become manipulated participants in dangerous and dissolute behaviour, exploited by drug pushers and criminals. Societies strive to improve life for people often at the expense of children, who seem not to be recognised as people with views, opinions and preferences. The importance and status given to the motor car in most countries overrides the safety of children. Children are often limited in their ability to roam and frequent their neighbourhood due to the hazards of roads and traffic. The play streets of the 1950s in England are largely gone and traffic calming in residential areas is often met with disdain as drivers regularly drive above the speed limit. That is not to say attempts are not being made to reduce the impact of traffic and some forward-thinking communities, such as Bristol, are bringing back the play streets of yesteryear.

Children ought to be active participants in their societies and communities and their needs and outcomes at the forefront of planning and policy-making considerations. Children have social capital invested in their communities and their ability to survive and thrive is affected by the decisions states and municipalities take on all manner of issues of rural and urban living. Decisions on open space use are crucial to children's experiences and optimal development, yet how many politicians supporting the coalition government thought about children's needs for open and play space when agreeing to free up restrictions on planning? I have yet to meet a prospective land developer or planning officer who has consulted with children in the locality about development plans for the area. In my locality a large, and somewhat contentious housing development is being proposed and extensive consultations have been undertaken – none, as far as can be ascertained, with children or advocates on their behalf. Yet the development will cover green and open land on the edge of the settlement and comprises family housing as part of the development. When asked about play space and early childhood facilities for play, care and education the planners advised that it was too early to consider.

As more and more people live in urban enclaves the development of cities needs to better consider children's involvement. The concept of child-friendly cities is being taken up by advocates across the world and there are many examples of good practice, as in the case study about the city of Melbourne. However, there are still mostly good intentions rather than practice, and professionals in planning, environmental health and architecture, among others, should ensure children are at the heart of landscape design.

A crucial aspect of environmental provision that has a serious impact on the quality of children's lives and their prospects for the future is housing. Children are losing out because of the lack of adequate housing. Many millions across the world are living in slums so squalid and lacking in basic amenities that it is surprising children survive at all. While some fail to survive due to the environmental and social toxicity of the place, virtually all fail to thrive. Children of slums become victims of ill-health, poor education and discrimination. Rather than romanticise such enclaves we should be concentrating on getting families into safe and adequate housing and razing these abominations to the ground. While the situation is at its worst for children living in sub-Saharan Africa, countries with extensive economic growth over the past decade or more still have large numbers of children living in slums and on the street. It is likely that the slum settlement in Dharavi, in Mumbai, brought to prominence by the film *Slumdog Millionaire* will be redeveloped. The idealist might say that is due to enlightenment of the authorities; the cynic might beg to differ and suggest it is because of the high value of the land upon which it sits. Slums are not the only issue for children when it comes to housing. Bad housing covers many elements from homelessness to overcrowding and suffering a lack of basic facilities to being structurally unsound. For children living in these circumstances the effects are injurious to their well-being, resulting in school failure, depression and chronic ill-health. Shelter estimates some 1.6 million children are living in inadequate housing in Britain today. This is surely an indictment for the sixth wealthiest nation in the world (*CIA world fact book*).

Further reading

B. Rice (2006) *Against the Odds*. London: Shelter.

> This report presents the findings of a Shelter investigation into what it means to be a child living in bad housing. It was carried out between April and August 2006. The investigation draws on the facts and figures related to housing conditions and listens to children's views of their housing situations and examines other studies and research to get the most complete picture possible. The report highlights the impact of bad housing on children, comparing the lives and life chances of children on either side of Britain's housing divide.

United Nations Human Settlements Programme (UN–HABITAT) (2012) *State of the World's Cities 2012/2013: Prosperity of Cities*. Nairobi: United Nations Human Settlements Programme (UN-HABITAT).

> The report considers the factors underlying the crises facing cities throughout the world and presents evidence of how a focus on financial prosperity alone has led to growing inequalities. It discusses the damage caused and what must be done to ensure sustainability. The report is a bridge between research and policy, with inputs from more than 50 cities.

World Health Organization (2008) *World Report on Child Injury Prevention*. Geneva: World Health Organization.

> This is a joint WHO/UNICEF world report on child injury prevention. It brings together current knowledge and data about the various types of child injuries and how to prevent them. It draws on examples of successful prevention initiatives that can be adapted for use elsewhere. The report is directed at researchers, academics and professionals. It provides some insightful information about an often neglected area of children's experiences in their homes and communities.

8 International issues in the early years

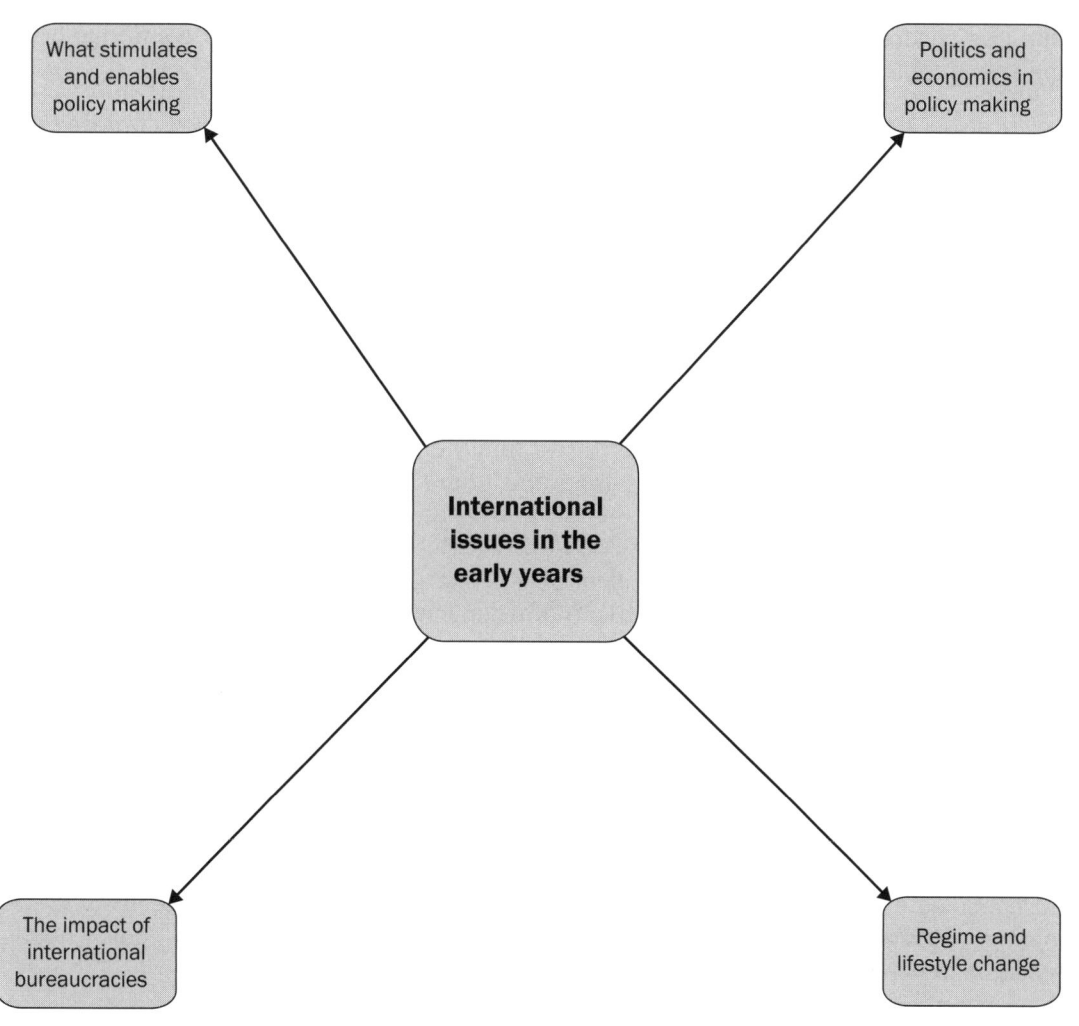

Introduction

Twenty-six per cent of the world's population are children under the age of 15. In many countries in Africa children make up approximately half the population whereas in Europe, which has become somewhat preoccupied with the increasing older population, it is closer to a fifth (Population Reference Bureau, 2012). Such numbers require serious consideration by policy-makers and influencers. Arguably children are a nation's most important asset as they represent the future prospects of a country. What happens to children throughout their childhood affects the ability of the state to grow and prosper or wither and decline. The chapter considers current trends, taking account of demographic data, in social and economic policy at an international and transnational level and the actual and potential impact on young children's lives. How the international community and nations view children and their role and status in society influences trends in economic and social policy. Children are members of nations and part of the international community and are affected by political and economic influences. Indeed, they may be more susceptible than other sectors of the population to the vagaries of policy-making as they have greater vulnerability due to age, developmental stage and relative powerlessness. There are no democracies in the world that give children the franchise and only a few, such as Brazil, that provide suffrage below the age of 18.

Policy at an international level tends towards the generic and is often slow to develop or change as it needs to reach a consensus across a broad church of political perspectives. Nationally, policy development and change is more direct and liable to fluctuation as policy emphasis shifts depending on the prevailing political and economic ideology of the time. For example, whether services are provided by private or public means will have a different impact on children and is largely influenced by the political views of the ruling party and current economic conditions. The chapter explores these political issues, such as regime and lifestyle changes.

The large bureaucracies that have authority in economic and social matters are seemingly very distant from the lives of children in their family and community settings but they can, and do, have an effect on children's lives and future prospects. For example, the World Bank's 'Heavily Indebted Poor Countries' (HIPC) initiative that seeks to help alleviate poverty and support welfare policy in poor countries is discussed later in the chapter. Knowing and understanding the effects of political beliefs and economic actions on the experience children have of their childhood, whether in the confines of the family, in their communities or their countries of residence, is essential in constructing policy. This chapter deliberates on the impact for children of such entities as the European Union, the United Nations, the International Monetary Fund and the World Bank.

By exploring some important demographic and social trends, such as the total fertility rates (TFR) in countries, which provide insight into the average numbers of children per mother, we can see how regimes contemplate the issues and gain a better understanding of how and what stimulates policy-making. Alongside social data, geographic, environmental and economic data create a richer picture of life for children throughout the world. In doing so it informs politicians, economists, bureaucracies and development agencies of policy needs, resource requirements and priorities for action.

What stimulates and enables policy-making?

The stimulus for policy-making operates in a variety of ways. Political parties are formed around a particular ethos or set of beliefs with an aim to achieve power within a nation to develop policy that reflect, such views. In democratic states politicians will seek office to promote their beliefs and party ethos. In other forms of government those taking or seeking power will come with an ideological perspective that influences the sort of policies that emerge. To develop policy on the basis of ideology and ethos alone is a somewhat hit and miss affair. For example, taking a philosophical stance on equality and diversity and developing legislation or principles that reflect it can be based on belief systems and little else. The principle of children's rights echoes such an approach. However, to develop rights into a set of articles to enable government and institutions to facilitate and support them and protect children from wrongs requires a more informed methodology based on knowledge and understanding of children's lives.

Without principled beliefs many important laws may never have come about, such as the abolition of slavery, women's equality with men and child protection. But for the most part it is a combination of principles and knowledge that provides good policy-making. Of course not all ideology is for the common good nor is knowledge gained always used for positive effect. The ethos of Nazism, for example, was aligned to that of fascism with specific elements of biological racism and anti-Semitism. Knowledge and informed data collection and analysis played little part in the development of the Nazi ideology but its persuasive rhetoric resulted in the most horrendous crimes against humanity.

Principles in policy-making

While holding a set of principles or aligning oneself to an ideology informs policy-making it is only part of the process. Policy-making related to children's rights and status and experience of childhood requires ethical decision-making. There are many elements required to make ethical decisions. The primary one is obtaining the facts of the matter, discussed later in the chapter. However, obtaining the facts does not convey how to proceed or what action to take. These decisions relate to the values given to the subject. Philosophers, from Aristotle to Kant, identify various approaches to moral decision-making. These are primarily:

- utilitarian;
- rights;
- fairness or justice;
- common-good;
- virtue.

The utilitarian approach identifies the benefits and harm of the various courses of action that could be taken and how many individuals and groups will be either positively or negatively affected. The ethical action is the one that provides the greatest good for the greatest number. The rights approach endorses individuals' freedom to make choices for themselves and for these to be respected by others. It raises a further moral question whether the rights of one person violate the rights of another and if so to what extent. The tension is often tempered by the notion of responsibilities running alongside rights. Notions of partiality and impartiality come into play when taking the fairness or justice stance. It raises questions on the fairness of the policy and the equity of treatment. The concept of the common good is based on membership of society and community that is concerned with what it wishes to become and how it can do so. It seeks to provide a society that benefits all its members. The virtue approach assumes a set of ideals that humanity pursues. Individuals measure their human achievement in the ethical attitudes and characters they convey. It is a reflective approach that requires the individual to pursue laudable traits such as honesty, integrity, courage and compassion (Velasquez et al, 2009).

Valasquez and his colleagues envisage a 'framework for ethical decision making' that encompasses:

* recognition of an ethical issue;

* getting the facts;

* evaluating alternative actions;

* making a decision and testing it;

* acting and reflecting on the outcome.

If we take the concept of social exclusion there are differences in approach to dealing with it depending on ideological perspectives. Three discourses dominate the discussion, highlighted in Pierson (2010).

* The political left viewpoint, which tends to emphasise the redistribution of wealth as the only effective way to alleviate poverty and is somewhat contemptuous of notions that individual behaviour and cultural circumstances create exclusion. Such a perspective is largely based on notions of fairness and justice.

* The political right outlook argues that moral weakness is engendered in enclaves of idleness, criminality and irresponsibility. It is linked to notions of an 'underclass' (Murray et al, 1996). This view leans towards a virtuous concept, expecting moral norms that if not met are not deserving.

* The political centre tends towards a more integrated approach, seeing work as an important facet of social inclusion and work creation and support of families to undertake it as a primary objective. This approach is inclined towards the notion of 'common good' with elements of utilitarianism in its implementation.

These differing perspectives provide very different explanations for the same phenomenon. Each discourse works from a particular set of assumptions and explanations of how the world works and incorporates its own set of values. When these differing perspectives are acted upon at the level of policy, then services to children and the impact on their lives will be very different.

Critical question

» *Consider an example of early years policy of the recent past and critically analyse the ethical and political ideology underpinning it. To test the principles discussed, review the area of policy using different ethical and ideological perspectives to create policy. What impact do these different approaches have on the policy?*

The importance of data in policy-making

Throughout the book we have discussed some of the specific conditions of young children's existence in the world today. These have included:

- family structures and status;

- cultural and social aspects of health and well-being;

- status and rights as political and policy influencers;

- education and care for early learning and development;

- poverty as part of the early years experience;

- the landscape of rural and urban living.

Credible data about the conditions children are dealing with daily have been invaluable in being able to critique past and current policy and evaluate potential approaches for best effect. It is essential that a comprehensive analysis is considered to maximise positive endeavours and minimise negative effects. For example, the ministerial proposal in the UK for demand-led early childhood education and care provision (Truss, 2012, discussed in Chapter 5, *Education and care for early learning and development*) is somewhat under-mined, once analysed in depth, by data that discredit many of the assumptions in support of the approach (Cooke and Henehan, 2012).

Insight grows as we consider additional, more complex social data. For example, to promote the importance of children having a voice it is helpful to know what percentage of the world's population are children. It enables high-level argument for some form of status and import-ance. However, it does nothing to tell us of the lives of these children and the conditions they experience. It does not assist in determining health and well-being or educational polices for example or how to implement rights policy. Once we begin to add to the basic information such as where children are living, for how long they are living and what familial relationships they have, we begin to gain insight into their needs and wants. For example, once it is known that the TFR (children born per woman) in Niger is 7.1 and in Singapore only 0.78 we can see that the policy discussion will be different for each country. In Niger, the health of the mother through pregnancy and childbirth is likely to be the most immediate issue whereas for Singapore the most likely topic is the inability to replace the population on current TFR and consequently a diminishing population. By exploring further it is clear that for Niger infant mortality is a serious issue, running at 110 per 1,000 live births, reinforcing the importance of maternity and infant healthcare and support, whereas Singapore has one of the lowest infant mortality rates in the world at 2.6 per 1,000 live births, which suggests good mater-nity and infant services. Already without knowing anything else about these two countries it becomes evident that one is a developed nation and the other a least developed one.

Prioritising policy

Demographic data are essential for nations to be able to adequately determine the prior-ity needs. An example is highlighted in Chapter 7, *The landscape of rural and urban living*, by the case study, Urban HEART in Nakuru, Kenya (Nyasani, 2009). It was essential to gather comprehensive data in the locality to interpret the high level data that sparked the initiative. By identifying exponential population growth and age distribution in the region it became apparent that a review of policy and resource needs was required. The local council then proceeded to interrogate the data and undertake further information gathering, to understand the population distribution, the residential demands and resource availability, which enabled it to determine the details of policy and resource allocation. Rather than adopting a scattergun approach it was able to focus policy on the greatest areas of need:

- provision of land, shelter, physical and social infrastructure and services for low income neighbourhoods and in the new settlements;

- creation of employment opportunities;

- development of a comprehensive municipal urban land-use policy to regulate the supply of land for urban development.

Without accurate and detailed data it is virtually impossible to ensure policy-making is able to meet expectations. The consequences can be catastrophic. Consider China's approach to curbing population growth by restricting family size to one child, without modelling the future and diverse consequences. The policy had the effect of reducing the rate of growth of the population, enabling the country to achieve economic growth. However, as a consequence, the population distribution now presents difficulties in terms of maintaining economic activity and growth. As the elderly non-wealth producing population expands as a percentage of the total population and the percentage of economically active adults contracts, sustaining economic and social expectations becomes problematic. China is not the only country facing problems with population distributions as expanding numbers of older people alongside lower TFR affect many developed nations. Short-term or narrow perspectives among policy-makers can result in policies that have immediate impact but not necessarily sustainability in the long-term.

Critical question

» *In the UK the media and politicians have engaged in some scaremongering about the problems caused by the population living longer and the difficulties this will create in the future for today's children. What is the basis for these claims and what evidence supports or challenges the claims? Test the rigour of the argument and evidence to take an informed perspective.*

Dearth of data about children

One of the main difficulties for policy-makers is the lack of detailed data related to stages of childhood. For example, the Organization for Economic Cooperation and Development (OECD) found that it was unable to collect sufficient cross-country data at various stages of children's lives due to lack of data between infancy and late childhood. It found a dearth of valid data for early and middle childhood, which prevented in-depth analysis related to child development. Data related to birth and infancy as well as vaccination data up to age two are well documented as is risk behaviour in late childhood but what is lacking is insightful comparative data related to children's health, well-being and developmental progress in between. OECD identifies a long list of data that would be helpful to enable it to compare children's well-being across OECD countries. These include:

*   child cognition and behavioural development at pre-school and school entry and at 8–10 years of age;

*   child nutrition, height and weight and oral hygiene at similar ages;

*   child poverty rates at different stages of childhood;

*   self-assessed satisfaction data from younger children;

*   physical health conditions;

*   parental time investment at different ages;

*   proportion of income spent on children. (OECD, 2009a)

The shortage of rich data about children's lives within and across countries means policy-makers are at the whim of speculation rather than informed knowledge, which results in policy that may or may not achieve the aims for which it was devised.

Politics and economics in policy-making

Moss and Petrie (2002) make it clear that the politics and economics of childhood are not static but shift in relation to economic and ideological trends. For example, as the demands for an increasingly educated workforce grow, the period of childhood extends to enable the fulfilment of these economic demands. This is evidenced by the massive expansion in young people continuing in full-time education beyond the minimum school leaving age. The concept of the child as an economic asset affects the larger discussion of the relationship between the family and the state's responsibility for children. The state, community and family may view children as primarily economic assets reared for their future productivity. This has been a commonly held view historically in Britain from the feudal system to the industrial revolution. Within this perspective the child is considered an economic resource essential to the well-being of the family and society. Child labour is an important issue when considering children as economic assets and identifies the tensions and complexity of policy-making for children.

Child labour

Doepke and Zilibotti (2005) suggest that changes to the economic asset model start to happen when fertility rates reduce resulting in fewer children to support and earn a living for the family thus producing a more stable family structure. Changing work demands also affect industrial practices that require ever more technical skills needing more knowledge and training of the potential workforce. Health and welfare reforms are also crucial in influencing policy in this area. When these situations prevail, legislators and policy-makers are likely to look at the need for education of the young and introduction of child labour restrictions. Such an approach is not always for altruistic reasons, such as to preserve childhood for children, but for pragmatic ones, when the workforce numbers reduce and adults are competing with children for jobs. Prior to the recognition of the value of an extended education, children were expected to contribute to their communities as early as possible rather than remain a cost through a prolonged period of childhood and not place undue burden on the resources of the state through personal or collective expectations of social welfare and care (Tomlinson in Jones et al, 2008).

The extent of a country's natural resources and ability to generate wealth runs alongside the means of wealth production and distribution. The use of child labour within a country demonstrates the intricacies of the political and economic axis. One obvious tension is the ever-increasing demand of the rich consumer in developed nations for cheap goods and the expectations of shareholders for increased profit that contrasts with the political rhetoric of politicians and public alike against exploitation of children. Direct action is full of good intent but does not always produce the desired outcomes. In recent years the international community has tried to tackle the issue largely by imposing sanctions on those countries where child labour persists. However, such an approach may be self-defeating as poor states become even poorer without the ability to manufacture goods for export. To close down the trade through lack of demand due to ethical concerns only results in greater poverty and consequently hardship for the children concerned. The research into child labour sanctions leads Doepke and Zilibotti (2005) to the following conclusion.

> Our theoretical analysis suggests that actions such as consumer boycotts, trade sanctions, or the imposition of international labor standards may undermine the prospects for further child-labor reform in developing countries ... We therefore conclude that international labor standards and trade sanctions are likely to be counterproductive measures that contribute to the persistence of the child-labor problem.
>
> (Doepke and Zilibotti, 2005, p 518)

The interrelationship between country economies historically, which has led to the unequal distribution of resources globally, provides a context within which we must try and understand the continuance of child labour. It is only by addressing the wider political and economic context of such practices together with the conditions in which children across the world live, that they may be overcome. The international community can support national initiatives to develop legislation against child labour exploitation but alongside, it is essential to consult closely with the children themselves and their families and support local initiatives aimed at preventing such exploitation and implementation of the law.

CASE STUDY

Domestic child labour

A recent estimate of the International Labour Organization is that over 350 million children worldwide are engaged in work. That means that over one fifth of the world's children aged 5–17 years are exploited by child labour in its different forms. Of these, a large percentage work as domestic servants.

Raju is from Saharsa, a remote town in the state of Bihar in eastern India. When Raju was two years old, his father died of tuberculosis. As a result the family became homeless. They left the village and went to Delhi in search of work. Raju's mother was hired to undertake domestic work in a private house. She worked from morning until night managing a big house. She was allowed to build a thatched hut for herself in the backyard of the house. Raju's brother was also doing domestic work in a house a few miles away. After several years Raju's mother became ill. Raju, then seven years old, took on the domestic work to support the family and pay back money borrowed from his employer for healthcare for his mother. It became obligatory for Raju to work in her place in order to repay the debt. For years, he continued working, experiencing bad treatment from his employer if he was ill or made a mistake.

After four years he was rescued by a rehabilitation agency. The agency reunited him with family and arranged for schooling and counselling. *Now, I am getting love and education*, he says. *My life has taken a completely new turn. I feel free, free from any pressure. I have learned how to speak and read well. My conduct has improved. I feel now I am getting more respect in the society and above all, I got to know about my right*s (adapted from Indian Matters!, 2011).

The complexity of Raju's plight goes beyond the exploitation of child labour. It relates to extensive areas of policy-making, including family law and entitlements, such as widow's welfare, healthcare and education and the rights of children. Even if the social welfare policies are in place it requires local implementation and policing to ensure they are effective. As Indian Matters! (2011) highlights:

> The challenge is to convince the parents that they should not force their children to work or beg on the streets ... Thus, it is essential that the economic conditions should be improved for the child labour to stop. When parents would have money, they would think of sending their children to schools as compared to mines and factories. But a social revolution at basic level is needed where every one of us should refuse to employ an underage domestic help.

The UNCRC recognises in Article 32 the right of the child

> to be protected from economic exploitation; and from any work that is likely to ... interfere with the child's education, or to be harmful to the child's health or physical, mental, spiritual, moral or social development.

The International Labour Organization (ILO) reinforced Article 32 by demanding action to eliminate the worst forms of child labour in 1999. This encouraged many states to draw up legislation against child labour. However, these have largely been in relation to some of the most hazardous work and within formal employment settings, such as industrial premises and public service industries. What remains are a significant number of children working in the informal sector, particularly household domestic work, who are subject to the vagaries of employers. There is little opportunity for collective action and support for such children and it is often difficult for agencies to track down exploitative employers. As with Raju, it can be years before help is at hand, if at all. De Silva-de-Alwis (2007) highlights the particular plight of girls in this area as most domestic workers are female. She concludes that a multifarious approach to policy reform is essential to make inroads into the problem and that not only should politicians consider the social welfare aspects, such as health and education, but also address inequalities and discriminatory practices relating to gender.

Critical question

» *Raju's situation highlights many of the elements that make the implementation of Article 32 of the UNCRC difficult to achieve. Use a PESTLE analysis to audit the range and complexity of Raju's family's situation and critically evaluate what are the options for change to facilitate the implementation of Article 32.*

A PESTLE analysis is a useful tool for understanding the 'big picture' of the environment in which an entity is operating. It is often used by business but is easily adaptable and viable in policy development and learning. Its six elements for analysis are as follows.

- **P**olitical. These drivers may be worldwide, regional and national/local conditions.

- **E**conomic. These factors may involve growth and output in and beyond the state involved, fiscal and welfare policies, funding mechanisms and streams and business and enterprise status.

- **S**ocial. These aspects include attitudes to education, cultural expectations and belief systems, status and equality, demographics and lifestyle circumstances.

- **T**echnology. What are the imperatives, changes and innovations in technological development that must be considered?

- **L**egal. Is there any current and impending legislation that might affect progress? This might be international, national or local.

- **E**nvironmental. What are the environmental considerations locally, nationally and internationally? These may be the results of some other elements of the PESTLE analysis such as political and social as well as natural circumstances.

Children as social assets

As well as being viewed as economic assets, some communities have recognised that children require their social needs to be addressed, including their health, welfare and education. Children are supported financially and emotionally within their families. Communities adapt environments to facilitate child development. The state supports the health, well-being and care of its children. In general, children are viewed as social assets. This happens to a greater or lesser extent in most developed countries, such as the UK. However, political ideologies and choices influence the extent of resources available and how they are distributed. As can be seen from the discussion on social exclusion earlier in the chapter and from health and education data, there are differentials in the quality and sufficiency of provision and services and their subsequent impact on children's lives. For example Barnado's (2013) data show that in the UK:

- three-year-olds in households with incomes below about £10,000 are 2.5 times more likely to suffer chronic illness than children in households with incomes above £52,000;

- infant mortality is 10 per cent higher for infants in the lower social group than the average;

- only half as many children who are eligible for free school meals achieved five or more A*–C grades at GCSE or equivalent compared to pupils not eligible;

- only 73 per cent of 5- to 6-year-olds from the most deprived areas achieved the expected level of writing, compared to 90 per cent of those in the least deprived.

(Adapted from 'Child poverty statistics and facts', Barnado's, 2013)

In developed countries economic, potential forms an important view of children, in relation to education and prospects for the future. However, in the social asset model the emphasis is on supporting their health, education and welfare without expectation of financial contribution throughout childhood. The child is socially valued beyond simply her or his economic worth and is seen as having the right to health, education and welfare.

Economics of childhood

De Vlyder (2001) in his contribution to a report for UNICEF makes a vigorous case for economic policy to orientate its thinking with a child-centred perspective. He considers much of the policy development in these areas to be ignorant of children's needs and wants; at best giving consideration to children through family strategy while, at worst, ignorant of the significant and differential impact of macro policy on the economic circumstances of children. For many interested in understanding childhood and working with children, it can seem a tenuous and tortuous connection from childcare and early years education to macroeconomics. Micklewright (2000) simplifies and clarifies the discussion by reminding us that economics is about improving the lives of people, and children are people, who we have seen, earlier in Chapter 4, are subject to some of the worst excesses of economic exploitation, for example trafficking and abuse. Such exploitation has an international economic context that requires a macroeconomic understanding and international action.

Intercountry adoption

The tendency is to consider the criminal margins of such exploitation, yet Smolin (2004) considers intercountry adoption as potentially a form of child trafficking. He does not suggest that all intercountry adoption is exploitative or unethical, but raises concerns about how market forces have become intertwined with law on intercountry adoption. Because the law in the past has tended to require a further testament to the sale of a person to call it trafficking, in the form of enslavement or exploitative labour, the sale of a child per se has not been viewed as trafficking. However, such a view is being challenged and while many intercountry adoptions are argued as in the best interests of the child there are others that are clearly a financial transaction, that is, the selling of a child. The arguments are well defined and tend to polarise opinion. There are those who decry the activity seeing it as people from developed nations using their wealth to exploit the poverty experienced by children in underdeveloped countries. This view promotes support to enable the lives of children in their home countries to be improved through economic growth and social welfare reforms. The proponents of intercountry adoption draw on the emotional distress of millions of children abandoned or living in dire circumstances needing the care and love of parents who can provide. (It is interesting to note that the large majority of intercountry adoptions into the USA are from China (Bureau of Consular Affairs, 2012). China was identified earlier in the chapter as experiencing a problem of population demographics due to low total fertility rates (TFR) over a lengthy period of time and is one of the tiger economies experiencing high levels of economic growth.) Intercountry adoption seems to be falling from a peak in 2005 to its lowest rate since 1999 in both the USA and UK. This trend may reflect Smolin's view that linking market transaction to intercountry adoption reinforces the perception of trafficking and as a result the behaviour will die out over time. The demise might, as likely, be a result of economic development in countries seen as a traditional source of adoptees as they achieve increased economic growth and prosperity. Longitudinal data show that as countries achieve economic prosperity and family incomes grow, living standards improve and health and social welfare services develop, TFR declines. Whether this will reduce the demand is another matter and where a vacuum is created between demand and supply it may be that transactions are even more related to market forces. Intercountry adoption demonstrates the disproportionate impact of global economic activity and policy on children who have little influence on the outcomes.

Critical question

» *The intercountry adoption example above raises many issues and dilemmas around the economics of adoption. Take both stances and use a cost–benefit analysis to enable informed evaluation of the issue and recommendations for future policy. Are there tensions with such an approach? For example, do some issues straddle both costs and benefits and if so how can they be reconciled? Do personal morality and beliefs play a part in determining the recommendations and if so how?*

Cost–benefit analysis is a technique for assessing the monetary social costs and benefits of a capital investment project over a given time period. However, it can be adapted to help determine social impact, as well as financial cost and value or otherwise, of a proposal that is social rather than financial. The principles of cost–benefit analysis (CBA) are straightforward.

* Calculate social costs and benefits, including:
    – tangible benefits and costs (those that are proximate and immediate to enable and implement the development);
    – intangible benefits and costs (those that are more remote and less immediate but will be a likely consequence of the action, often called the 'knock-on effects');
    – searching analysis of events occurring. How likely is it that the benefits and costs identified will happen?
* Compare the costs and benefits to determine the net social rate of return. This helps evaluate the development or policy.
* Compare net rate of return to consider the value or otherwise of proceeding with the development or policy.

Economic trends

Macroeconomic trends at the end of the twentieth century show evidence of increasing differentiation between children who benefit most from the growing affluence of the developed world and those who benefit least. As highlighted in the introduction, children form a substantial minority of the world's population and in some countries are the majority. This in itself raises important economic and political issues when it is set alongside data showing the significant impact of children on households. Figures 8.1 and 8.2 show the percentage of children in poor households across selected countries in the OECD and the average income of children across the same countries. They provide some stark and surprising information that raises important questions of national social and economic policy.

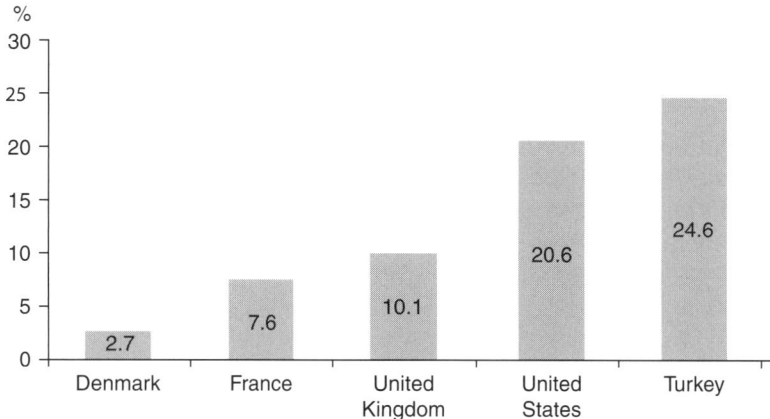

Figure 8.1 Percentage of children in poor households

Source: Adapted from OECD Income Distribution database, developed for OECD, in OECD, 2009b.

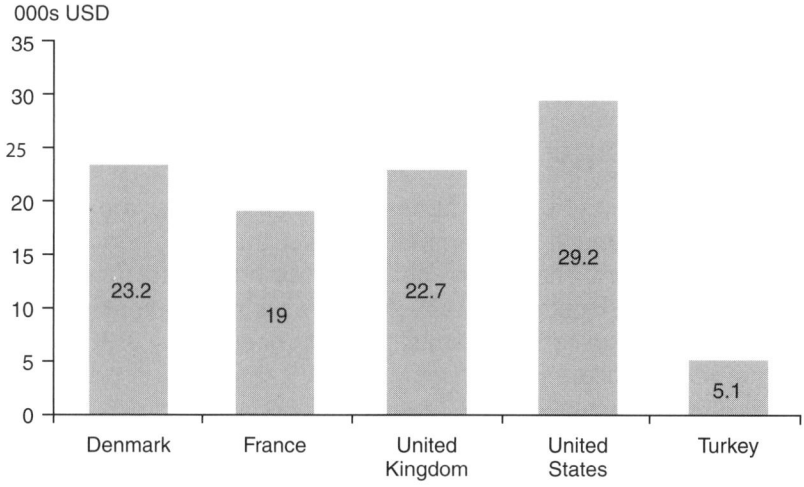

Figure 8.2 Average family income for children aged 0–17 years

Source: Adapted from OECD Income Distribution database, developed for OECD, in OECD, 2009b.

The graphs show the tremendous differential of children in poverty across the countries, with poverty nine times higher in Turkey than in Denmark. In Turkey, perhaps in line with expectations when poverty is high, the average income for children is low. However, the United States which has the highest average income second only to Luxembourg, also has one of the highest percentages of children in poverty of all OECD countries and more than double that of the average (12.4 per cent). This contradicts the more typical expectation that high average income generally correlates with low incidence of child poverty. Gorman (2013) in a paper for the National Bureau of Economic Research (NBER) suggests that poverty persists alongside increases in average income in the United States for two main reasons. She concludes that:

Taken together, the results suggest that the lack of improvement in the poverty rate reflects a weakened relationship between poverty and the macroeconomy. The lack of progress despite rising living conditions is attributable to the stagnant growth in median wages and to increasing inequality. Holding all else equal, changes in female labor supply should have reduced poverty, but an increase in the rate of female-headed families may have worked in the opposite direction. Other factors often cited as having important effects on the poverty rate do not appear to play an important role – these include changes in the number and composition of immigrants and changes in the generosity of anti-poverty programs.

(Gorman, 2013)

Such analysis demonstrates the value of wage and benefits policy that links to economic indices, such as a retail price index or inflation if children are to minimise the vagaries of economic downturn or growth. It also highlights the importance of equality in relation to population diversity of wage and labour legislation, if the population as a whole is to benefit from the economic wealth of a nation.

Critical question

» *Turkey has applied for European Union membership. If successful, what political and economic issues would the EU need to consider and address given the parlous extent of child poverty in Turkey?*

Regime and lifestyle change

Children experience firsthand the impact of political upheaval and unrest. They are subject to the vagaries of lifestyle choices of adults and communities. Yet they have very little, if any, choice or influence in these matters. The Syrian conflict, for example, has affected up to 2 million children according to UNICEF estimates (UN, 2013), resulting in homelessness, injury and ill-health, family loss and termination of education and healthcare. UNICEF has highlighted the devastation of war on children:

Children are always among the first affected by armed conflict. Even if they are not killed or injured, they can be orphaned, abducted or left with psychological and psychosocial distress from direct exposure to violence, dislocation, poverty or the loss of loved ones.

(UNICEF, 2004, p 39)

Unscrupulous political regimes and rebel armies use children to maintain conflict. This may be as soldiers, runners and messengers or for sexual exploitation.

CASE STUDY

Agnes's story

Agnes was only 10 when she was abducted from her home in Uganda by members of the Lord's Resistance Army. She was forced to kill another child, on pain of her own death, by the rebels. When she was 12 she was taken as a wife and raped by one of the commanders. When she was 13 she escaped with the help of a local farmer. She is now 18 and says, *At night I dream about what I have done and I wake up crying.*

Source: Adapted from War Child UK (2013).

The case study underlines the horrendousness of such experiences and the subsequent long-term effects. Joseph Kony is leader of this rebel group which lost any credibility it might once have had and now roams beyond Uganda, striking particularly at children. Although wanted for war crimes, along with his senior commanders, he has so far avoided capture. The difficult terrain and lack of resources are the main reasons cited for him being still at large. It is not only the rebel groups that use sexual violence as a weapon. The Congolese army is widely acknowledged to do so too. Discipline within the army is poor and most soldiers do not get paid regularly. Like the rebel groups, they survive by exploiting local resources and use similar tactics to do so, such as keeping the local population scared and compliant through barbarous acts, including rape. The United Nations has a special force in the region but recognises that without commitment to human rights by the region's governments and armed forces it is unlikely to bring stability and peace to the region. Thus children in countries such as Democratic Republic of Congo continue to be at risk of abduction and abuse (MONUSCO, 2013).

Not all regime change is as dramatic or destructive as that of Uganda and Syria. In the United Kingdom there has been significant change in the focus of political and economic policy affecting children in recent years. Before 1997, through the 1980s and early 1990s, the notion of poverty within government had virtually disappeared with euphemistic phrases such as 'low income families' taking over. In the government of the day's report to the UNCRC there was no mention of poverty – in spite of 4.1 million children living below the poverty line (based on half average income after housing costs). From 2000 the then Chancellor of the Exchequer's speeches were peppered with concerns about children in poverty and alleviating the burden, and the emphasis moved to 'social exclusion', which tended to divert attention from growing inequalities in wealth. In any event, children became more visible in many aspects of economic policy.

CASE STUDY

The 'Baby Bond'

The Children's Trust Fund which was rolled out in 2005 is a clear example of the move towards child focused policy-making. Although the fund, commonly known at the time as the 'Baby Bond', was a new and relatively small financial investment in children, the emphasis was on motivating parents to 'save' money for their children rather than simply delivering state benefits to children. The payment was to the newborn child and could not be used by the adults of the family. Payment was housed in a bank account and held until the child reached 18. The Trust was a significant shift in policy-making towards asset building as part of anti-poverty strategy. It was much more in line with Narayan's (2000) research, which is discussed in Chapter 6, and highlights a focus on assets not simply income for alleviation of poverty. In January 2011 the coalition government scrapped the Child Trust Fund.

Critical question

» *The two examples of regime change seem wildly different in scale and importance yet both are influenced by the politics of the state. Critically compare and contrast the politics of these situations and use a force field analysis to identify potential solutions.*

Force field analysis is a tool to help identify the driving and restraining forces for change and consideration of ways of increasing positive, driving forces and reducing the negative, resisting forces. It is a useful tool for visualising the various forces and identifying actions to support the implementation of change. The following assertions apply.

*   Increasing the driving forces results in an increase in the resisting forces. Thus, the current equilibrium is maintained but under increased tension.

*   Reducing resisting forces is preferable because it allows movement in the desired direction without increasing tension.

*   Group norms are an important force in resisting and shaping organisational change.

A force field analysis usually involves the development of a diagram. The driving forces and resisting forces are identified and then indicated pictorially with lines of differing strengths indicating the relative importance of each aspect (Lewin, 1951)

Lifestyle and politics

Lifestyle changes also have an impact on children. As UNICEF stresses:

> *HIV/AIDS is tearing at the very fabric of childhood. Around 15 million children under the age of 18 had been orphaned by the pandemic by the end of 2003.*
> (UNICEF, 2004, p 67)

When one or more parents in a family are infected with HIV/AIDS, a child's life can be devastated. By 2003, 15 million children under the age of 18 had been orphaned by HIV/AIDS. Eight out of 10 of these children live in sub-Saharan Africa. Culture and politics play a large part in the spread or curtailment of HIV/AIDS. In some cultures the inequality and subservience of women together with tolerated promiscuity of men has had a significant impact on the spread of the disease. Lifestyle rejection of use of protection as part of safe sex also encourages the spread of the disease. But perspectives of government have an impact too.

CASE STUDY

South Africa HIV/AIDS policy

> *In South Africa HIV/AIDS is the leading cause of death in children under the age of 5 and there are 1.9 million AIDS orphans. In most instances the virus was transmitted from the child's mother. Consequently, the HIV-infected child is born into a family where the virus may have already had a severe impact on health, income, productivity and the ability to care for each other.*
> (Ubuntu Africa, 2013)

The timeline below shows how the personal views of politicians can influence the development of policy and the consequent impact on the population they represent.

*   1998. A battle begins for the provision of anti-retroviral drugs (ARVs) by the South African government that would last for much of the following decade. Health Minister Dlamini-Zuma openly opposes the drug, and declares the South African government's policy focus on prevention rather than treatment.

- 2000. The National Integrated Plan (NIP) for children infected and affected by HIV and AIDS promotes three interventions: life skills education for youth, home/community-based care, and support for HIV-positive children through NIP funds. The HIV/AIDS/STD National Strategic Plan promotes two primary goals of reducing new infections and the impact of HIV/AIDS on individuals, families and communities. There are no plans for large-scale provision of ARV drugs included in either programme.

- 2001. President Mbeki states his belief that HIV does not cause AIDS. Health Minister Tshabalala-Msimang refuses to contradict the claims of the President. The South African government successfully protects a law to allow the domestic production of cheaper, generic brand medicines, including ARVs.

- 2002. The South Africa High Court orders the government to make the antenatal drug Nepravine available to HIV-positive pregnant women. The South African cabinet officially confirms the policy that 'HIV causes AIDS' to stop further speculation by government officials.

- 2003. The South African cabinet approves a plan for universal ARV treatment.

- 2004. The programme begins.

- 2005. The target of the 2003 plan is met for at least one service point for AIDS related care and treatment in each of the country's 53 districts. The number of people receiving ARV treatment remains far below the plan's objectives. The government responds with a new policy framework declaring a commitment to improving public access to ARVs. Health Minister Manto Tshabalala-Msimang promotes an alternative treatment campaign based on nutrition and palliative care, advocating the consumption of African foods as a viable alternative to ARV treatment in preventing the onset of AIDS. She continues to make public statements insinuating that ARVs are toxic.

- 2006. The Health Department initiates the development of a new five-year National Strategic Plan (NSP).

- 2007. The plan is launched. It focuses on four key priority areas: (1) prevention; (2) treatment, care and support; (3) human and legal rights; and (4) monitoring, research and surveillance. It contains greater emphasis on ARV provision but ARV treatment falls short.

- 2008. President Mbeki resigns from office. An interim president is put in place, and the Health Minister is replaced.

- 2009. President Zuma's cabinet publicises a commitment to test all children exposed to HIV and provide all HIV-positive children with ARVs. Target is set for 95 per cent coverage of HIV-positive mothers with AZT treatment by 2010. Transmission from mothers to their children is reduced to just 3.5 per cent.

- 2010. Only 55 per cent of people who need ARV treatment are receiving it, falling short of the government's goal of 80 per cent coverage. Only 36 per cent of South African children eligible for HIV treatment have access to ARVs, leaving 196,000 HIV-positive children without the drugs they need.

- 2011. Health Minister Motsoaledi proudly announces that 11.9 million South Africans were being tested for HIV every year.

Source: Adapted from McNeil (2013).

The case study shows the importance of government knowledge and commitment to deal with lifestyle issues that detrimentally affect children. The lengthy delays between realisation of the problem, acceptance of it and implementation of a strategy to deal with it can lead to devastating outcomes for children and families. For South Africa, delay and ignorance at the highest level of government have led to untimely death and loss of family for millions of children.

Critical question

» *Persuasion and knowledge are important facets in a professional's attributes. How would you seek to persuade and influence the political policy agenda to the benefit of young children? You might want to revisit the issue of supply- versus demand-led early childhood education and care (ECEC) discussed in Chapter 5, and critically explore how you might encourage the policy-makers to adopt a supply-led approach to ECEC, as in the Denmark model, rather than the demand-led model preferred by the coalition government.*

The impact of international bureaucracies

Young children's lives are directly affected by global activity on a daily basis, for example by global communication that is available in many children's homes and communities via satellite television, the internet and mobile phones. A simple perusal of the weekly shopping basket of families across the UK shows the extent of world trade, with produce from Kenya, Costa Rica and India being commonplace. Children experience events taking place in international politics on a daily basis directly or through their television screens. Thus, at both a micro and macro level children see and feel the impact of global activity. Young children are not immune to decisions made on the international stage.

Economic management and growth

Deliberations of the International Monetary Fund (IMF) have a direct impact on the economic conditions of children and their families and the prospects for their future life experiences. The IMF was set up as an independent organisation at the behest of the United Nations and as a result of financial crisis after the Second World War. Its role is threefold: it keeps a watchful eye on the economic situations of member countries and how they are managing their financial affairs; it provides assistance to low and middle income countries with management of their economies; and it provides loans for countries that are struggling to meet financial commitments and obtain finance to support economic growth. It also provides loans to countries in need of social and welfare support for vulnerable communities. For example the IMF in 2013 is involved in a number of specific initiatives to alleviate the impact of the world financial crisis on children. These include the following.

- In Haiti, launching a comprehensive free and compulsory education programme to bring all children aged 6 to 12 to school for free over a period of four years and a food production and distribution programme in poor neighbourhoods.

- In Kenya, with IMF support, the government has expanded cash transfers programmes to orphans and other vulnerable children.

- In Latvia the guaranteed minimum income allocated to families was increased by 22 per cent for children. Families whose income is below the subsistence level are eligible for cash transfers equal to the difference between the sum of the subsistence levels and the actual family income (IMF, 2013).

The IMF comments on the economic policies of its members and holds some sway in influencing policy review and change. In April 2013 the IMF questioned the British government's strategy for UK recovery and suggested a lessening of austerity measures to encourage growth. Such deliberations may seem a long way from the provision of early years services but higher rates of employment and increases in wealth across families do increase demand for early childhood education and care. It can create further differentials in income if social welfare reforms are not aligned to it and therefore greater demands on social and remedial services. So how a government reacts and responds to IMF suggestions is highly relevant to future policy review.

International debt

The United Nations suggests that the impact of world events on children is intense and at times disproportionate to other sectors of the population. The demographics of childhood imply that children are in the majority of those facing some of the many awful situations across the world. Christian Aid (2001) argued that there was little chance of eradicating child poverty among the poorer nations of the world until the economic agencies of the rich developed countries were politically coerced to write off Third World debt. In the 2004 Spending Review, the UK Chancellor of the Exchequer announced a large increase in the United Kingdom's aid budget. He announced that by 2007–8, total United Kingdom aid would rise to nearly £6.5 billion a year. Part of the increase in the Department for International Development's (DFID) budget was specifically earmarked for the provision of multilateral debt relief. Gordon Brown, in a DFID press release (2004) said:

> Too many countries are still being forced to choose between servicing their debts and making the investments in health, education and infrastructure that would allow them to achieve the millennium development goals and so we must do more.

The World Bank and the IMF have been influential in tackling the debt problem and helped facilitate the 'Heavily Indebted Poor Countries' (HIPC) initiative, which acknowledged that debt relief was needed on multilateral debts. HICP has provided debt relief worth $54 billion to 27 heavily indebted poor countries. The initiative is open to the world's poorest countries with a number of provisos, including *a proven track record in implementing strategies focused on reducing poverty and building the foundation for sustainable economic growth* (World Bank, 2013). By September 2006, 40 countries were identified as potentially qualifying for HIPC assistance.

However, while desirable this in itself will not improve children's lives unless the political will to do so prevails in respective nations of the world. Those who use and abuse children for political and economic gain will not necessarily cease to do so because the strait-jacket of poverty through debt has been lifted. Within this context, any consideration of political and economic influences on childhood requires us to take an international and global perspective. The World Bank adopts such an approach and links debt relief to anti-poverty policy and implementation:

It is important to maintain standards for policies and procedures as a prerequisite for sustainable economic growth and high-impact poverty reduction programs. The standards are designed to make sure that maximum benefits are attained through the Initiative and that the freed-up money is used well and reaches the poor.

(World Bank, 2013, 2013)

Enabling political rights

The promotion and protection of the rights of the child is one of the objectives of the EU on which the Treaty of Lisbon (2009) has put further emphasis. The treaty was ratified by each of the EU's 27 members and came into force on 1 December 2009. It defines what the EU can and cannot do, and what means it can use. It alters the structure of the EU's institutions and how they work. Its objective is to make the EU more democratic and ensure its core values are supported. The inclusion of children's rights in the treaty is an important step to providing political status for children and ensuring their rights are considered in policy-making at European and national levels. The Europe 2020 Strategy, a response to the global economic crisis, reinforces the importance of education and alleviation of poverty as part of its plan for what it describes as smart, sustainable and inclusive growth. The Charter of Fundamental Rights of the European Union (2010) iterates confirmation of the adoption of the articles of the UNCRC. Together, these important documents set the context for policy development and implementation, resulting in action by the European Commission to *move up a gear on the rights of the child and to transform policy objectives into action* (European Commission, 2011, p 3). The Commission has concluded that to ensure implementation across the EU and in nation states all EU policies that either directly or indirectly affect children should be *designed, implemented and monitored* to ensure that the best interests of the child are addressed (European Commission, 2011, p 3). The Commission is also working with justice systems to provide sound protection for children who are victims of, or accused of, committing crimes. It is concerned with parental responsibility and safeguarding particularly vulnerable children, such as those from marginalised ethnic groups and those who go missing. The strategy goes into detail on a host of issues from internet safety to violence against children.

The three examples of international intervention and action discussed in this section indicate the extent to which decisions, policies and strategies affect children's daily lives.

Table 8.1 *Enhanced SWOT analysis*

Translate into plan	Strengths	Weaknesses
Opportunities	Use the strengths to build the opportunities	Overcome weaknesses that prevent take up of opportunities
Threats	Use the strengths to reduce the impact of the threats	Overcome the weaknesses that make threats a reality

Source: Adapted from Jisc infoNet (www.jiscinfonet.ac.uk, 2013).

Critical question

» *Consider any one of the strategies discussed in this section and critically evaluate its strengths, weaknesses, opportunities and threats using a SWOT analysis (see Table 8.1). Taking account of the analysis, consider what different or additional approaches you would recommend to the institution responsible for the initiative and explain why.*

Critical reflections

From global action to local impact

As indicated earlier, the impact of world events on children is intense and of disproportionate impact on the wider population. Micklewright (2000, p 1) concludes that *key economic variables on which economic policy operates can all be given a child dimension*. When considering the impact of European Monetary Union, Atkinson (1998) suggests that the focus has been on business and monetary matters rather than children and families. He argues for children being centre stage in all macroeconomic discussions as children are direct recipients of economic policy-making. He suggests that:

> *Macroeconomics in OECD countries has tended to become a remote and abstract subject, discussed in aggregate terms that seem far removed from the everyday experience of families.*
>
> (Atkinson, 1998, p 2)

It is clear that international politics and macroeconomics have real significance for children, who have been largely invisible in forums where these matters are discussed, perhaps with the exception of the United Nations. Bureaucracies such as the World Bank and IMF are beginning to focus on the economics of childhood, and institutions such as the European Union are engaging with the politics of childhood. Academics are raising the quality of the debate articulating a clear rationale for focusing on children, who due to their life-stage may be particularly vulnerable to economic measures and swings and political disturbances. For example, poverty in childhood has repercussions for life chances in the future (see Chapter 6, *Poverty as part of the early years experience*). Atkinson (1998) proposes a number of changes in monitoring economic performance that would support a child-centred approach to economic policy-making and strategy. These include:

* a child-focused unemployment rate;

* a price index for families with children;

* a measure of the cost of borrowing for families with children.

He suggests that such measures would demonstrate the effect of economic conditions on children within states and enable policy-making to be more sensitive to the circumstances and needs of children. He claims that s*uch developments are necessary ... to put children centre stage in the policy debate* (Atkinson, 1998, p 17).

It is also true that political decision-making and action has a direct, and potentially disproportionate, impact on children's lives. For the children caught up in the tension of the HIV/

AIDS political machinations in South Africa, childhood was lost and family life destroyed. And for children in poor families a start in adult life with some assets, however small, is of value. Moves by the European Union to require that all policy of relevance to children should ensure compliance with the articles of UNCRC is a step in the right direction.

It is imperative that professionals involved with the welfare of young children have the knowledge and appreciation of the effects of political and economic conditions on children's experience and consequent professional practice. If, as an early years educator or family health worker, you meet with children and families seeking refuge from corrupt regimes, you will need some appreciation of their past experiences. As a social worker involved with poor children and families, understanding the social and welfare policies of the day are paramount in identifying support and care. Whatever the context of work with children, professional practice requires awareness of the political and economic complexities of children's lives and knowledge of the impact for them of political and economic decisions across the world.

Further reading

A. B. Atkinson (1998) *EMU, Macroeconomics and Children.* Innocenti Occasional Papers, Economic and Social Policy Series 68.

> This paper provides a good introduction to a child-focused economic approach. It clarifies the rationale for such an approach using the example of European Monetary Union in its analysis. It demonstrates the link between macroeconomic analysis and family welfare, in particular for children. The paper examines the relation between employment, wage levels, take-home pay, interest rates, consumer prices and public services. It proposes new indicators of economic performance that are sensitive to the needs of families and children.

Rangita de Silva-de-Alwis (2007) *Legislative Reform on Child Domestic Labour: A Gender Analysis*, Legislative Reform Initiative Paper Series. New York: UNICEF.

> The study poses a gender perspective to critically explore the need for reform of legislation in the area of child domestic labour. The paper analyses the need for a holistic approach to law-making in this area and sets out a methodology to create a legal policy and programme framework to regulate and protect the domestic child worker. The paper argues that child domestic labour requires consideration of many facets of policy, including social welfare and education and gender equality.

David M. Smolin (2004) Intercountry Adoption as Child Trafficking. *Valparaiso University Law Review*, 39: 281–325.

> The paper provides a reasoned debate about the law in relation to intercountry adoption and the impact of market forces. It raises contentious issues and provides a focus for further analysis and critical discussion of a sensitive issue.

References

Chapter 1

Aldrich, R. (2002) *A Century of Education*. London: Routledge

Alexander, R. (2009) *Children, their World, their Education: Final Report and Recommendations of the Cambridge Primary Review*. London: Routledge

Allen, G. (2011) *Early Intervention: The Next Steps*. London: HM Government

Anning, A. (1991) *The First Years at School*. Bristol: Open University

Asylum (1836) *Eighth annual report of the board of managers of the Merchant-Seamen's Orphan Asylum for the board, clothing, and education of the children of merchant-seamen deceased, read at the annual meeting held at the City of London Tavern on the 28th August, 1835, with a list of governors and donors and the constitution of the Asylum*

Bergen, B. H. (1982) Only a Schoolmaster: Gender, Class, and the Effort to Professionalize Elementary Teaching in England, 1870–1910. *History of Education Quarterly*, 22(1): 1–21

Blackstone, T. (1974) Some Issues Concerning the Development of Nursery Education in Britain. *Paedagogica Europaea*, 9(1), Pre-School Education in Europe / L'Enseignement Pré-Scolaire en Europe / Vorschulerziehung in Europa (1974): 172–83

Board of Education (1905) Reprinted. *Reports on Children Under Five Years of Age in Public Elementary Schools by Women Inspectors of the Board of Education*. London: HM Stationery Office

Bradburn, E. (1976) *Margaret McMillan: Framework and Expansion of Nursery Education*. Surrey: Denholm House Press

Brewer, M., Crawford, C. and Dearden, L. (2005) Reforms to Childcare Policy. Chapter 9. Available at: www.ifs.org.uk/budgets/gb2005/05chap9.pdf [accessed 3 May 2012]

Cameron, C. (2007) *Men in the Nursery Revisited: Issues of Male Workers and Professionalism*. London: University of London. Available at: http://eprints.ioe.ac.uk/4811/1/Cameron2007MenCIEC7_1.pdf [accessed 2 May 2012]

Carneiro, P. and Heckman, J. (2003) Human Capital Policy, in Heckman, J. and Krueger, A. (eds) *Inequality in America*

Report from the Committee of the Parochial Schools of St. Mary Islington, to the subscribers; rules and regulations, list of subscribers, &c. Source: Hume Tracts. UCL Library Services Stable. Available at: www.jstor.org/stable/60211613 [accessed 1 May 2013]

Children's Workforce Development Council (CWDC) (2006) *Early Years Professional Prospectus*. Leeds: CWDC. Available at: http://webarchive.nationalarchives.gov.uk/20120119192332/http:/cwdcouncil.org.uk/

Children's Workforce Development Council (CWDC) (2009) *Memorandum Submitted by the Children's Workforce Development Council*. Leeds: CWDC. Available at: www.parliament.uk [accessed 16 April 2012]

Children's Workforce Development Council (CWDC) (2011) *CWDC News Release 9th December 2011*. Leeds: CWDC. Available at: http://webarchive.nationalarchives.gov.uk/20120119192332/http:/cwdcouncil.org.uk/

Cottrell, S. (2005) *Critical Thinking Skills*. Basingstoke: Palgrave Macmillan

David, T. and Britain, G. (2003) *Birth to Three Matters: A Review of the Literature*. London: Department for Education and Skills

Department for Children, Schools and Families (DCSF) (2009a) *Draft Code of Practice on Provision of the Free Early Education Entitlement for 3 and 4 year olds*, paragraph 1.2

Department for Children, Schools and Families (DCSF) (2009b) *Draft Code of Practice on Provision of the Free Early Education Entitlement for 3 and 4 year olds*, paragraph 1.3

Department for Children, Schools and Families (DCSF) (2009c) *Draft Code of Practice on Provision of the Free Early Education Entitlement for 3 and 4 year olds*, paragraph P.18

Department for Education (DfE) (2011a) *Evaluation of Graduate Leader Fund, Final Report*. London: DfE. Available at: www.education.gov.uk/publications/RSG/publicationDetail/Page1/DFE-RR144 [accessed 16 April 2012]

Department for Education (DfE) (2011b) *Graduate Leaders in Early Years: EYPS Explained*. London: DfE. Available at: www. education.gov.uk/childrenandyoungpeople/earlylearningandchildcare/delivery/b00201345/graduate-leaders/eyps [accessed 1 May 2012]

Department for Education (DfE) (2011c) *Supporting Families in the Foundation Years*. Available at: http://media. education.gov.uk/assets/files/pdf/s/supporting%20families%20in%20the%20foundation%20years.pdf [accessed 3 May 2012]

Department for Education (DfE) (2012a) *Graduate Leaders in Early Years: Changes to the EYPS Programme*. Available at: www. education.gov.uk/childrenandyoungpeople/earlylearningandchildcare/delivery/b00201345/graduate-leaders/ eyps/changes [accessed 2 May 2012]

Department for Education (DfE) (2012b) *School Workforce in England: Statistical First Release*. Available at: www.education. gov.uk/researchandstatistics/statistics/allstatistics/a00205723/school-workforce-in-england-provisional-nov-2011 [accessed 1 May 2012]

Department for Education and Employment (2000) *Curriculum Guidance for the Foundation Stage*. London. QCA also available at: www.smartteachers.co.uk/upload/documents_32.pdf [accessed 2 May 2012]

Department for Education and Skills (DfES) (2002) *Birth to Three Matters*. Available at: www.education.gov.uk/ publications/standard/publicationDetail/Page1/Birth#downloadableparts [accessed 3 May 2012]

Department for Education and Skills (DfES) (2003) *National Standards for Under Eights Day Care and Childminding*. Available at: www.legislation.gov.uk/uksi/2003/1996/contents/made [accessed 2 May 2012]

Department for Education and Skills (DfES) (2006) The Childcare Act 2006. Available at: www.legislation.gov.uk/ ukpga/2006/21/contents [accessed 6 May 2012]

Education Act (1902) Available at: www.parliament.uk/about/living-heritage/transformingsociety/livinglearning/school/ overview/reform1902–14/ [accessed 1 April 2012]

Education Act (1944) c31. London: HMSO

Education Bill HC Deb (13 March 1918) vol 104 cc335–447. Available at: http://hansard.millbanksystems.com/ commons/1918/mar/13/education-bill [accessed 1 April 2012]

Education in England: The Acland Report (1908) Available at: www.educationengland.org.uk/documents/acland1908/

English Indices of Deprivation (2010) Available at: www.communities.gov.uk/documents/statistics/pdf/1871208.pdf [accessed 2 April 2012]

EPPE Project. Available at: www.education.gov.uk/childrenandyoungpeople/earlylearningandchildcare/evidence/ a0068162/effective-provision-of-pre-school-education-eppe [accessed 19 March 2012]

Field, F. (2010) *The Foundation Years: Preventing Poor Children Becoming Poor Adults. The Report of the Independent Review on Poverty and Life Chances*. London: HM Government

Fisher, A. (2001) *Critical Thinking: An Introduction*. Cambridge: Cambridge University Press

Fleer, M. (2003) Early Childhood Education as an Evolving 'Community of Practice' or as Lived 'Social Reproduction': Researching the 'Taken-for-Granted'. *Contemporary Issues in Early Childhood*, 4(1): 64–79

Gelder, T. V. (2005) Teaching Critical Thinking: Some Lessons from Cognitive Science. *College Teaching*, 53(1): 41–48

Gillard, D. (2006) *The Hadow Reports: An Introduction*. Available at: www.educationengland.org.uk/articles/24hadow. html [accessed 2 May 2012]

Gove, M. (2013) Education Secretary Speech. Available at: www.gov.uk/government/speeches/what-does-it-mean-to-be-an-educated-person [accessed 10 May 2013]

Great Britain: Board of Education (1905) Introductory Memorandum by Cyril Jackson. *Reports on Children under 5 Years of Age in Public Elementary Schools, by Women Inspectors of the Board of Education*. Great Britain: Board of Education

Hadfield, M., Jopling, M., Royle, K. and Waller, T. (2010) *First National Survey of Practitioners with Early Years Professional Status*. Walsall: CeDare and University of Wolverhampton. Available at: www.wlv.ac.uk/PDF/sed-res-cwdcfinal.pdf [accessed 2 April 2012]

Hadfield, M., Jopling, M., Royle, K. and Waller, T. (2011) *First National Survey of Practitioners with EYPS*. Walsall: CeDare and University of Wolverhampton

Hadow Report (1923) *Differentiation of the Curriculum for Boys and Girls*. Report of the Consultative Committee. London: HMSO

Hadow Report (1933) *Infant and Nursery Schools*. Available at: www.educationengland.org.uk/documents/hadow1933/ [accessed 1 May 2012]

Hadow, W.H. and Harris, H.A. (1931) *Report of the consultative committee on the primary school*. HM Stationery Office

Halpern, D. F. (1996) *Thought and Knowledge: An Introduction to Critical Thinking*. Mahwah, NJ: Lawrence Erlbaum Associates

Hammond, M. and Collins, R. (1991) *Self-Directed Learning: Critical Practice*. East Brunswick, NJ: Nichols

Hargreaves, L., Cunningham, M., Everton, T., Hansen, A., Hopper, B., McIntyre, D., Maddock, M., Pell, T., Rouse, M., Turner,

P. and Wilson, L. (2006) *The Status of Teachers and the Teaching Profession: Views from Inside and Outside the Profession: Interim Findings from the Teacher Status Project*. Research Report. London: Department for Education and Skills

Health Protection Agency (HPA) (2011) *Infection Prevention and Communicable Disease Control Guidance for Early Years and School Settings*. Version 2. Available at: www.hpa.org.uk/webc/HPAwebFile/HPAweb_C/1194947365864 [accessed 1 March 2013]

Heckman, J. (2003) *What Role for Human Capital Policies?* Cambridge, MA: MIT Press

Hevey, D., Lumsden, E. and Moxon, S. (2007) Early Years Professional Status: Pilot Evaluation and Issues. Paper presented at *Seeds for Change*, International conference of the Centre for Early Childhood Development and Education, February, Dublin

HM Treasury (2005) *Choice for Parents, the Best Start for Children: A Ten Year Strategy for Childcare.* London: HM Treasury

House of Commons (HC) Debates (1944) vol 396, cc207–322207. Available at: www.parliament.uk/about/living-heritage/transformingsociety/livinglearning/school/overview/educationact1944/ [accessed 19 March 2012]

House of Commons (HC) (2006) CM Select Committee on Public Accounts. Available at: www.publications.parliament.uk/pa/cm200607/cmselect/cmpubacc/261/7012208.htm [accessed 1 May 2012]

House of Commons (HC) (2011) Autumn Statement to the House of Commons delivered by the Rt Hon George Osborne MP, Chancellor of the Exchequer. Available at: http://nds.coi.gov.uk/content/Detail.aspx?ReleaseID=422279&NewsAreaID=2 [accessed 7 May 2012]

House, R. (2012) *Why I Believe the Plans for EYFS Reform Don't Make the Grade*. Available at: www.nurseryworld.co.uk/article/1111210/why-i-believe-plans-eyfs-reform-dont-grade [accessed 3 May 2013]

Isaacs, S. (1965) *The Children We Teach*. London: University of London Press

Jensen, J. J. and Hansen, H. K. (2003) Danish National Report for Workpackage Seven: Care Work in Europe, in Cameron, C. (2007) *Men in the Nursery Revisited: Issues of Male Workers and Professionalism.* London: University of London. Available at: http://eprints.ioe.ac.uk/4811/1/Cameron2007MenCIEC7_1.pdf [accessed 2 May 2012]

Jozwiak, G. (2013) Government Scraps Plans to Change Child Care Ratios. *Children & Young People Now*, 5 June. Available at: www.cypnow.co.uk/cyp/news/1077411/breaking-news-government-scraps-plans-change-ratios [accessed 5 June 2013]

King, A. (1995) Designing the Instructional Process to Enhance Critical Thinking across the Curriculum. *Teaching of Psychology*, 22(1): 13–17

Kliebard, H. M. (1987) *The Struggle for the American Curriculum 1893–1958*. New York: Routledge & Kegan Paul

Lawrence, E. (1969 and 2011) *Friedrich Froebel and English Education*. London: Routledge

Lumsden, E. (2010) The New Early Years Professional in England. *International Journal for Cross-Disciplinary Subjects in Education (IJCDSE)*, 1(3): 253–62

Lumsden, E. (2012) The Early Years Professional: A New Professional or a Missed Opportunity? Extended Research Overview. PhD Thesis, Northampton University

Mail Online (2011) *Testing for Two-Year-Olds: Now Every Tot at Nursery Will Have Their Progress Rated*. Available at: www.dailymail.co.uk/news/article-2011709/Every-year-old-nursery-receive-compulsory-progress-tests.html [accessed 1 June 2013]

McGurk, H., Mooney, A. et al (1995) *Staff-Child Ratios in Care and Education Services for Young Children*. London: HMSO

McMillan, M. (1911) School Nursing in England. *The American Journal of Nursing*, 11(6): 459–64

Montessori, M. (2004) *The Discovery of the Child*. Delhi: Aakar Books

Moss, P. (1999) Renewed Hopes and Lost Opportunities: Early Childhood in the Early Years of the Labour Government. *Cambridge Journal of Education*, 29(2): 229–38

Munton, T., Mooney, A. et al (2002) *Research on Ratios, Group Size and Staff Qualifications and Training in Early Years and Childcare Settings*. Next Steps for Early Learning and Childcare DCSF-00173–2009. Available at: www.education.gov.uk/publications/standard/publicationDetail/Page1/DCSF-00173–2009 [accessed 2 April 2012]

Nursery World (14–27 June 2011) EYPS Future in Question (p 10). Available at: http://cde.cerosmedia.com/1V4df5ed30452b9012.cde/page/10 [accessed 1 May 2012]

Nursery World (13 Dec 2011) Enormous Shortfall in 2 Year Old Places Predicted. Available at: www.nurseryworld.co.uk/news/1108829/Enormous-shortfall-two-year-old-places-predicted/?DCMP=ILC-SEARCH [accessed 3 March 2012]

Nursery World (16 April 2012) EYPS Review. Available at: www.nurseryworld.co.uk/news/rss/1112215/EYPS-review-CWDC-proposes-move-just-eight-standards/ [accessed 2 May 2012]

Nursery World (25 June 12) EYPS Wonder Where They Fit into the Nutbrown Vision. Available at www.nurseryworld.co.uk/article/1137748/eyps-wonder-fit-nutbrown-vision [accessed 2 May 2013]

Nursery World (6 Aug 2012) EYPS and the Nutbrown Review: Threat or Opportunity? Available at www.nurseryworld.co.uk/article/1144212/eyps-nutbrown-review-threat-opportunity [accessed 2 May 2013]

Nutbrown, C. (2012) *Review of Early Education and Childcare Qualifications: Interim Report*. London: Department for Education.

Owen, C. (2004) Personal Communication. In Cameron, C. (2007) *Men in the Nursery Revisited: Issues of Male Workers and Professionalism*. London: University of London. Available at: http://eprints.ioe.ac.uk/4811/1/Cameron2007MenCIEC7_1.pdf [accessed 2 May 2012]

Roche, P. (2007) *Unloved: The True Story of a Stolen Childhood*. London: Penguin

Rogoff, B. (1990) *Apprenticeship in Thinking: Cognitive Development in Social Context*. New York: Oxford University Press

Sylva, K., Melhuish, E. et al (2004) *The Effective Provision of Pre-School Education (EPPE) Project: Findings from Preschool to End of Key Stage 1*. Available at: http://eppe.ioe.ac.uk/ [accessed 10 March 2012]

Teaching Agency (2012) *Graduate Leaders in Early Years*. Available at: www.education.gov.uk/childrenandyoungpeople/earlylearningandchildcare/delivery/b00201345/graduate-leaders/eyps [accessed 1 May 2012]

Teather, S. (2011) *Sarah Teather in 'Nursery World' on Graduate Funding for Early Years Workforce*. Available at: www.education.gov.uk/inthenews/articles/a0073741/sarah-teather-in-nursery-world-on-graduate-funding-for-early-years-workforce [accessed 2 May 2012]

Tickell, C. (2011) *The Early Years: Foundations for Life, Health and Learning*. London: Department for Education

Twigg, S. (2013) Childcare Policy, House of Commons Debate, ITN. Available at: www.guardian.co.uk/money/video/2013/may/09/elizabeth-truss-childcare-plans-video [accessed 9 May 2013]

Vygotsky, L. (1978) *Mind in Society: The Development of Higher Psychological Processes*. Cambridge, MA: Harvard University Press

Whitbread, N. (1972) *The Evolution of the Nursery-Infant School: A History of Infant and Nursery Education in Britain, 1800–1970*. London: Routledge & Kegan Paul

Wood, E. (2004) A New Paradigm War? The Impact of National Curriculum Policies on Early Childhood Teachers' Thinking and Classroom Practice. *Teaching and Teacher Education*, 20: 361–74

Chapter 2

Allen, G. (2011) *Early Intervention: The Next Steps*. London: HM Government

Beaumont, J. (n.d.) *Households and Families* (Social Trends No. 41). Office of National Statistics

Bronfenbrenner, U. (1979) *The Ecology of Human Development: Experiments by Nature and Design*. Cambridge, MA: Harvard University Press

Bryson, C., Kazimirski, A. and Southwood, H. (2006) *Childcare and Early Years Provision: A Study of Parents' Use, Views and Experiences*. London: National Centre for Social Research

Daniel, P. and Ivatts, J. (1998) *Children and Social Policy*. Basingstoke: Palgrave Macmillan

Daycare Trust (2012) *Childminders in the Netherlands*. London: Daycare Trust

De Gioia, K. (2009) Parent and Staff Expectations for Continuity of Home Practices in the Child Care Setting for Families with Diverse Cultural Backgrounds. *Australasian Journal of Early Childhood*, 34

del Boca, D. and Wetzels, C. (eds) (2007) *Social Policies, Labour Markets and Motherhood: A Comparative Analysis of European Countries*. Cambridge: Cambridge University Press

Department for Education and Skills (DfES) (2006) *Social Mobility: Narrowing Social Class Educational Attainment Gaps*. London: DfES

Department for Work and Pensions (DWP) (2010) *Flexibility for the Future: The Government's Response to the Recommendations of the Family Friendly Working Hours Taskforce*. London: DWP

Department for Work and Pensions (DWP) (2012) *Social Justice: Transforming Lives*. London: DWP

Department for Work and Pensions (DWP) (2013) *Universal Credit: Local Support Services Framework*. London: DWP

Eydal, G. B. and Olafsson, S. (2003) *Social and Family Policy: The Case of Iceland*. Third report, Welfare Policy and Employment in the Context of Family Change. University of Iceland, Faculty of Social Sciences

Family Friendly Working Hours Taskforce (n.d.) *Flexible Working: Working for Families, Working for Business*. A report by the Family Friendly Working Hours Taskforce

Family and Parenting Institute (2013) *Quick Facts from Family Trends*. Available at: www.familyandparenting.org. URL www.familyandparenting.org/ our_work/future-families/Family-Trends/ Quick-Facts-from-Family-Trends

Field, F. (2010) *The Foundation Years: Preventing Poor Children Becoming Poor Adults*. The Report of the Independent Review on Poverty and Life Chances. London: HM Government

Finch, N. (n.d.) *Demographic Trends in the UK* (First report for the project). Welfare Policy and Employment in the Context of Family Change. University of York, Social Policy Research Unit

Finch, N. (2003) *Family Policy in the UK* (No. 3). Welfare Policy and Employment in the Context of Family Change. University of York, Social Policy Research Unit

Garvin, D. and Lewis, E. (2012) *Making Work Pay*. New Left Project. Available at: www.newleftproject.org/index.php/site/article_comments/making_work_pay

Gingerbread (2010) *Statistics*. Available at: www.gingerbread.org.uk/content/365/Statistics

Glenndenning, J. (2011) *Children Looked After in England (Including Adoption and Care Leavers) year ending 31 March 2011.* Department for Education

Goodman, A. and Greaves, E. (2010) *Cohabitation, Marriage and Child Outcomes*. London: Institute for Fiscal Studies

Harker, L. (2006) *Chance of a Lifetime: The Impact of Bad Housing on Children' Lives*. London: Shelter

Harkness, S. (1980) The Cultural Context of Child Development. *Anthropological Perspectives on Child Development: New Direction for Child Development*, 8: 7–18

Hartas, D. (2010) Families' Social Backgrounds Matter: Socio-Economic Factors, Home Learning and Young Children's Language, Literacy and Social Outcomes. *British Educational Research Journal*, 37: 893–914

Henricson, C. (2012a) *A Revolution in Family Policy*. RSA. Available at: http://comment.rsablogs.org.uk/2012/08/28/revolution-family-policy/

Henricson, C. (2012b) *A Revolution in Family Policy: Where We Should Go from Here*. Bristol: Policy Press

Hill, M. and Tisdall, K. (1997) *Children & Society*. Upper Saddle River, NJ: Prentice Hall

HM Revenue and Customs (2013) *Giving up Your Right to Pay Reduced National Insurance*. Available at: www.hmrc.gov.uk/ni/reducedrate/ givingupright.htm

Lloyd, E. (2009) *Childcare Markets in England and The Netherlands: A Comparative Study*. International Centre for Study of the Mixed Economy of Childcare, University of East London

McCulloch, S. M. (2006) Welfare to Work: Have Policy Initiatives, such as the New Deal for Lone Parents Impacted Upon the Experiences of Lone Mothers in Employment? *International Journal of Urban Labour and Leisure*, 7

Munro, E. (2011) *The Munro Review of Child Protection (Final Report)*. London: The Stationery Office

National Statistics (2011) *Children Looked After by Local Authorities in England: year ending 31 March 2011*

Office of National Statistics (2011a) *Civil Partnerships in the UK, 2010*

Office of National Statistics (2011b) *Families and Households in the UK, 2001 to 2010*

Office of National Statistics (2011c) *Frequently Asked Questions: Births & Fertility*

Office of National Statistics (2012a) *Births and Deaths in England and Wales, 2011 (Final)*

Office of National Statistics (2012b) *Conceptions in England and Wales, 2010*

Office of National Statistics (2012c) *Families and Households, 2012*

Office of National Statistics (2012d) *Marriages in England and Wales, 2010*

Office of National Statistics (2013) *Cohort Fertility, England and Wales 2011*

Owen, T. M., Ware, A. M. and Barfoot, B. (2000) Caregiver–Mother Partnership Behaviour and the Quality of Caregiver–Child and Mother–Child Interactions. *Early Childhood Research Quarterly*, 15: 413–28

Plantenga, J. and Remery, C. (2009) *The Provision of Childcare Services: A Comparative Review of 30 European Countries*. European Commission's Expert Group on Gender and Employment Issues (EGGE), European Commission

Reeves, R. (2013) *The Symmetrical Family, Families@30*. 4Children

Robinson, K. H. and Jones Diaz, C. (2007) *Diversity and Difference in Early Childhood Education. Issues for Theories and Practice*. Maidenhead: Open University Press

Spicer, P. (2010) *Cultural Influences on Parenting*. ZERO TO THREE

Thomas, C. (1998) Culture Defined: A Twenty-First Century Perspective. *Educational Horizons*, 76: 121–26.

Vygotsky, L. S. (1978) *Mind in Society: The Development of Higher Psychological Processes*. Cambridge, MA: Harvard University Press

Wilson, K., Sinclair, I., Taylor, C., Pithouse, A. and Sellick, C. (2004) *Fostering Success: An Exploration of the Research Literature in Foster Care*. London: Social Care Institute for Excellence (SCIE)

Zumpe, J., Jefferies, J. and Dormon, O. (2012) *Childbearing Among UK Born and non-UK Born Women Living in the UK*. Office of National Statistics

Chapter 3

Ashforth, B. E. and Lee, R. T. (1990) Defensive Behavior in Organizations: A Preliminary Model. *Human Relations*, 43: 621–48

Audit Commission (2010a) *Giving Children a Healthy Start* (Health report February). London: Audit Commission

Audit Commission (2010b) *Healthy Balance: A Review of Public Health Performance and Spending* (Health briefing March). London: Audit Commission

Balls, E. (Secretary of State for Children, Schools and Families) and Burnham, A. (Secretary of State for Health) (2009) *Government Response to the Social Work Task Force*

Batty, D. (2003) Catalogue of Cruelty. *The Guardian*, 27 January

Blom-Cooper, L., Beal, J., Brown, B., Marshall, P. and Mason, M. (1985) *A Child in Trust. The Report of the Panel of Inquiry into the Circumstances Surrounding the Death of Jasmine Beckford.* London Borough of Brent

C4EO (2011) *Briefing Paper: Delivering Children's Services in the UK and other Parts of the World – a Short Policy Context*

Cabinet Office (2013) *Big Society – Overview.* Available at: www.cabinetoffice.gov.uk/content/big-society-overview

Central Inspection Group, Social Services Inspectorate (1998) *Inspection of Child Protection Services.* Cambridgeshire County Council, Department of Health

Chief Nursing Officers (2010) *Midwifery 2020: Delivering Expectations*

Churchill, H. (2011) *Wither the Social Investment State? Early Intervention, Prevention and Children's Services Reform in the New Policy Context.* Presented at the Social Policy Association international conference *Bigger Societies, Smaller Governments?* University of Lincoln

CIA (2013) *The World Factbook.* Washington, DC: CIA

Commission on Social Determinants of Health (2008) *Closing the Gap in a Generation: Health Equity through Action on the Social Determinants of Health.* Final report of the Commission on Social Determinants of Health. Geneva: World Health Organization

Corsini, C. A. and Viazzo, P. P. (1993) *The Decline of Infant Mortality in Europe 1800–1950: Four National Case Studies.* New York: UNICEF

CYP (Children and Young People's health outcomes forum) (n.d.) *Report of the Long Term Conditions, Disability and Palliative Care Subgroup*

CYP (Children and Young People's health outcomes forum) (2012) *Report of the Children and Young People's Health Outcomes Forum*

Department for Children, Schools and Families (DCSF) (2007a) *Narrowing the Gap: Providing for all Children*

Department for Children, Schools and Families (DCSF) (2007b) *The Children's Plan: Building Brighter Futures.* London: The Stationery Office

Department for Children, Schools and Families (DCSF) (2010) *Working Together to Safeguard Children: A Guide to Inter-Agency Working to Safeguard and Promote the Welfare of Children*

Department for Education (DfE) (2011) *A Child-Centred System: The Government's Response to the Munro Review of Child Protection*

Department for Education (2012a) *The Children's Safeguarding Performance Information Framework.* Available at: www.education.gov.uk/childrenandyoungpeople/safeguardingchildren/protection/b00209694/perf-info

Department for Education (DfE) (2012b) *Local Safeguarding Children Boards.* Available at: www.education.gov.uk/childrenandyoungpeople/safeguardingchildren/protection/b00219380/lscb

Department for Education (DfE) (2012c) *Support and Aspiration: A New Approach to Special Educational Needs and Disability. Progress and Next Steps*

Department for Education (DfE) (2013) *Children and Families Bill*

Department for Education and Skills (DfES) (2004) *Every Child Matters: Change for Children*

Department of Health (2012a) *Health Visiting Programme: Supporting Implementation of the New Service Model 1: Health Visiting and Midwifery Partnership – Pathway for Pregnancy and Early Weeks*

Department of Health (2012b) *Maternity: Children, Families and Maternity* e-bulletin. Edition 74 Gateway Ref: 18581

Hallsworth, M., Farrands, A., Oortwijn, W. J. and Hatziandreu, E. (2007) *The Provision of Neonatal Services: Data for International Comparisons* (Technical report for National Audit Office). Rand Europe

Hatem, M., Sandall, J., Devane, D., Soltani, H. and Gates, S. (2009) *Midwife-led versus Other Models of Care for Childbearing Women (Review).* The Cochrane Collaboration. Chichester: John Wiley

HM Government (2004) Children Act 2004

HM Government (2010) *The Coalition: Our Programme for Government*

Human Rights Watch (2010) *A State of Isolation: Access to Abortion for Women in Ireland*

Lambert, A. (2013) 'Social services criticised over murder of girl: killing of child "could have been prevented"'. *Independent*, 13 December 1993

Laurance, J. (2003) Reports Linked by Familiar Failings. *The Independent*, 29 January

Lord Laming (2003) *The Victoria Climbié Inquiry.* London: The Stationery Office

Lord Laming (2009) *The Protection of Children in England: A Progress Report.* London: The Stationery Office

Marmot, M. (2010) *Fair Society, Healthy Lives: A Strategic Review of Health Inequalities in England post 2010*. Department of Health

Morris, N. (2013) 100,000 Assaults. 1,000 Rapists Sentenced. Shockingly Low Conviction Rates Revealed. *The Independent*, 10 January

Munro, E. (1999) *Common Errors of Reasoning in Child Protection Work*. LSE Research Articles Online

Munro, E. (2011) *The Munro Review of Child Protection (Final Report).* London: The Stationery Office

Munro, E. R. and Lushey, C. (2012) *The Impact of More Flexible Assessment Practices in Response to the Munro Review of Child Protection: Emerging Findings from the Trials.* London: Childhood Well-Being Research Centre

National Health Service (2012) *Arrangements to Secure Children's and Adult Safeguarding in the Future NHS: The New Accountability and Assurance Framework – interim advice*

National Institute for Clinical Excellence (2010) *Antenatal Care: Clinical Guideline 62*

NSPCC (2010) *The Child Protection System in the UK*. Factsheet

NSPCC (2012) *An Introduction to Child Protection Legislation in the UK*. Factsheet

NSPCC (2013) *Statistics on Looked After Children*. Available at: www.nspcc.org.uk/Inform/resourcesforprofessionals/lookedafterchildren

Oestergaard, M. Z., Inoue, M., Yoshida, S., Mahanani, W. R., Gore, F. M., Cousens, S., Lawn, J. E. and Mathers, C. D. (2011) Estimation, on behalf of the U.N.I.G. for C.M. Group, the C.H.E.R., Neonatal Mortality Levels for 193 Countries in 2009 with Trends since 1990: A Systematic Analysis of Progress, Projections, and Priorities. *PLoS Med* 8: e1001080

Parton, N. (2003) From Maria Colwell to Victoria Climbié: Reflections on a Generation of Public Inquiries into Child Abuse. Presented at the BASPCAN conference, Child Abuse Review, 2004

Parton, N. (2011) Child Protection and Safeguarding in England: Changing and Competing Conceptions of Risk and their Implications for Social Work. *British Journal of Social Work, 41*: 854–75

Payne, L. (n.d.) *The Healthy Child Programme (HCP), VSS – Policy Briefing*. NCB

Rowlands, J. (2010) Services Are Not Enough: Child Well-Being in a Very Unequal Society. *Journal of Children's Services*, 5: 80–88

Royal College of Midwives (2012) *State of Maternity Services Report 2012*

Royal College of Psychiatrists (n.d.) *An Overview of the Children Act 1989*

Shaw, R. (2011a) *The Cleveland Report by Judge Elizabeth Butler-Sloss*. Children Webmag

Shaw, R. (2011b) *The Maria Colwell Report: Chaired by T. G. Field-Fisher*. Children Webmag

Shribman, S. and Billingham, K. (2009) *Healthy Child Programme – Pregnancy and the First Five Years.* Department of Health

Social Work Reform Board (2012) *Building a Safe and Confident Future: Maintaining Momentum – Progress Report from the Social Work Reform Board*. Department for Education

Social Work Task Force (2009) *Building a Safe, Confident Future* (The final report of the Social Work Task Force). Department for Children, Schools and Families

Steele, L. (2001) Child Murder Report Reveals Poor Communication and Cooperation. *The Guardian*, 8 March

Stein, R. E. and Jessop, D. J. (1982) A Noncategorical Approach to Chronic Childhood Illness. *Public Health Report,* 97(4): 354–62

UNICEF (1989) *A Summary of the UN Convention on the Rights of the Child*. New York: UNICEF

UNICEF (2004) *Progress for Children: A Child Survival Report Card* (Volume 1). New York: UNICEF

Chapter 4

Anti-Slavery International (2013) *What is Child Labour?* Available at: www.antislavery.org/english/slavery_today/child_labour.aspx

Archard, D. (1993) *Children, Rights and Childhood*. Abingdon: Routledge.

Aspinall, A. and Watters, C. (2010) *Refugees and Asylum Seekers: A Review from an Equality and Human Rights Perspective* (Research report 52). London: Equality and Human Rights Commission

Aviezer, O., Van Uzendoorn, M. H., Sagi, A. and Schuengel, C. (1994) 'Children of the Dream' Revisited: 70 Years of Collective Early Child Care in Israeli Kibbutzim. *Psychological Bulletin*, 116: 99–116

Bruns, B., Mingat, A. and Rakotomalala, R. (2003) *Achieving Universal Primary Education by 2015: A Chance for Every Child*. Washington, DC: World Bank

Children are Unbeatable Alliance (2004) *Research Review*. Briefing 6

Children's Bureau (2011) *Child Maltreatment 2011*. US Department of Health & Human Services Administration for Children and Families Administration on Children, Youth and Families

Craig, G. (2010) *Child Slavery Now: A Contemporary Reader*. Bristol: Policy Press

Department for Education (DfE) (2012) *Framework Agreement Document between the Department for Education and the Children's Commissioner*

Department for Education (DfE) (2013) *Office of the Children's Commissioner*. Available at: www.education.gov.uk/childrenandyoungpeople/healthandwellbeing/a0074780/office-of-the-childrens-commissioner

Department of Health (1989) *An Introduction to the Children Act 1989*. London: The Stationery Office

Elliman, D. and Lynch, M A. (2000) The Physical Punishment of Children. *Archives of Disease in Childhood*, 83: 196–98

End Corporal Punishment (2012) *Global Progress*. Available at: www.endcorporalpunishment.org/pages/progress/prohib_states.html

Foster, P. (1999) Most Parents in Favour of Smacking Children. *Daily Telegraph*, 2 August

Franklin, B (ed) (2002) *The New Handbook of Children's Rights*. London: Routledge

Harker, R. (2012) *Children in Care in England: Statistics*. House of Commons Library

Harvey, R. (2001) *Children and Armed Conflict*. The Children and Armed Conflict Unit, University of Essex

Home Office (2012) *Children in Detention*. Available at: www.homeoffice.gov.uk/publications/science-research-statistics/research-statistics/immigration-asylum-research/immigration-q3–2012/detention-q3–2012

International Programme on the Elimination of Child Labour (IPEC) (2002) *Statistical Information and Monitoring Programme on Child Labour (SIMPOC). Every Child Counts: New Global Estimates on Child Labour*. Geneva: International Labour Organization

Innocenti Report Card, No. 4 (2002) 'A league table of educational disadvantage in rich nations'. UNICEF

Jones, P., Moss, D., Tomlinson, P. and Welch, S. (eds) (2008) *Childhood: Services and Provision for Children*. Harlow: Pearson Education

London Organising Committee of the Olympic Games and Paralympic Games (2013) *International Inspiration: Annual Review 2011–12* (London 2012's international legacy programme)

Lundy, L., Kilkelly, U., Byrne, B. and Kang, J. (2012) *The UN Convention on the Rights of the Child: A Study of Legal Implementation in 12 Countries*. UNICEF UK and Queen's University, Belfast

Machel, G. (2000) The Impact of Armed Conflict on Children. Presented at the international conference on War Affected Children. Winnipeg, Canada

Marshall, K., Lewsley, P., Towler, K. and Aynsley-Green, A. (2008) *UK Children's Commissioners' Report to the UN Committee on the Rights of the Child*. UK Children's Commissioners

Mazurana, D. and Carlson, K. (2006) *The Girl Child and Armed Conflict: Recognizing and Addressing Grave Violations of Girls' Human Rights*. United Nations Division for the Advancement of Women

McCarthy, E. (2012) *Universal Children's Day. Action on Armed Violence*. Available at: www.aoav.org.uk/news/21/34/Universal-Children-s-Day

Mollins, J. (2012) More than 70 pct of war casualties civilian in 2011 – report. Available at: www.trust.org/item/?map=more-than-70-pct-of-war-casualties-civilian-in-2011-report

Munro, E. (2001) *Empowering Looked After Children*. London: LSE Research Articles Online

Munro, E. (2011) *The Munro Review of Child Protection (Final Report)*. London: The Stationery Office

Office for Standards in Education (Ofsted) (2003) *The Education of Asylum Seeker Pupils*. Manchester: Ofsted

Olusoga, Y. (2008) *Childhood: Services and Provision for Children*. Harlow: Pearson Education

Omaar, R. (2007) *The World of Modern Child Slavery*. BBC News. Available at: http://news.bbc.co.uk/1/hi/programmes/this_world/6458377.stm

Pruthi, P. (2013) *New Health Centres Help India Battle High Infant Mortality Rates*. Available at: www.unicef.org/infobycountry/india_67695.html

Refugee Council (2013) *The Truth About Asylum*. Available at: www.refugeecouncil.org.uk/

Report of the Director-General (2006) The End of Child Labour: Within Reach (Global Report under the Follow-up to the ILO Declaration on Fundamental Principles and Rights at Work). International Labour Office, International Labour Conference 95th Session

Royal College of Paediatrics and Child Health (2009) *Significant Harm – The Effects of Administrative Detention on the Health of Children, Young People and their Families*. Intercollegiate Briefing Paper

Rutter, J. (2006) *Refugee Children in the UK: Education in an Urbanised Society*. Maidenhead: Open University Press

Seymour, D. (2009) *Twenty Years of the CRC*. UNICEF UK blog

Smith, L. (2008) *Child Labour: An Overview*

Teather, S. (n.d.) *Government Response to Consultation on Establishing a New Office of the Children's Commissioner for England* (OCCE)

The Guardian (2011) What Stops Children in Rural Areas Going to School? 21 April

Turk, V. (2012) Judge Freed Mother for Smacking Children, but it Should be Banned Completely. *The Independent*, 5 October

UK Parents Back Right to Smack (1999) BBC News, 2 August

UN Department of Public Information (2010) *Millennium Development Goals: Achieve Universal Primary Education.* High-Level Plenary Meeting of the General Assembly. Presented at the United Nations Summit, New York

UNESCO (2000) Education for All: Meeting Our Collective Commitments. Presented at the World Education Forum, Dakar, Senegal

UNHCR (2006) *The State of the World's Refugees 2006: Human Displacement in the New Millennium*

UNHCR (2013) *Future Remains Bleak for Democratic Republic of the Congo.* Available at: www.unhcr.org/513a176e9. html

UNICEF (1989) *A Summary of the UN Convention on the Rights of the Child.* New York: UNICEF

UNICEF (2005) Convention on the Rights of the Child. Available at: www.unicef.org/crc/index_30229.html

UNICEF (2012a) *The State of the World's Children: Children in an Urban World.* New York: UNICEF

UNICEF (2012b) *UNICEF Emergency Report for 2011.* New York: UNICEF

UNICEF (2013) *Child Protection from Violence, Exploitation and Abuse: Child Trafficking.* Available at: www.unicef.org/protection/57929_58005.html

UNICEF Child Protection Section Programme Division (2006) *Children without Parental Care.* Child Protection Information Sheet. New York: UNICEF

UNICEF UK (2012c) *The World We Want after 2015.* London: UNICEF UK

UNICEF, UN Global Compact and Save the Children (2012) *Children's Rights and Business Principles.* New York: UNICEF

United Nations (1948) The Universal Declaration of Human Rights

Watters, C. (2008) *Refugee Children: Towards the Next Horizon.* London: Routledge

Westerbeek, S. (2013) *African Leadership for Child Survival Meeting in Ethiopia Charts Map for Reducing Child Deaths.* New York: UNICEF. Available at: www.unicef.org/infobycountry/ethiopia_67656.html

World Bank Group (2012) *Trading Economics.* Available at: www.tradingeconomics.com/india/indicators

World Health Organization and UNICEF (2006) *Meeting the MGD Drinking Water and Sanitation Challenge: The Urban and Rural Challenge of the Decade.* Geneva: WHO and UNICEF

Chapter 5

Alakeson, V. and Hurrell, A. (2012) *Counting the Costs of Childcare.* London: Resolution Foundation

Barnett, B. and Frede, E. (2009) *Federal Early Childhood Policy Guide for the First 100 Days.* New Brunswick, NJ: NIEER

BBC News (2013) *Nursery Ratios Raised 'To Improve Standards'.* Available at: www.bbc.co.uk/news/education-21232270

Benchmarking Group (2007) *Early Childhood Studies.* Quality Assurance Agency for Higher Education

Bostrom, M. (2002) *The Whole Child: Parents and Policy – A Meta-Analysis of Opinion Data Concerning School Readiness, Early Childhood and Related Issues.* Prepared for the Frameworks Institute

Centre for Economic & Social Inclusion (2006) *Qualifications, Pay and Quality in the Childcare Sector.* UNISON submission to the Low Pay Commission

CESifo Group (2010) *The Quality of Childcare Services – A Comparative View* (DICE report). Munich: IFO

Children in Scotland (2011) *Early Childhood Education and Care: Developing a Fully Integrated Early Years System.* Special report No. 2, September

Children's Workforce Development Council (CWDC) (2009) *Business Plan 2009–2010: Leading Change for a Better Future*

Children's Workforce Development Council (CWDC) (2012) *Review of the Early Years Professional Status Standards*

Chowdry, H. and Sibieta, L. (2011) *Trends in Education and Schools Spending,* October. London: Institute for Fiscal Studies

Conolly, L.H. and Lyon, N. (2007) *Families with children in Britain: findings from the 2005 Families and Children Study (FACS), (Research Report No. 424).* DWP, Leeds: CDS.

Cooke, G. and Henehan, K. (2012) *Double Dutch: The Case against Deregulation and Demand-Led Funding in Childcare.* London: Institute for Public Policy Research

Council of the European Union (2011) *Council Conclusions on Early Childhood Education and Care: Providing all our Children with the Best Start for the World of Tomorrow.* Official Journal of the European Union

Daycare Trust (2012) *Childminders in the Netherlands.* London: Daycare Trust

Department for Children, Schools and Families (DCSF) (2008) *Statutory Framework for the Early Years Foundation Stage: Setting the Standards for Learning, Development and Care for Children from Birth to Five*

Department for Children, Schools and Families (DCSF) (2010) *Breaking the Link between Disadvantage and Low Achievement in the Early Years*

Department for Education (DfE) (2010) *Sure Start Children's Centres, Statutory guidance* (DFE-00020-2011)

Department for Education (DfE) (2011) *Early Years Evidence Pack*

Department for Education (DfE) (2012a) *Early Years Foundation Stage (EYFS): Learning and Development Consultation Report*

Department for Education (DfE) (2012b) *Reforming the Early Years Foundation Stage (the EYFS): Government Response to Consultation*

Department for Education (DfE) (2012c) *Statutory Guidance for Local Authorities on the Delivery of Free Early Education for Three and Four Year Olds and Securing Sufficient Childcare*

Department for Education (DfE) (2013a) *Improving the Quality and Range of Education and Childcare from Birth to 5 Years*

Department for Education (DfE) (2013b) *More Great Childcare: Raising Quality and Giving Parents More Choice*

Department for Education and Department of Health (2011a) *Families in the Foundation Years Evidence Pack*

Department for Education and Department of Health (2011b) *Supporting Families in the Foundation Years*

Early Years Stakeholder Group (2008) *Report to the Children's Minister*

European Commission (2011) *Early Childhood Education and Care: Providing all our Children with the Best Start for the World of Tomorrow* (COM(2011) 66 final). Brussels: European Commission

Hadfield, M., Jopling, M., Royle, K. and Waller, T. (2011) *First National Survey of Practitioners with Early Years Professional Status*. CWDC, CeDARE, University of Wolverhampton

Hanson, K. (2012) Early Years Professionals Deserve More Recognition. *The Guardian*, 18 September

HM Government (2010) *Securing Sufficient Childcare*. London: DCSF

HM Treasury (2005) *Choice for Parents, the Best Start for Children: A Ten Year Strategy for Childcare*. London: HM Treasury

Hoxhallari, L., Conolly, A. and Lyon, N. (2007) *Families with Children in Britain: Findings from the 2005 Families and Children Study (FACS)* (Research Report No. 424). Department for Work and Pensions

International Child Development Steering Group (2007) Strategies to Avoid the Loss of Developmental Potential in more than 200 Million Children in the Developing World. *The Lancet*, 369: 229–42

Kilpatrick, W. H. (2009) *Froebel's Kindergarten Principles Critically Examined*. Newcastle: Cambridge Scholars Publishing

Lloyd, E. and Penn, H. (2010) Why Do Childcare Markets Fail? Comparing England and the Netherlands. *Public Policy Research*, 17: 42–48

Lloyd, E. and Penn, H. (eds) (2012) *Childcare Markets: Can They Deliver an Equitable Service?* Bristol: Policy Press

Lumsden, E. (2010) The New Early Years Professional in England. *International Journal for Cross-Disciplinary Subjects in Education (IJCDSE)*, 1: 253–62

MacMillan, M. (2009) *The Nursery School*. Charleston, SC: Bibliolife

Mathers, S., Ranns, H., Karemaker, A., Moody, A., Sylva, K., Graham, J. and Siraj-Blatchford, I. (2011) *Evaluation of the Graduate Leader Fund*. Research Report DFE-RR144. London: DfE

Mathers, S., Singler, R. and Karemaker, A. (2012) *Improving Quality in the Early Years: A Comparison of Perspectives and Measures*. Daycare Trust, A+ Education and University of Oxford

Moylett, H. and Stewart, N. (2011) *Development Matters in the Early Years Foundation Stage (EYFS)*. London: Early Education

Nutbrown, C. (2012) *Foundations for Quality: The Independent Review of Early Education and Childcare Qualifications*. London DfE

OECD (2000) *Early Childhood Education and Care Policy in Finland*. Background report prepared for the OECD Thematic Review of Early Childhood Education and Care Policy. Paris: OECD

OECD (2006a) *Starting Strong II: Early Childhood Education and Care. Executive summary*. Paris: OECD

OECD (2006b) *Starting Strong II: Early Childhood Education and Care UK. Summary Annex E*. Paris: OECD

OECD (2008) *Babies and Bosses: Balancing Work and Family Life*. Policy Brief. Paris: OECD

OECD (2011) *Divided We Stand: Why Inequality Keeps Rising*. Paris: OECD

OECD (2012) *Starting Strong III: A Quality Toolbox for Early Childhood Education and Care*. Paris: OECD

Ofqual (2012) *Comparing Qualifications Levels*. Available at: www.ofqual.gov.uk/help-and-advice/comparing-qualifications/

Ofsted (2012) *Requirements for the Childcare Register: Childcare Providers on Non-Domestic or Domestic Premises – a childcare factsheet*

Owen, S. (2008) *Childminders: The Road to Professionalism*. London: National Children's Bureau

Peisner-Feinberg, E. S. (2004) Child Care and Its Impact on Young Children's Development, in Tremblay, R. E. et al (eds) *Encyclopedia on Early Childhood Development*. Montreal: Centre of Excellence for Early Childhood Development. Available at: www.child-encyclopedia.com/documents/Peisner-FeinbergANGxp.pdf

Pre-School Learning Alliance (2010) *A History of the Pre-school Learning Alliance*. Available at: www.pre-school.org.uk/document/599

PriceWaterhouseCoopers (2006) DfES *Children's Services The Childcare Market*.

Pugh, G. and Duffy, B. (eds) (2010) *Contemporary Issues in the Early Years*, 5th edn. London: Sage Publications

QAA (2007) *Early childhood studies*. Quality Assurance Agency Benchmarking Group.

Rock, L. (2012) What Britain Could Learn from Denmark's Childcare Model. *The Observer*, 18 February

Scottish Government (2008) *The Early Years Framework*

Siraj-Blatchford, I., Sylva, K., Muttock, S., Gilden, R. and Bell, D. (2002) *Researching Effective Pedagogy in the Early Years*. London: DfES

Sylva, K., Melhuish, E., Sammons, P., Siraj-Blatchford, I. and Taggart, B. (2008) *Final Report from the Primary Phase: Pre-school, School and Family Influences on Children's Development during Key Stage 2 (Age 7–11)* (Research Report No DCSF-RR061), Effective Pre-school and Primary Education 3–11 Project (EPPE 3–11). London: DCSF

Taguma, M., Litjens, I. and Makowiecki, K. (2012a) *Quality Matters in Early Childhood Education and Care: Finland*. Paris: OECD

Taguma, M., Litjens, I. and Makowiecki, K. (2012b) *Quality Matters in Early Childhood Education and Care: United Kingdom (England)*. Paris: OECD

Taguma, M., Litjens, I. and Makowiecki, K. (2013) *Quality Matters in Early Childhood Education and Care: Sweden*. Paris: OECD

Tamsin (2012) *The History of Childminding*. Available at: www.childminding-success.co.uk/registration/history-of-childminding/

Teaching Agency (2012a) *Early Years Professional Status Standards*

Teaching Agency (2012b) *Graduate Leaders in Early Years: Early Years Professional Status (EYPS) Explained*. Available at: www.education.gov.uk/h00201345/graduate-leaders/eyps

Tickell, C. (2011) *The Early Years: Foundations for Life, Health and Learning* (An Independent Report on the Early Years Foundation Stage to Her Majesty's Government). Department for Education

Tickell, C. (2012) *Statutory Framework for the Early Years Foundation Stage.* Department for Education

Truss, E. (2012) *Affordable Quality: New Approaches to Childcare*. Centre Forum

UCAS (2012) Course lists. Available at: http://unistats.direct.gov.uk/searchresults/

Chapter 6

Anon (n.d.) *The Normative Theory of Social Exclusion: Perspectives from Political Philosophy*. Available at: www.ucl.ac.uk/~ucesswo/IJSSP%20ms.doc

Antonioni, P. and Masaki Flynn, S. (2010) *Economics For Dummies: UK Edition*. Chichester: John Wiley

Banerjee, A. and Duflo, E. (2011) *Poor Economics: Barefoot Hedge-fund Managers, DIY Doctors and the Surprising Truth about Life on Less than $1 a Day*. London: Penguin Books

Banerjee, A. and Duflo, E. (2012) *Poor Economics: A Radical Rethinking of the Way to Fight Global Poverty*. New York: PublicAffairs

Bradbury, B., Jenkins, S. P. and Micklewright, J. (eds) (2001) *The Dynamics of Child Poverty in Industrial Countries*. Cambridge: Cambridge University Press

Bradshaw, J., Kemp, P., Baldwin, S. and Rowe, A. (2004) *The Drivers of Social Exclusion: A Review of the Literature for the Social Exclusion Unit, Breaking the Cycle*. London: Office of the Deputy Prime Minister

Brewer, M., Browne, J. and Joyce, R. (2011) *Child Poverty and Working Age Poverty from 2010 to 2020,* IFS Commentary C121. London: Institute for Fiscal Studies

Brooks-Gunn, J. and Duncan, G. J. (1997) The Effects of Poverty on Children. *The Future of Children: Children and Poverty*, 7(2): 55–71

Cabinet Office (2010a) *The Coalition: Our Programme for Government*. HM Government

Cabinet Office (2010b) *Context for Social Exclusion Work*. Social Exclusion Task Force. Available at: http://webarchive.nationalarchives.gov.uk/ and www.cabinetoffice.gov.uk/social_exclusion_task_force/context.aspx

Cameron, D. (2012) Welfare speech. Available at: www.number10.gov.uk/news/welfare-speech/

Centre Services (2012) Clifton Children's Centre. Available at: www.clifton-childrens-centre.co.uk/services

Child Poverty Action Group (CPAG) (ed) (2012) *Ending Child Poverty by 2020: Progress Made and Lessons Learned*. London: CPAG

Confederation of British Industry (CBI) (2012) *First Steps: A New Approach for our Schools*. London: CBI

Department for Work and Pensions and Department for Education (2012) *Child Poverty in the UK: The Report on the 2010 Target Presented to Parliament Pursuant to Section 1(1) of the Child Poverty Act 2010*. London: The Stationery Office

Dickie, D. (2012) *What Happened to UK Child Poverty?* Scotland: Child Poverty Action Group

Eisenstadt, N. (2011) *Providing a Sure Start: How Government Discovered Early Childhood*. Bristol: Policy Press

Eisenstadt, N. (2012) Sure Start and Child Poverty: What Have We Learned? in Child Poverty Action Group (ed) *Ending Child Poverty by 2020: Progress Made and Lessons Learned*. London: CPAG

European Communities (2008) *Thematic Study on Policy Measures Concerning Child Poverty* (Policy Studies Findings No. 10). Brussels: EU Social Protection and Social Inclusion Process

Fairbanks, M. and Fal, M. (eds) (2009) *In the River They Swim: Essays from Around the World on Enterprise Solutions to Poverty*. West Conshohocken, PA: Templeton Press

Field, F. (2010) *The Foundation Years: Preventing Poor Children Becoming Poor Adults*. The report of the Independent Review on Poverty and Life Chances (Field Report). London: HM Government

Gates Foundation (2009) *Polio Strategy Overview 2009*. Global Health Program. Bill & Melinda Gates Foundation

Gaunt, C. (2012) Expansion of Free Early Years Places for Two-Year-Olds to Start in the Autumn. *Nursery World*, 30 May

Gillard, D. (2006) *Infant and Nursery Schools – The Hadow Reports: An Introduction*. Education in England. Available at: www.educationengland.org.uk

Golden, O. (2006) *Young Children after Katrina: A Proposal to Heal the Damage and Create Opportunity in New Orleans*. Washington, DC: The Urban Institute

Hadfield, M., Jopling, M., Needham, M., Waller, T., Coleyshaw, L., Emira, M. and Royle, K. (2012) *Longitudinal Study of Early Years Professional Status: An Exploration of Progress, Leadership and Impact, Final Report*. University of Wolverhampton

HM Government (2011) *A New Approach to Child Poverty: Tackling the Causes of Disadvantage and Transforming Families' Lives*. Crown copyright

HM Government (2012) *Guide to Child Trust Funds*. Available at: www.gov.uk/child-trust-funds/overview

International Child Development Steering Group (2007) Strategies to Avoid the Loss of Developmental Potential in more than 200 Million Children in the Developing World. *The Lancet*, 369: 229–42

Johnson, B. (2012) London Mayor Speech. The Living Wage Foundation. Available at: www.livingwage.org.uk/home

Johnson, P. and Kossykh, Y. (2008) *Early Years, Life Chances and Equality: A Literature Review*. Frontier Economics. Manchester: Equality and Human Rights Commission

Joyce, R. (2009) *Child Poverty during the Recession and Beyond*. London: Institute for Fiscal Studies

Kakuta Ole Maimai (2012) *Mission Statement, Maasai Association*. Available at: www.maasai-association.org/mission.html

Karlan, D. and Appel, J. (2011) *More Than Good Intentions: Improving the Ways the World's Poor Borrow, Save, Farm, Learn, and Stay Healthy*. New York: Penguin Books

Kiernan, K. E. and Huerta, M. C. (2008) Economic Deprivation, Maternal Depression, Parenting and Children's Cognitive and Emotional Development in Early Childhood. *The British Journal of Sociology*, 59: 783–806

Lake, A. (2012) *The Global Crisis You've Never Heard Of: Stunting*. Available at: http://ideas.time.com/2012/01/31/the-global-crisis-youve-never-heard-of/

Lelkes, O. and Gasior, K. (2011) *Income Poverty in the EU: Situation in 2007 and Trends* (based on EU–SILC 2005–2008). Policy Brief European Centre No. 1

Matthew, E. and Melmed, J. D. (2007) Statement of Zero to Three Policy Center submitted to the Committee on Ways and Means, US House of Representatives

Murray, C. et al (1996) *Charles Murray and the Underclass: The Developing Debate*. London: IEA Health and Welfare Trust

Narayan, D. (2000) *Voices of the Poor*. Volume 1: *Can Anyone Hear Us?* Oxford: Oxford University Press for the World Bank

Narayan, D., Chambers, R., Shah, M. K. and Petesch, P. (2000) *Voices of the Poor: Crying Out for Change*. Oxford: Oxford University Press for the World Bank

National Center for Children in Poverty (1999) *Poverty and Brain Development in Early Childhood*. Columbia University

Peace, R. (2001) Social Exclusion: A Concept in Need of Definition? Robin Peace Knowledge Management Group, Ministry of Social Policy. *Social Policy Journal of New Zealand*, 16 (July)

Percy-Smith, J. (2000) *Policy Responses to Social Exclusion: Towards Inclusion?* Maidenhead: Open University Press

Piachaud, D. and Sutherland, H. (2000) *How Effective is the British Government's Attempt to Reduce Child Poverty?* CASE Paper 38. Centre for Analysis of Social Exclusion

Robb, C. M. (2001) *Can the Poor Influence Policy? Participatory Poverty Assessments in the Developing World*, 2nd edn. Washington, DC: World Bank

Scottish Affairs Committee (2000) *Poverty in Scotland* (Parliamentary Committee No. 1). House of Commons

Shonkoff, J. P. and Phillips, D. A. (eds) (2000) *From Neurons to Neighborhoods: The Science of Early Childhood Development*. National Academy of Sciences, Committee on Integrating the Science of Early Childhood Development, Board on Children, Youth, and Families

Simon, J. and Nobes, C. (2012) *Economics of Taxation (2011/12)*, 11th edn. Birmingham: Fiscal Publications

Social Protection Committee (2012a) Annex to the *SPC Ad-Hoc Group Advisory Report Tackling and Preventing Child Poverty, Promoting Child Well-Being*. Brussels: European Commission

Social Protection Committee (2012b) *SPC Advisory Report to the European Commission on Tackling and Preventing Child Poverty, Promoting Child Well-Being B*. Brussels: European Commission

Sylva, K., Melhuish, E., Siraj-Blatchford, I. and Taggart, B. (2007) *Promoting Equality in the Early Years*. Report to the Equalities Review, Cabinet Office

Thatcher, M. (1987) Interview with Douglas Keay. *Woman's Own*, 23 September

Trickle Up (2012) *Trickle Up's 2007–2012 Strategic Plan*. Available at: www.trickleup.org/about/About-Trickle-Up.cfm

UNICEF (2012a) *Breastfeeding Can Help Save Lives and Prevent Stunting*. The Baby Friendly Initiative. Available at: www.unicef.org.uk/BabyFriendly/

UNICEF (2012b) *Rakhine State, Myanmar*. Available at: www.unicef.org/infobycountry/myanmar_66426.html

UNICEF (2012c) *The State of the World's Children: Children in an Urban World*. New York: UNICEF

Chapter 7

Allan, J. and Catts, R. (eds) (2012) *Social Capital, Children and Young People: Implications for Practice, Policy and Research*. Bristol: Policy Press

Brown, F. (2012) Playwork, Play Deprivation and Play: An Interview with Fraser Brown. *American Journal of Play*, 4: 267–84

Carrera, S. and Beaumont, J. (2010) *Income and Wealth*. Social Trends (No. 41). Office for National Statistics

CIA world fact book. www.cia.gov/library/publications/the-world-factbook/ (accessed September 2013)

City of Melbourne (2010) *The Children's Plan: Children's Rights, Children's Voices, Municipal Early Years Plan 2010–2013*. City of Melbourne

Department for Communities and Local Government (2006) *A Decent Home: Definition and Guidance for Implementation (Update)*. Department for Communities and Local Government

Department for Culture, Media and Sport (2011) *Business Plan 2011–2015*

Edgington, M. (2013) *Supporting Young Children to Engage with Risk and Challenge*. Teaching Expertise. Available at: www.teachingexpertise.com/articles/supporting-young-children-to-engage-with-risk-and-challenge-2089

Fields in Trust (2012a) *Guiding You through the Planning Process*. Available at: www.fieldsintrust.org/Upload/file/FIT_Planning.pdf

Fields in Trust (2012b) *Loss of Sites*. Available at: www.fieldsintrust.org. URL www.fieldsintrust.org/Loss_of_Sites.aspx

Grant, R., Shapiro, A., Joseph, S., Goldsmith, S., Rigual-Lynch, L. and Redlener, I. (2007) The Health of Homeless Children Revisited. *Advances in Pediatrics*, 54: 173–87

Harker, L. (2006) *Chance of a Lifetime: The Impact of Bad Housing on Children's Lives*. London: Shelter

Harpham, T. (2002) *Measuring the Social Capital of Children*. Working Paper No. 4. Young Lives: An International Study of Childhood Poverty

International Secretariat for Child Friendly Cities (2013) *Child Friendly Cities – Brazil*. Available at: www.childfriendlycities.org/en/building-a-cfc/indicators-criteria-for-cfc/brazil

Jacobson, M. (2007) *8 Incredible Facts about Mumbai*. National Geographic

Keep, M. (2013) *Reported Road Accident Statistics*. Available at: www.parliament.uk

Kelly, A. (2012) Traffic Accidents are 'Biggest Killer of Young People Worldwide', Report Says. *The Guardian*, 2 May

Leonard, M. (2005) Children, Childhood and Social Capital: Exploring the Links. *Sociology*, 39: 605–22

Lindon, J. (2011) *Too Safe for Their Own Good: Helping Children Learn About Risk and Lifeskills*, 2nd edn. London: NCB

Lister, R. (ed) (1996) *Charles Murray and the Underclass: The Developing Debate, Choice in Welfare*. London: Institute of Economic Affairs

Lunn, S. (2006) Modern Urban Planning is No Child's Play. *The Australian*, 31 October

Maplethorpe, N., Chanfreau, J., Philo, D. and Tait, C. (2010) *Families with Children in Britain: Findings from the 2008 Families and Children Study* (FACS) (Research Report No. 656). Department for Work and Pensions

Mitchell, F. et al (2004) *Living in Limbo: Survey of Homeless Households Living in Temporary Accommodation*. London: Shelter

Muñoz, S. A. (2009) *Children in the Outdoors: A Literature Review*. Sustainable Development Research Centre

Muriel, S. (2013) *Toughest Place to be a … Taxi Driver*. BBC2, 10 March

Nyasani, I. B. (2009) *Kenya's Experience on Urban Health Issues. Final Report on the Urban Heart Pilot-Testing Project*. Geneva: World Health Organization

Parliamentary Office of Science and Technology (2011) *Housing and Health* (Postnote No. 371)

Planning Institute of Australia (PIA) (2013) *Child Friendly Communities: Why Develop a Child Friendly Communities' Policy?* Available at: www.planning.org.au/policy/child-friendly-communities

Presland, A. (2013) *Statutory Homelessness: October to December Quarter 2012: England, Housing Statistical Release*. Department for Communities and Local Government

Rice, B. (2006) *Against the Odds*. London: Shelter

Riggio, E. and Kilbane, T. (2000) The International Secretariat for Child-Friendly Cities: A Global Network for Urban Children. *Environment & Urbanization*, 12(2): 201–5

Shackell, A., Butler, N., Doyle, P. and Ball, D. (2008) *Design for Play: A Guide to Creating Successful Play Spaces*. London: Play England

Shelter (2003) *Listen Up: The Voices of Homeless Children*. London: Shelter

Shelter (2009) *Improving Outcomes for Children and Young People in Housing Need: A Benchmarking Guide for Joint Working Between Services*. London: Shelter

Shelter (2013) *What is it Like to be Homeless?* Available at: http://england.shelter.org.uk

Stewart, G. (2013) *Bang! A History of Britain in the 1980s*. London: Atlantic Books

The Times of India (2013) High-Rises Elbow Children Out of Play Areas, 7 April

UN–Habitat (2003) *The Challenge of Slums: Global Report on Human Settlements 2003*. London: Earthscan Publications

UN–Habitat (2010) Development Context and the Millennium Agenda. Chapter 1 of the *Global Report on Human Settlements*

UNICEF (2012) *The State of the World's Children: Children in an Urban World*. New York: UNICEF

United Nations (2009) *Child-Friendly Cities: Working to Fulfil the Rights of Children*. United Nations special session on children

United Nations (2013) *Population: Vital Statistics*. Available at: www.un.org/en/globalissues/briefingpapers

United Nations Human Settlements Programme (UN–HABITAT) (2012) *State of the World's Cities 2012/2013: Prosperity of Cities*. Nairobi: United Nations Human Settlements Programme (UN–HABITAT)

Whitelegg, J. and Haq, G. (2006) *VISION ZERO: Adopting a Target of Zero for Road Traffic Fatalities and Serious Injuries*. Stockholm Environment Institute

World Health Organization (WHO) (2008) *World Report on Child Injury Prevention*. Geneva: WHO

World Health Organization (WHO) (2010) *Injuries and Violence: The Facts*. Geneva: WHO

World Health Organization (WHO) and UN–Habitat (2010) *Hidden Cities: Unmasking and Overcoming Health Inequities in Urban Settings*. Geneva: WHO

Chapter 8

Atkinson, A. B. (1998) *EMU, Macroeconomics and Children*. Innocenti Occasional Papers, Economic and Social Policy Series 68

Barblett, L., Hydon, C. and Kennedy, A. (2008) *The Code of Ethics: A Guide for Everyday Practice*. Research in Practice Series. Early Childhood Australia

Barnado's (2013) *Child Poverty Statistics and Facts*. Available at: www.barnardos.org.uk.

Barroso, J. M. (2010) *Europe 2020: A European Strategy for Smart, Sustainable and Inclusive Growth*. Brussels: European Commission

Chaudhuri, S. (2009) *Labour Market Reform and Incidence of Child Labour in a Developing Economy*. Calcutta University

Cooke, G. and Henehan, K. (2012) *Double Dutch: The Case against Deregulation and Demand-Led Funding in Childcare*. London: Institute for Public Policy Research

de Silva-de-Alwis, R. (2007) *Legislative Reform on Child Domestic Labour: A Gender Analysis.* Legislative Reform Initiative Paper Series. New York: UNICEF

de Vlyder, S. (2001) 'A macroeconomic policy for children in the era of globalization' in Cornia, G.A. (ed) *Harnessing globalisation for children: a report to UNICEF*. Florence: UNICEF

Doepke, M. and Zilibotti, F. (2005) The Macroeconomics of Child Labor Regulation. *American Economic Review*, 95: 1492–1524

Doepke, M. and Zilibotti, F. (2009) International Labor Standards and the Political Economy of Child-Labor Regulation. *Journal of the European Economic Association*, 7: 508–18

Elsass, P. M. and Veiga, J. F. (1994) Acculturation in Acquired Organizations: A Force-Field Perspective. *Human Relations*, 47: 431–43

European Commission (2011) *Communication from the Commission to the European Parliament, the Council, the European Economic and Social Committee and the Committee of the Regions: An EU Agenda for the Rights of the Child* (COM (2011) 60 final). Brussels: The Commission to the European Parliament

European Union (2010) *Charter of Fundamental Rights of the European Union*. Official Journal of the European Union C: 389–403

Gorman, L. (2013) *Why Poverty Persists*. Available at: www.nber.org/digest/jun06/w11681.html

Indian Matters! (2011) *Child Labour: A Case Study*. Available at: http://indianmatters.in/index.php?Page=eyeopner/eomaster&inter=E0110110001_5

International Labour Convention (1999) Worst Forms of Child Labour (Convention No. 182)

International Monetary Fund (2013) *The IMF's Role in Helping Protect the Most Vulnerable in the Global Crisis*. Washington, DC: IMF

Jones, P., Moss, D., Tomlinson, P. and Welch, S. (eds) (2008) *Childhood: Services and Provision for Children*. Harlow: Pearson Education

Lewin, K. (1951) *Field Theory in Social Science: Selected Theoretical Papers*. New York: Harper

Lustig, N. C. (2000) *Crises and the Poor: Socially Responsible Macroeconomics* (Sustainable Development Department, Poverty and Inequality Advisory Unit No. Working Paper No. 108). Washington, DC: Inter-American Development Bank

McNeil, J. (2013) *A History of Official Government HIV/AIDS Policy in South Africa*. Available at: www.sahistory.org.za/topic/history-official-government-hivaids-policy-south-africa

Micklewright, J. (2000) *Macroeconomics and Data on Children*. Innocenti Working Papers, Economic and Social Policy Series

MONUSCO (2013) *Mandate*. Available at: http://monusco.unmissions.org/Default.aspx?tabid=10766&language=en-US

Moss, P. and Petrie, P. (2002) *From Children's Services to Children's Spaces*. London: Routledge/Falmer

Murray, C. et al (1996) *Charles Murray and the Underclass: The Developing Debate*. London: Institute of Economic Affairs

Nuffield Council on Bioethics (2006) *Critical Care Decisions in Fetal and Neonatal Medicine*, Chapter 2: Decision Making: The Ethical Issues. London: Nuffield Council on Bioethics

Nyasani, I. B. (2009) *Kenya's Experience on Urban Health Issues. Final Report on the Urban Heart Pilot-Testing Project*. Geneva: WHO

OECD (2009a). *Doing Better for Children*. Paris: OECD

OECD (2009b) *Growing Unequal: Income Distribution and Poverty in OECD Countries*. Paris: OECD

Pierson, J. (2010) *Tackling Social Exclusion*, 2nd edn. London: Routledge

Population Reference Bureau (2012a) *2012 World Population Data Sheet*. Washington, DC: Population Reference Bureau

Population Reference Bureau (2012b) *Population under Age 15 (Percent) 2012*. Available at: www.globalhealthfacts.org/data/topic/map.aspx?ind=82

Smolin, D. M. (2004) Intercountry Adoption as Child Trafficking. *Valparaiso University Law Review*, 39: 281–325

Ubuntu Africa (2013) *HIV/AIDS and Children*. Available at: http://ubafrica.org. URL http://ubafrica.org/about-us/the-need/hivaids-and-children/

UN News Centre (12 March 2013). *Syrian Conflict Risks Leaving Entire Generation of Children 'Scarred for Life'* – UNICEF

UNICEF (2004) *The State of the World's Children: Childhood under Threat*. New York: UNICEF

Velasquez, M. et al (2009) *Thinking Ethically: A Framework for Moral Decision Making*. Santa Clara, CA: Santa Clara University. Available at: www.scu.edu/ethics/practicing/decision/thinking.html

World Bank (2013) *Economic Policy and Debt*. Available at: http://web.worldbank.org/WBSITE/EXTERNAL/TOPICS/EXTDEBTDEPT/0,,contentMDK:20259564~pagePK:64166689~piPK:64166646~theSitePK:469043,00.html

Index